The Observer Atlas of World Affairs

A Guide to Major Tensions and Conflicts

Edited by ANDREW WILSON

Visual Aids by DIAGRAM

George Philip and Son Limited

A Mitchell Beazley book

Produced by Mitchell Beazley Ltd
41 King Street London WC2
and first published 1971 in Great Britain by
George Philip & Son Ltd
Victoria Road London NW10
In association with *The Observer*

All other maps and diagrams
devised and drawn by
DIAGRAM
145 Wardour Street London W1

ISBN 0540 05160 8

Filmset, Printed and Bound by
Sir Joseph Causton and Sons Ltd
Eastleigh Hampshire

Introduction

by ANDREW WILSON

The function of *The Observer Atlas of World Affairs* is to bring together in a readily appreciable form the chief factors affecting world crisis areas, and to provide a concise background reference book to current events. The material has been chosen for its relevance to political, military, economic, and social issues. It does not attempt to assess all the problems raised by its subject matter: in dealing with differences of race, language, culture, and standards of living some degree of selectivity is inevitable. But its impartial analysis should make it indispensable to all students of current affairs in school or college, and give it wide appeal to the general public.

Particular attention has been given to military matters, underlining the grim reality that supports the present structure of international relations. Military technology and defence hardware is rarely encountered by the average citizen, but it both defends and threatens him, and cannot be ignored.

For ease of use as well as to present a compact treatment of specific areas, the atlas is divided into six sections: The World, The Americas, Europe, The Middle East, Africa, and Asia.

The statistics represented in the numerous thematic maps and diagrams are the latest available. Some, those on population and resources, for example, may be taken as valid over a period of years; others, relating, say, to military forces, may change more abruptly.

A concise statistical profile for every nation is included at the end of the book for reference, and to enable direct comparisons to be made outside the specific relationships treated within the atlas sections.

The text that accompanies each section deals with those aspects of an area or situation that do not lend themselves to graphic representation. It thus provides, wherever necessary, a counterbalance to conclusions that might otherwise be drawn from a too simple reading of diagrams. It is designed, however, to be read continuously, with the maps and diagrams as illustrations to the text.

In compiling a work of this kind, the editor and publishers are indebted to innumerable publications, organizations, and individuals for information and advice concerning both the text and the illustrations. To name every source is impossible, but the producers would like especially to acknowledge the help given by the United Nations and its various agencies; the Royal Institute of International Affairs, London; the Institute of Strategic Studies, London; and the Stockholm International Peace Research Institute. Publications issued by these authorities have been among the most important of the many sources consulted in the compilation of the maps, diagrams, and statistical data.

Last, but by no means least, the producers wish to thank Richard Gott, the journalist and writer, whose expert knowledge of the developing countries —particularly those of Latin America—has been a major contribution; and Professor W. H. Morris-Jones, Professor of Commonwealth Affairs and Director of the Institute of Commonwealth Studies, University of London, whose advice and comments have proved invaluable.

Andrew Wilson

Andrew Wilson is the Defence Correspondent of The Observer

Contents

The world rich and poor

World exports: how total is shared

Figures in $1000 million

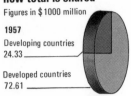

1957
Developing countries 24.33
Developed countries 72.61

1962
Developing countries 27.76
Developed countries 91.16

1967
Developing countries 37.45
Developed countries 141.25

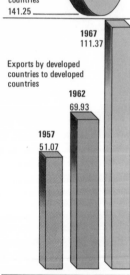

Exports by developed countries to developed countries

1957 51.07
1962 69.93
1967 111.37

Exports by developed countries to developing countries

21.54 21.83 29.88

Exports by developing countries to developed countries

18.10 20.77 29.04

Exports by developing countries to developing countries

6.23 6.39 8.41

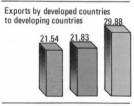
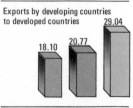

The wealth gap

One of the most fundamental and dangerous divisions in the world is that between the rich nations and the poor, the developed and the developing.

In the long run this division along the poverty line is a greater threat to peace than the old cold war division between East and West, or the increasing polarization of whites and non-whites. This is not so much because of the threat of a rich-poor war—which the poor countries are in no position to undertake—but because of the internal instabilities of the poor world, which the richer powers are constantly tempted to exploit.

And although there are parts of the world, the Middle East, for example, where the two super powers (the Soviet Union and the United States) and the former colonial powers (Great Britain and France) have a mutual interest in reducing tension, both may encounter great difficulty when faced with the determination of those whom they are pledged to protect or support.

Another potential cause of instability in the developing world is the possibility that the poor countries will bind themselves to their technologically most advanced, and most militant member— China—and seek to redress their position. Lin Piao, the Chinese defence minister and officially named in 1969 as Mao Tse-tung's successor, has suggested that as in a revolutionary guerrilla war it is possible for the countryside to strangle the towns, so the poor countries will eventually be able to join together to deprive the rich of the vital raw materials on which the wealth of their societies is based.

But the feasibility of such a move is doubtful. Russia and the United States account for more than 40 per cent of the world's production of wheat, iron, copper, and oil. Nevertheless, the increasing wealth gap between rich and poor makes local explosions of popular resentment inevitable. Nor is the wealth gap confined to relations between countries. Poor countries often have a wealthy class with a standard of living way above the average in the United States.

Income differences

Self-interest suggests that greater efforts to reduce the wealth gap would save the developed nations some of the huge expenditure on military operations that are undertaken to protect trade and commercial interests overseas. But in the end many people would recognize the problem of the wealth gap as a moral one. The dramatic differences in living standards indicated on this and the following pages speak for themselves. Income per capita in North America is $2675 a year, which is some 20 times the figure for Africa ($120), six times that for Latin America ($420), and twice that for Europe ($1235). (For national income per capita, see p. 10.)

More serious than the gap itself is the alarming speed at which it is widening. The origins are mainly historical. In the advanced countries science has been developing at an ever-increasing rate for the last 200 years, resulting in a huge growth in knowledge and in the numbers of scientifically educated people. Living conditions in Europe, America, Russia and Japan, for instance, have been transformed. Every year the discrepancy between standards of living in rich and poor countries grows more marked. And nothing can reduce the imbalance except an immense, sustained effort by the advanced nations to solve the age-old problems of poverty, illiteracy, ignorance, and disease. This disparity in living standards is a fairly new phenomenon in history. The foundations of Western economic supremacy derive in the end from the progress made in the 17th, 18th, and 19th centuries, particularly in the rapid exploitation of the natural resources of Africa, Asia, and Latin America. (Before that, differences in living standards between one part of the world and another tended to be largely marginal.) Native economies were forced to develop on lines that satisfied European rather than local needs, while poor countries were often flooded with cheap mass-produced goods from Europe and America.

Vicious circle

Economic growth becomes possible only when a nation makes efficient use of all its resources in people, land, and capital. But in the developing world, because people are poor, hungry, and uneducated they seem to have no chance of catching up with the advanced countries. They remained trapped in a vicious circle of disease and poverty.

Although the political aspects of the pre-1939 colonial system have now been generally removed, except by Portugal, the economic aspects have more often survived. The poor, ex-colonial countries must still sell their products on a world market over which they have very little control. They still rely, as they always have done, on access to the markets of the rich countries.

Attempts to escape from this situation have proved very difficult. For although exports of primary products from the poor countries have risen, the prices have frequently declined. For example:

1. Two thirds of Ghana's exports are cocoa. Between 1953 and 1961, cocoa exports increased by 71 per cent, but the revenue rose by only 23 per cent. In the same period European goods shipped to West Africa went up 25 per cent in cost. So a piece of machinery that cost Ghana the equivalent of 10 tons of cocoa in 1953 cost 25 tons of cocoa in 1961.
2. Half Brazil's exports consist of coffee. Between 1953 and 1961 coffee exports increased by 90 per cent in volume, but the revenue dropped by 35 per cent.
3. Half the exports of the Malay peninsula are rubber. Between 1950 and 1961 rubber exports increased by 4 per cent in volume, but the revenue fell by 35 per cent.

Low-cost imports from the poor countries often appear to threaten the domestic industries of the rich. So the rich often impose subsidies to protect their industry. The British sugar beet industry, for example, gets such a subsidy, and some European countries are even planning to export their subsidized sugar production.

Commodity agreements

Frequently, commodity agreements are introduced in an attempt to give developing countries a better chance; but whenever the poor countries look like making a serious breakthrough, the rich usually call for the agreement to be renegotiated. A few years ago Brazil succeeded in capturing 14 per cent of the United States market in soluble coffee by setting up its own processing factories. The United States then threatened not to renew the International Coffee Agreement, which maintains stable prices, and talked of cutting aid to Brazil. Due to pressure from North American coffee-processing firms, Brazil (in March 1968) was forced to give way. The Brazilian government promised to impose an export tax on powdered coffee, and so made their own product as expensive as the North American in the United States domestic market.

The poor countries need to increase their exports in order to buy goods from the advanced industrialized world, both for consumption and in order to service their own industries. But because of the Western lead in economic development, the new industries that have grown up in the developing countries are so structured that their continuation and expansion have depended largely on European (or American) skills and machinery exports. They are often foreign-owned and are usually capital-intensive—employing very few people. They aggravate, rather than alleviate, the growing problem of unemployment and under-employment. (In Latin America, where the population is doubling every 24 years, about a quarter of the continent's total work force—about 25 million men—are without proper jobs.)

The developing countries have tried to diversify exports, but this strategy meets with little success. When India and Pakistan, who produce cheap textiles, showed signs of capturing a large part of the British textile market, the British government (under pressure from domestic producers) imposed quotas on low-cost (i.e. poor countries') goods. Similarly, electronic goods made in Singapore face insurmountable tariff barriers in Australia.

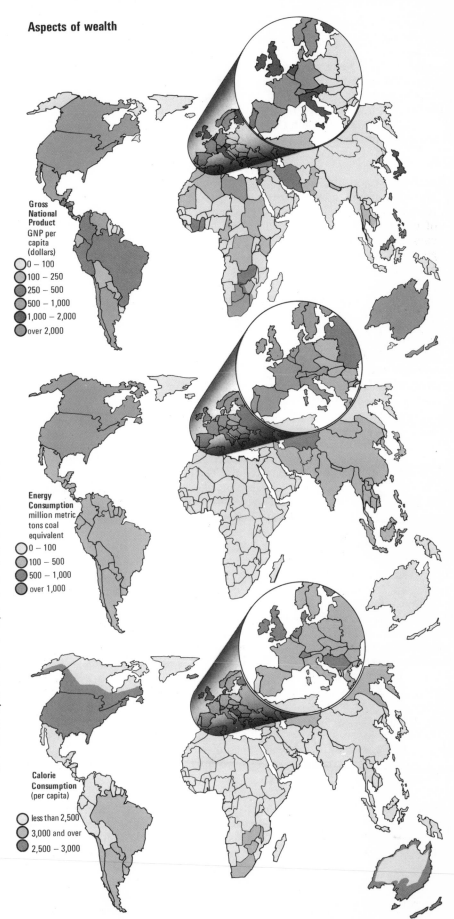

Aspects of wealth

Gross National Product
GNP per capita (dollars)
- 0 – 100
- 100 – 250
- 250 – 500
- 500 – 1,000
- 1,000 – 2,000
- over 2,000

Energy Consumption
million metric tons coal equivalent
- 0 – 100
- 100 – 500
- 500 – 1,000
- over 1,000

Calorie Consumption (per capita)
- less than 2,500
- 3,000 and over
- 2,500 – 3,000

The world aid and population

Loans and assistance

While the rich countries spend money on space programmes (pp. 18–19) and on complex weapon systems (pp. 20–22), the poor countries are forced to grapple with more immediate problems: how to speed up capital accumulation, how to slow down population growth, how to grow more food.

In an effort to maintain their ability to import, the poor countries have borrowed funds from the rich, accepted aid, and courted private investment. But that has only served to reinforce their economic dependence. As time goes by, they are obliged to borrow more and more to repay old loans. Already repayments on such loans amount to the equivalent of two thirds of all aid going to the developing countries; and it is estimated that by 1980 the aid given will be entirely offset by repayments—unless aid is sharply increased, which is highly unlikely.

Although the rich countries make much play with their allocation of overseas aid, such aid may fall far short of what is needed. The poorer countries are left to finance about 80 per cent of their investment themselves. For example, India needs an investment of some $3000 million a year to fulfil its current Five-Year Plan. It gets 25 per cent of this from outside; the rest must come from its own people.

In real money terms the aid given by the rich to the poor nations has gone down every year since 1961. In 1969 the American aid budget, although the world's largest, was the smallest since America started giving aid after World War II. (The graph on page 31 plots the gradual decline in the volume of US foreign aid in the years since 1949; but the scale is too small to indicate the microscopic increase that occurred in the 1970 budget.)

Most overseas aid has strings attached, often military and political as well as economic. They may involve the lease of military bases in the recipient's territory or its adherence to a certain political line that will be reflected in its voting at the United Nations. Often the recipient finds it must buy goods with aid money from the original aid donor. Sometimes the strings acquire more sinister overtones. In 1967 the United States offered Peru a $25 million standby loan provided Peru bought American subsonic military aircraft instead of French supersonic jets. The bargain also demanded that United States ships should be allowed to fish in Peruvian territorial waters, and that the government of Peru should stop its attempts to gain a large share in the profits of the International Petroleum Company—an American firm. The Peruvians rejected the bargain.

The Soviet Union also uses aid to exert political pressure. Russian aid to Cuba has often been used as a lever in the attempt to make Fidel Castro toe Russia's ideological line.

Population growth: history and forecast

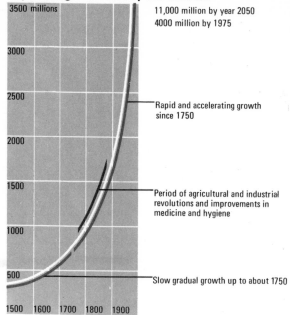

11,000 million by year 2050
4000 million by 1975

Rapid and accelerating growth since 1750

Period of agricultural and industrial revolutions and improvements in medicine and hygiene

Slow gradual growth up to about 1750

Population explosion

Some 8000 years ago the world had a population of about 5 million people. It rose to 1000 million by 1850, to 2000 million by 1930, and is expected to reach 4000 million by 1975. If current rates continue, the total could be as high as 11,000 million by the year 2050. Yet in the 1940s, demographers saw little cause for alarm, and thus little was done to deal with a chronic problem whose enormous dimensions were not really understood.

The world population explosion has been caused almost entirely by the rapid drop in mortality; the birth rate itself has remained almost unchanged. The drop in mortality has occurred partly through the improved storage and distribution of food. But it has mainly been brought about by the tremendous improvement in public health measures, particularly the virtual eradication of malaria, and the suppression of major epidemics. Bubonic plague, for instance, has almost disappeared (though there have been outbreaks at Saigon and Da Nang during the Vietnam war); smallpox and cholera have been much reduced, and tuberculosis is also on the wane. More people, too, are living longer than ever before. In Mexico, for instance, between 1930 and 1964, life expectancy rose from 36 to 60. In Mauritius it improved from 38 to 58 between 1940 and 1960. And in Taiwan it climbed from 45 to 65 during the same period. It was not until the 1960s that the rate of world population growth was widely recognized as a threat to living standards in the developing countries. Not till 1966 did China (with over 750 million people) take the

Future population

	Population (1969)	Percentage under 15 years of age	Doubling time (years)
AFRICA			
Nigeria	54m	43%	28
Egypt	32m	43%	24
Ethiopia	24m		35
ASIA			
China	750m		50
India	537m	41%	28
Pakistan	128m	45%	21
AMERICAS			
USA	203m	30%	70
Brazil	92m	43%	25
Mexico	49m	46%	21
EUROPE			
USSR	241m	32%	70
W. Germany	58m	23%	117
UK	56m	23%	175

Above, left: World population will double in less than 40 years if the present annual rate of growth continues. Some experts have even suggested a figure of 30,000 million by the year 2050. But—as Thomas Malthus pointed out in 1798—population increases geometrically, whereas agriculture increases arithmetically. In the end, population *must* face the limit of a food barrier.

Top: Table gives the three most populated countries of each continent, plus the percentage (where available) of the population now under 15 years of age, and the estimated number of years needed for the present population to double.

Population growth by continents
figures in millions

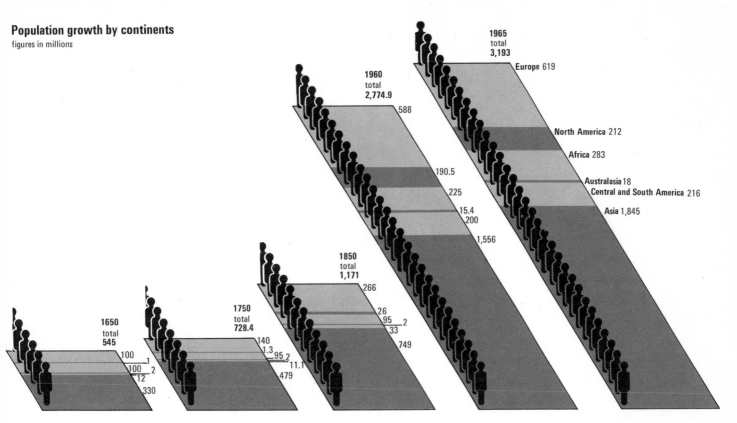

1965 total **3,193**
Europe 619
North America 212
Africa 283
Australasia 18
Central and South America 216
Asia 1,845

1960 total **2,774.9**
588
190.5
225
15.4
200
1,556

1850 total **1,171**
266
26
95
2
33
749

1750 total **728.4**
140
1.3
95
2
11.1
479

1650 total **545**
100
1
100
2
12
330

unprecedented step of announcing that families must be restricted to not more than three children. Only in 1965 did the US Congress allocate a sizeable sum within its aid budget ($34·7 million) to be devoted specifically to population control. Yet compared with the needs of a country such as India (540 million people), where numbers are increasing at the rate of more than one million a month, this sum is tiny.

India's position is most serious. Despite the 20 years of government-sponsored family planning, the population growth rate has in fact more than doubled, from 1·3 per cent in 1951 to the present figure of 3 per cent. It has been estimated that to prevent 35 to 45 million births over 10 years would cost the country $250 million. And even if fertility rates were to decline by 50 per cent tomorrow, in 20 years the rate of growth would still be the same as it is now. Many of the now developed countries earlier experienced periods when there was a big drop in their mortality figures. But that was accompanied by intensive industrialization and by the rapid development of world food markets and an international economy. Eventually, too, fertility in these countries declined. No such decline has yet appeared in the developing world; the only notable exceptions being in some Latin American countries with a high percentage of European immigrants, and in a few Asian countries, especially Japan and Singapore.

Thus the developing world threatens to be overwhelmed by its ever-growing numbers. Most countries have been slow to respond to such a challenge, for a variety of reasons. Resistance to contraception, sterilization, and abortion is deeply ingrained in some societies. Where the mass of the people are poor, large families are regarded as an insurance against old age. In Latin America, where the population is doubling every 24 years, Catholics and Communists have combined to oppose birth control, the former on Biblical grounds, the latter in the apparent belief that an unchecked population explosion will benefit the cause of world revolution. (In Brazil, where the population has in 25 years soared from 50 million to 90 million and where nearly half the people are under the age of 14, the advertising and sale of contraceptives is forbidden.)

New techniques—oral contraception (the Pill), for example, and the intra-uterine device (IUD)— are beginning to offer some chance of bringing population control within the realm of practical politics. But an immense, worldwide campaign is needed, involving huge expenditures of money, if the situation is to be saved before it is too late. The dramatic check to population growth rates achieved by Japan and by Singapore in recent years show that population control can be made to work. Perhaps spreading education and affluence are the necessary prerequisites to a really successful population policy.

The world standards of living

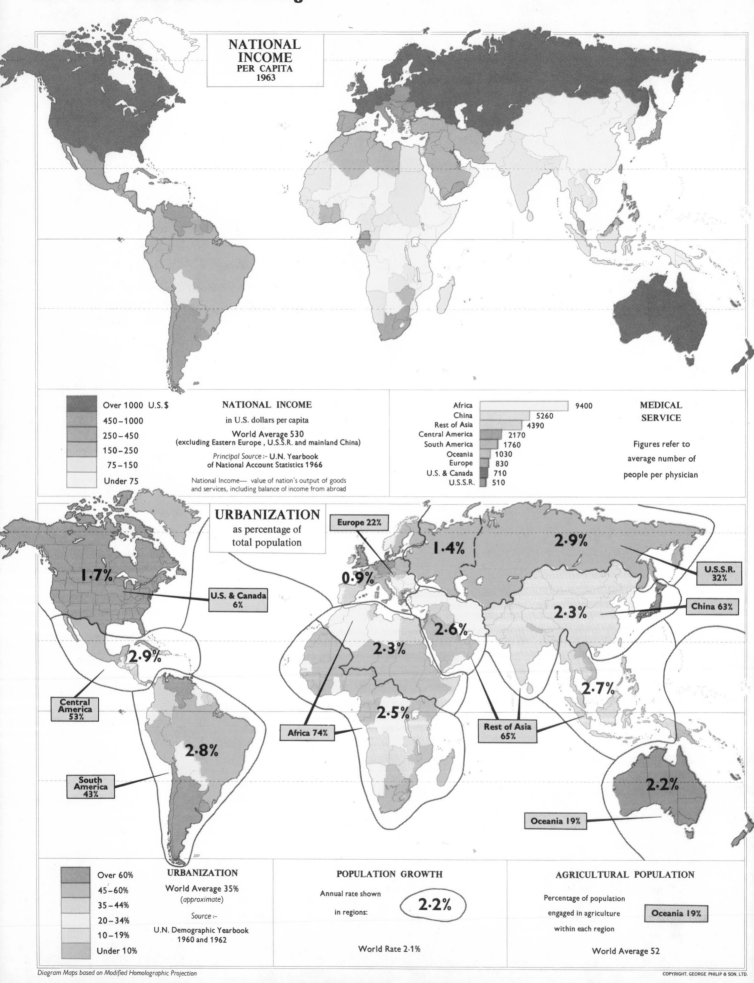

NATIONAL INCOME PER CAPITA 1963

NATIONAL INCOME
in U.S. dollars per capita

World Average 530
(excluding Eastern Europe, U.S.S.R. and mainland China)

Principal Source :- U.N. Yearbook of National Account Statistics 1966

National Income— value of nation's output of goods and services, including balance of income from abroad

Colour	Value
	Over 1000 U.S. $
	450 – 1000
	250 – 450
	150 – 250
	75 – 150
	Under 75

MEDICAL SERVICE

Figures refer to average number of people per physician

Africa	9400
China	5260
Rest of Asia	4390
Central America	2170
South America	1760
Oceania	1030
Europe	830
U.S. & Canada	710
U.S.S.R.	510

URBANIZATION
as percentage of total population

Europe 22%
U.S. & Canada 6%
U.S.S.R. 32%
China 63%
Central America 53%
Rest of Asia 65%
South America 43%
Africa 74%
Oceania 19%

1·7%
0·9%
1·4%
2·9%
2·6%
2·3%
2·3%
2·9%
2·5%
2·3%
2·7%
2·8%
2·2%

URBANIZATION

World Average 35%
(approximate)

Source :-
U.N. Demographic Yearbook
1960 and 1962

Colour	Value
	Over 60%
	45 – 60%
	35 – 44%
	20 – 34%
	10 – 19%
	Under 10%

POPULATION GROWTH

Annual rate shown in regions:

2·2%

World Rate 2·1%

AGRICULTURAL POPULATION

Percentage of population engaged in agriculture within each region

Oceania 19%

World Average 52

Diagram Maps based on Modified Homolographic Projection

COPYRIGHT. GEORGE PHILIP & SON. LTD.

Equatorial Scale 1:170,000,000

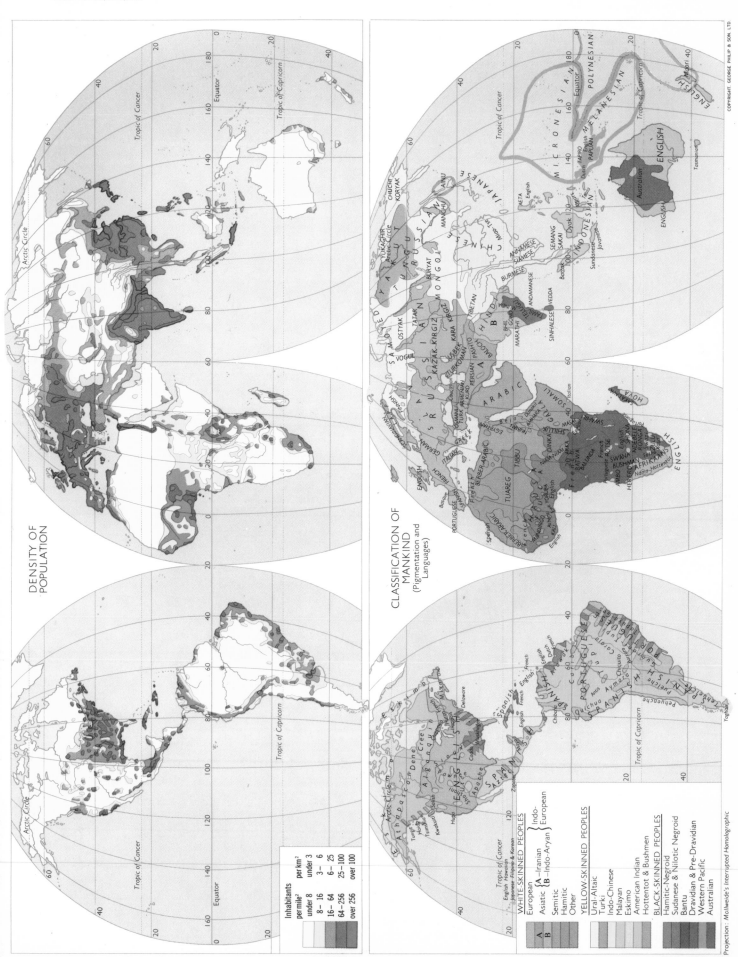

Scale 1:148,000,000

DENSITY OF POPULATION

CLASSIFICATION OF MANKIND
(Pigmentation and Languages)

Inhabitants

per mile²	per km²
under 8	under 3
8 – 16	3 – 6
16 – 64	6 – 25
64 – 256	25 – 100
over 256	over 100

WHITE-SKINNED PEOPLES
European
Asiatic { A—Iranian { Indo-
        { B—Indo-Aryan { European
Semitic
Hamitic
Other

YELLOW-SKINNED PEOPLES
Ural-Altaic
Turki
Indo-Chinese
Malayan
American Indian
Eskimo
Hottentot & Bushmen

BLACK-SKINNED PEOPLES
Hamitic-Negroid
Sudanese & Nilotic Negroid
Bantu
Dravidian & Pre-Dravidian
Western Pacific
Australian

Projection: Mollweide's Interrupted Homolographic

The world industry and agriculture

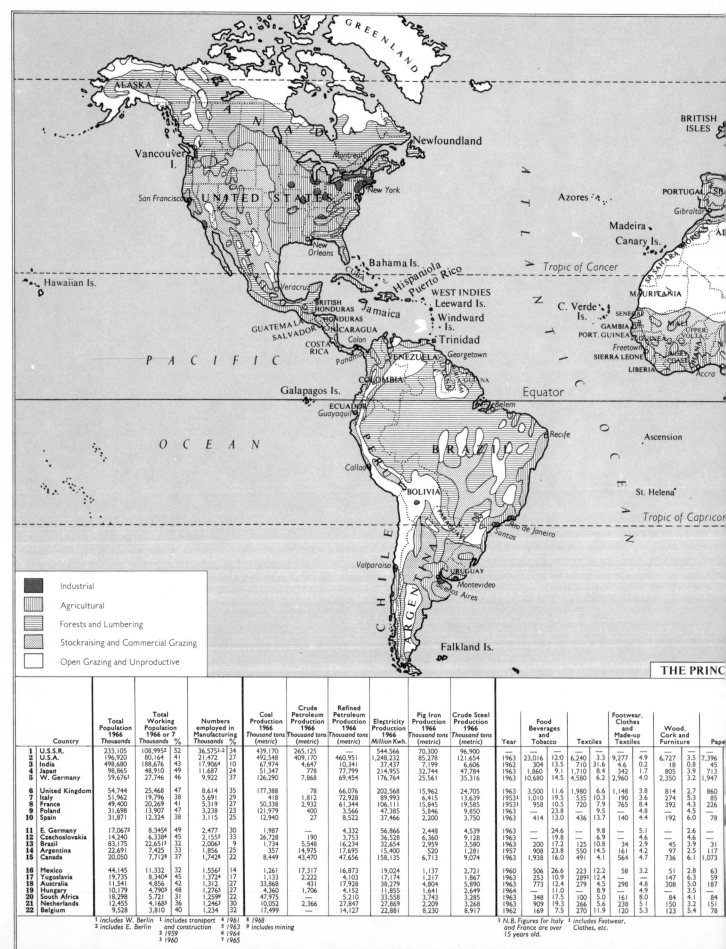

Legend:
- Industrial
- Agricultural
- Forests and Lumbering
- Stockraising and Commercial Grazing
- Open Grazing and Unproductive

THE PRINC...

#	Country	Total Population 1966 Thousands	Total Working Population 1966 or 7 Thousands	%	Numbers employed in Manufacturing Thousands	%	Coal Production 1966 Thousand tons (metric)	Crude Petroleum Production 1966 Thousand tons (metric)	Refined Petroleum Production 1966 Thousand tons (metric)	Electricity Production 1966 Million Kwh.	Pig Iron Production 1966 Thousand tons (metric)	Crude Steel Production 1966 Thousand tons (metric)	Year	Food Beverages and Tobacco		Textiles		Footwear, Clothes and Made-up Textiles		Wood, Cork and Furniture		Paper
1	U.S.S.R.	233,105	108,995[2]	52	36,575[1,2]	34	439,170	265,125	—	544,566	70,300	96,900	—	—		—		—		—		—
2	U.S.A.	196,920	80,164	41	21,472	27	492,548	409,170	460,951	1,248,232	85,278	121,654	1963	23,016	12.0	6,240	3.3	9,277	4.9	6,727	3.5	7,396
3	India	498,680	188,676	43	17,906[4]	10	67,974	4,647	10,341	37,437	7,199	6,606	1962	304	13.5	710	31.6	46	0.2	18	0.8	45
4	Japan	98,865	48,910	49	11,687	24	51,347	778	77,799	214,955	32,744	47,784	1963	1,860	9.1	1,710	8.4	342	1.7	805	3.9	713
5	W. Germany	59,676[1]	27,746	46	9,922	37	126,290	7,868	69,454	176,764	25,561	35,316	1963	10,680	14.5	4,580	6.2	2,960	4.0	2,350	3.2	1,947
6	United Kingdom	54,744	25,468	47	8,614	35	177,388	78	66,076	202,568	15,962	24,705	1963	3,500	11.6	1,980	6.6	1,148	3.8	814	2.7	860
7	Italy	51,962	19,796	38	5,691	29	418	1,812	72,928	89,993	6,415	13,639	1953[1]	1,010	19.5	535	10.3	190	3.6	274	5.3	85
8	France	49,400	20,269	41	5,319	27	50,338	2,932	61,344	106,111	15,845	19,585	1953[1]	958		720	7.9	765	8.4	392	4.3	226
9	Poland	31,698	13,907	47	3,238	23	121,979	400	3,566	47,385	5,846	9,850	1963	—	23.8	—	9.5	—	4.8	—	4.5	—
10	Spain	31,871	12,324	38	3,115	25	12,940	27	8,522	37,466	2,200	3,750	1963	414	13.0	436	13.7	140	4.4	192	6.0	78
11	E. Germany	17,067[2]	8,345[6]	49	2,477	30	1,987	—	4,332	56,866	2,448	4,539	1963	—	24.6	—	9.8	—	5.1	—	2.6	—
12	Czechoslovakia	14,240	6,338[4]	45	2,155[5]	33	26,728	190	3,753	36,528	6,360	9,128	1963	—	19.8	—	6.9	—	4.6	—	4.6	—
13	Brazil	83,175	22,651[5]	32	2,006[3]	9	1,734	5,548	16,234	32,654	2,959	3,580	1963	200	17.2	125	10.8	34	2.9	45	3.9	31
14	Argentina	22,691	7,425	33	1,856	25	357	14,975	17,695	15,400	520	1,281	1957	908	23.8	550	14.5	161	4.2	97	2.5	117
15	Canada	20,050	7,712[8]	37	1,742[8]	22	8,449	43,470	47,656	158,135	6,713	9,074	1963	1,938	16.0	491	4.1	564	4.7	736	6.1	1,073
16	Mexico	44,145	11,332	32	1,556[3]	14	1,261	17,317	16,873	19,024	1,137	2,721	1960	506	26.6	223	12.2	58	3.2	51	2.8	63
17	Yugoslavia	19,735	8,340[4]	45	1,372[4]	17	1,133	2,222	4,103	17,174	1,217	1,867	1963	253	10.9	289[1]	12.4	—	—	147	6.3	59
18	Australia	11,541	4,856	42	1,312	27	33,868	431	17,928	38,279	4,804	5,890	1963	773	12.4	279	4.5	298	4.8	308	5.9	187
19	Hungary	10,179	4,790[5]	48	1,276[5]	27	4,360	1,706	4,152	11,855	1,641	2,649	1964	—	11.0	—	8.9	—	4.9	—	3.5	—
20	South Africa	18,298	5,721	31	1,259[7]	22	47,975	—	5,210	33,558	3,743	3,285	1963	348	17.5	100	5.0	161	8.0	84	4.1	84
21	Netherlands	12,455	4,168[3]	36	1,246[3]	30	10,052	—	27,847	27,869	2,209	3,268	1963	909	19.3	266	5.6	238	5.1	150	3.2	151
22	Belgium	9,528	3,810	40	1,234		32	17,499	—	14,127	22,881	8,230	8,917	1962	169	7.5	270	11.9	120	5.3	123	5.4	78

[1] includes W. Berlin
[2] includes E. Berlin
[1] includes transport and construction
[2] 1959
[3] 1960
[4] 1961
[5] 1963
[6] 1964
[7] 1965
[8] 1968
[9] includes mining

[1] N.B. Figures for Italy and France are over 15 years old.
[1] includes Footwear, Clothes, etc.

Diagram Map based on Modified Homolographic Projection

Equatorial Scale 1:95,000,000

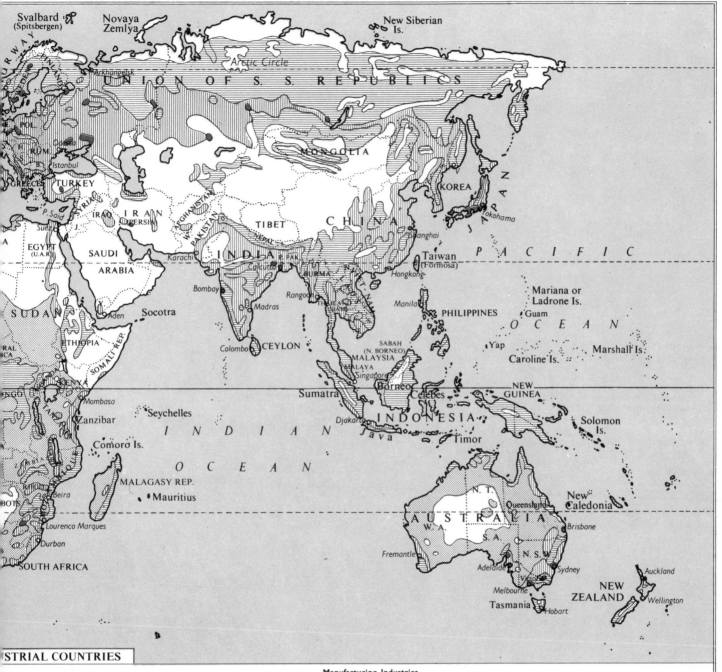

...STRIAL COUNTRIES

Manufacturing Industries

This table shows the total value added by manufacture, and the value added in particular types of industry³. (In Million U.S. dollars)

Printing and Publishing		Rubber and Leather		Chemicals, including Coal and Petrol Manufacturing		Non-metallic Manufacture		Basic Metal Industries		Machinery, Elect. appliances and Transport Equipment		Total	Index of Employment in Manufacturing 1966 1963=100	Index of Manufacturing 1966 1963=100	Index of Agricultural Production 1966 1952-6=100	Gross Domestic Product¹ 1966 Total in U.S. dollars	G.D.P. per capita in dollars	Origin % Agric.	Origin % Indust.	Origin % Other	Annual growth rate of G.D.P. 1960–66 (%)	Annual rate of population increase 1963–67 (%)	
,476	5.5	3,700	1.9	24,168	12.6	7,044	3.7	15,068	7.9	69,554	36.4	191,391	114	127	118	213,997m²	—	22	61³	17	6.5⁴,⁵	1.2	1
57	2.5	65	2.9	246	10.9	101	4.5	215	9.6	460	20.4	2,251	107	115	123	690,004m	3,504	4	39	57	5.0	1.3	2
980	4.8	417	2.0	2,530	12.4	1,010	4.9	1,700	8.3	7,380	36.5	20,500	107	138	137	41,907m	84	51	18	31	2.9	2.4	3
762	1.0	322	0.4	5,370	7.3	1,100	1.5	4,070	5.6	34,620	47.1	73,500	102	118	127	90,822m	919	12	37	51	9.8	1.0	4
																103,862m	1,740	4	53	43	4.5	1.0	5
,540	5.1	650	2.2	3,150	10.4	1,180	3.9	2,318	7.7	11,860	39.3	30,180	103	113	146	89,992m	1,644	3	48	49	3.0	0.6	6
182	3.5	117	2.2	780	15.0	226	4.4	461	8.9	1,240	24.0	5,180	95	118	130	54,022m	1,040	13	40	47	5.1	0.8	7
286	3.1	214	2.3	906	10.0	312	3.4	417	4.6	3,250	35.8	9,100	99	116	135	117,077m	2,370	8	47	45	5.2	1.0	8
—	0.7	—	2.3	—	10.2	—	3.9	—	10.7	—	27.2	—	112	129	—	32,900m²	636³	23	60³	17	6.6⁴	1.0	9
88	2.8	90	2.8	444	13.9	215	6.8	284	8.9	634	19.9	3,180	120	142	140	24,600m	636³	21	36	43	8.0	0.8	10
—	0.8	—	2.9	—	12.4	—	2.5	—	4.8	—	27.8	—¹	100	120	—	37,200m²	—	10	70³	20	3.6⁴	-0.2	11
—	0.7	—	1.3	—	8.4	—	4.4	—	10.7	—	33.6	—¹	106	121	—	24,166m²	—	13	74³	13	3.3⁴	0.6	12
27	2.3	29	2.5	154	13.3	56	4.8	137	11.8	212	18.2	1,160	—	112	157	22,720m	273	25	25	50	4.3	3.0	13
114	3.0	133	2.5	433	11.3	157	4.0	214	5.6	940	24.6	3,840	—	128	119	17,360m	765	16	44	40	2.8	1.5	14
605	5.0	237	2.0	1,154	9.6	434	3.6	1,172	9.7	3,310	27.4	12,100	116	127	144	46,947m	2,341	6	40	54	5.6	1.9	15
61	3.3	49	2.7	320	17.4	101	5.5	125	6.8	229	12.5	1,835	—	135	182	21,376m	484	17	36	47	6.0⁵	3.5	16
73	3.1	104	4.5	392	16.8	47	2.0	232	10.0	613	26.4	2,330	111	134	182	24,487m²	—	29	45³	26	7.7⁴	1.2	17
233	3.8	132	2.1	501	8.1	280	4.5	58	0.9	1,879	30.0	6,200	109	115	153	22,774m	1,973	14	40	46	6.0	1.9	18
	1.1		2.4		7.0		5.1		11.0		36.6	—¹	105	124	—	14,211m²	—	20	68³	12	5.1⁴	0.3	19
85	4.2	63	3.1	234	11.6	123	6.1	189	9.5	530	26.8	1,995	129	130	145	11,560m	559	10	41	49	6.2	2.4	20
232	4.9	71	1.5	692	14.7	183	3.9	194	4.1	1,410	29.9	4,710	100	121	136	18,657m	1,498	8	41	51	4.5	1.3	21
129	5.7	37	1.6	251	11.1	181	8.0	—	—	906¹	40.0	2,264	103	118	118	15,882m	1,667	6	42	52	4.7	0.8	22

the 'value added' is the gross value of the manufacture less the cost of the raw materials and fuel used in the manufacture.

¹ including Basic Metal Industries.

¹ as no satisfactory exchange rate can be used, only the percentage contribution by each type of industry to the total value added is given.

¹ the Gross Domestic Product, for purposes of comparison, is a measure of a country's total production of goods and services.
² the Net Material Product. This is not strictly comparable with the G.D.P., differing slightly in content.

³ includes Mining
⁴ N.M.P.
⁵ 1960-65

The world **political**

Projection: Hammer Equal Area

Scale 1:80,000,000

ARCTIC OCEAN

Franz Joseph Ld.
Novaya Zemlya
Severnaya Zemlya
Kotelny New Siberian Is.
Barents Sea
Kara Sea
Taymyr Pen. Khatanga
Laptev Sea
East Siberian Sea
Arctic Circle
North C.
Hammerfest
Murmansk
Kolguyev I.
G. of Ob
Novvy Port
Igarka
Verkhoyansk
Nizhne-Kolymsk Kolyma
Anadyr

FINLAND
White Sea
Arkhangelsk
Vorkuta
Salekhard
Lower Tunguska
Tiksi
S i b e r i a
Yakutsk REPUBLIC
Magadan
Bering Sea
Komandorskiye Is.

Helsinki
Ladoga
N. Dvina
Kotlas
Stony Tunguska Yenisey
Lena
Shelekhov G.
Kamchatka
Near Is.
Rat Is.

Stockholm
Leningrad
Gorkiy
Kazan
Perm
Sverdlovsk
UNION OF SOVIET SOCIALIST REPUBLICS
Tunguska
Vilyuysk
Okhotsk
Petropavlovsk-Kamchatskiy
L. Lopatka

Baltic Sea
Riga
Moscow
Kuybyshev
Chelyabinsk
Novosibirsk
Omsk
Tomsk
Krasnoyarsk
RUSSIAN SOVIET FEDERAL SOCIALIST
Angara
L. Baykal
Chita
Blagoveshchensk
Khabarovsk
Komsomolsk
Nikolayevsk
Sea of Okhotsk
Sakhalin

POLAND
Warsaw
Minsk
Voronezh
Saratov
Ufa
Magnitogorsk
Ishim
Barnaul
Semipalatinsk
Novokuznetsk
Yenisey Irkutsk
Ulan Ude
Selenga
Ulan Bator
Amur
Vladivostok
Sapporo
Kuril Islands

Wroclaw
Kiev
Kharkov
Donetsk
Rostov
Volgograd
Orenburg
Karaganda
Hovd
Ulyasutay
MONGOLIA
Harbin
Changchun
Mukden
Hokodate
Sendai
JAPAN

Budapest
RUMANIA
Odessa
Krasnodar
Astrakhan
Aral Sea
L. Balkhash
Syr Darya
Alma Ata
Urumchi
INNER MONGOLIA
Peking
Tientsin
Liu-ta
Pyongyang
Seoul
Kyōto
Tokyo
Yokohama

Belgrade
BULGARIA
Black Sea
Tbilisi
Baku
Caspian Sea
UZBEKISTAN
Tashkent
KIRGIZIA
SINGKIANG
Taiyuan
Tsinan
Pusan
Kōbe
Nagoya
Osaka

YUGOSLAVIA
Bucharest
Istanbul
Georgia
Grozny
Samarkand
UIGUR
CHINA
Tsingtao
Kitakyūshū

Naples
Sardinia
GREECE
Ankara
Yerevan
TURKEY
TURKMENISTAN
Dushanbe
Soche (Yarkand)
Tarim
Lanchow
Sian
Nanking
Shanghai
RYŪKYŪ Is.
PACIFIC

Sicily
MALTA
Athens
CYPRUS
Izmir
Tabriz
Ashkhabad
Mashhad
AFGHANISTAN
KASHMIR
TIBET
Chengtu
Wuhan
East China Sea
Bonin Is.
Tropic of Cancer

Mediterranean Sea
Crete
SYRIA
Aleppo
Beirut
Mosul
Tehran
IRAN
Kabul
Rawalpindi
Srinagar
Indus
Lhasa
Chungking
Changsha
Foochow
20

Tripoli
Benghazi
Tel Aviv-Jaffa
Damascus
Amman
IRAQ
Baghdad
Euphrates
(PERSIA)
Esfahan
Abadan
Quetta
Lahore
NEPAL
Brahmaputra
Kunming
Canton
Taipei
TAIWAN (FORMOSA)

Alexandria
Cairo
Jerusalem
Shiraz
Zahidan
PAKISTAN
Agra
Delhi
Kanpur
Lucknow
Varanasi
Dacca
Hankow
Hongkong

LIBYA
EGYPT (U.A.R.)
Asyut
Nejd
Kuwait
Bahrain
QATAR
TRUCIAL OMAN
Karachi
Ahmadabad
INDIA
Calcutta
BURMA
Hanoi
VIET-NAM
Hué
South China Sea
Mariana or Ladrone Is.
Wake I. (U.S.)

Libyan Desert
Aswan
Medina
Riyadh
Muscat
Bombay
Nagpur
Bay of Bengal
Mandalay
Wake I.

NIGER
CHAD
Hejaz
Mecca
SAUDI ARABIA
OMAN
Arabian Sea
Poona
Hyderabad
Rangoon
Vientiane
THAILAND (SIAM)
Bangkok
Manila
PHILIPPINES
Guam (U.S.)
Marshall Is.

Sahara
SUDAN
Omdurman
Khartoum
Atbara
Port Sudan
YEMEN
SOUTH YEMEN
Aden
G. of Aden
Bangalore
Madras
Andaman Is.
CAMBODIA
Phnom Penh
G. of Siam
Saigon-Cholon
Cebu
Yap
Palau
Caroline Is.
(U.S. Trust Territory)
OCEAN

NIGERIA
L. Chad
Ft. Lamy
El Obied
Blue Nile
TALT. (Fr.)
Djibouti
SOMALI REP.
Berbera
Ras Asir (C. Guardafui)
Laccadive Is. (India)
Tiruchchirappalli
Nicobar Is. (India)
Georgetown
MALAYSIA
SABAH
Truk
Ponape
Jaluit

CAMEROON
Douala
CENTRAL AFRICA
Bangui
Addis Ababa
ETHIOPIA
Berbera
SOMALI
Colombo
CEYLON
Dondra Hd.
Kuala Lumpur
MALAYA
Kuching
SARAWAK
Brunei
Gilbert Is. (Br.)

RIO MUNI
GABON
CONGO
Kisangani
UGANDA
KENYA
Kampala
Kismayu
Maldive Is.
Medan
Singapore
Borneo
Nauru

Yaoundé
Brazzaville
Kinshasa
Kasai
RWANDA
BURUNDI
Nairobi
Equator
Sumatra
INDONESIA
Bandjarmasin
Sulawesi
Moluccas
TERR. OF NEW GUINEA (Australian Trust Territory)
Admiralty
Sukarnapura
New Ireland

Luanda
Luluabourg
Kigoma
TANZANIA
Dar-es-Salaam
Zanzibar
Mombasa
Amirante Is. (Br.)
Seychelles (Br.)
Chagos Arch.
INDIAN
Palembang
Makasar
New Guinea
Rabaul
NEW BRITAIN

ANGOLA
Lubumbashi
Llongwe
MALAWI
BRITISH INDIAN OCEAN TERR. Diego Garcia
Djakarta
Java
Bandung
Surabaja
Sunda Islands
PAPUA
Port Moresby
C. York
Solomon Is.
Ellice Is. Funafuti

Benguela
ZAMBIA
Lusaka
Zambesi
Salisbury
OCEAN
Cargados Garajos (Br.)
Timor
Timor Sea
Arafura Sea
Torres Str.
Louisade Arch.
Santa Cruz Is. (Br.)
Rotuma (Br.)

Ossamedes
Comoro Is. (Fr.)
MALAGASY REPUBLIC
Tamatave
Cocos or Keeling Is. (Australia)
Christmas I. (Australia)
Darwin
Coral Sea
New (Br.-Fr.) Hebrides
Vanua Levu
Fiji Is.
Viti Levu
Suva

C. Fria
RHODESIA
Bulawayo
Mozambique
Madagascar
Rodriguez
Réunion (Fr.)
Mauritius
NORTHERN TERRITORY
Cairns
New Caledonia
Nouméa

S.W. AFRICA
BOTSWANA
Windhoek
Gaberones
Beira
Mt. Isa
Townsville
Norfolk I. (Australia)
Lord Howe I. (Australia)

Walvis Bay
Kalahari
Pretoria
Johannesburg
SWAZ.
Tropic of Capricorn
North West C.
WESTERN AUSTRALIA
Meekatharra
Alice Springs
L. Eyre
QUEENSLAND
Rockhampton
20

Luanda
ANGOLA
Orange
Lourenço Marques
Delagoa B.
Geraldton
Perth
Kalgoorlie
SOUTH AUSTRALIA
Brisbane
NEW SOUTH WALES
Newcastle

C. Agulhas
SOUTH AFRICA
Durban
Amsterdam (Fr.)
St. Paul (Fr.)
Fremantle
AUSTRALIA
Sydney

Cape Town
C. of Good Hope
Port Elizabeth
East London
C. Leeuwin
Great Australian Bight
Albany
Adelaide
Murray
VICTORIA
Canberra
C. Howe
North C.
Auckland

Pr. Edward Is. (South Africa)
Crozet Is. (Fr.)
Kerguelen (Fr.)
Melbourne
Bass Str.
Tasman Sea
NEW ZEALAND
Wellington

McDonald I. Heard I. (Australia)
TASMANIA
Hobart
Christchurch
South I.
North I.

SOUTHERN OCEAN
Stewart I.
Dunedin
Antipodes Is. (N.Z.)
Auckland I. (N.Z.)

King Haakon VII Sea
Enderby Land
Antarctic Circle
Wilkes Land
S. Magnetic Pole 1965
Macquarie I. (Australia)
Campbell I. (N.Z.)
Bounty Is.

DEPENDENCY
AUSTRALIAN DEPENDENCY
20 40 60 80 100 120
from Greenwich
ADELIE LAND
Balleny Is.
Ross Sea

The world political, religious, and colonial aspects

The world: alliances and alignments

NATO
North Atlantic Treaty Organization

Belgium	Italy
Canada	Luxembourg
Denmark	Netherlands
France	Norway
Germany	Portugal
(Federal Republic)	Turkey
Greece	United Kingdom
Iceland	United States

Warsaw Pact

Bulgaria
Czechoslovakia
Germany
(Democratic Republic)
Hungary
Poland
Rumania
Soviet Union

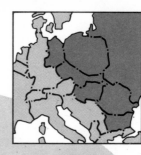

NATIONAL ALIGNMENTS

- ⬤ Western, or countries linked by military agreements with West
- ⬤ Countries officially non-aligned but with strong links with West
- ⬤ Non-aligned
- ⬤ Non-aligned countries having close links with the communist bloc
- ⬤ Communist

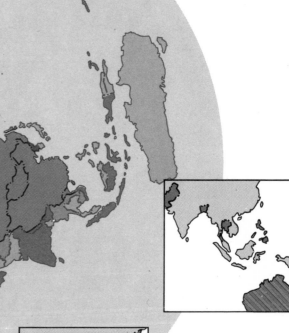

OAS
Organization of American States

Argentina	Honduras
Barbados	Mexico
Bolivia	Nicaragua
Brazil	Panama
Chile	Paraguay
Colombia	Peru
Costa Rica	Trinidad & Tobago
Dominican Republic	United States
Ecuador	Uruguay
El Salvador	Venezuela
Guatemala	
Haiti	

OAU
Organization of African Unity

All states of Africa except
South Africa and Rhodesia.
(Also excluded are the
Portuguese territories of Angola,
Mozambique, and Portuguese Guinea)

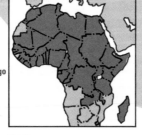

COLOMBO PLAN + ASEAN

Colombo Plan

Afghanistan	Laos
Australia	Malaysia
Bhutan	Maldive Islands
Burma	Nepal
Cambodia	New Zealand
Canada	Pakistan
Ceylon	Philippines
India	Singapore
Indonesia	Thailand
Iran	United Kingdom
Japan	United States
S. Korea	S. Vietnam

ASEAN
Association of South-East
Asian Nations

Indonesia	Malaysia
Thailand	Singapore
Philippines	

SEATO + ANZUS
South East Asia Treaty Organization

Australia	Philippines
France	Thailand
New Zealand	United Kingdom
Pakistan	United States

ANZUS Treaty

Australia
New Zealand
United States

CENTO
Central Treaty Organization

Iran
Pakistan
Turkey
Britain
United Kingdom
United States

Arab League

Algeria	Libya
Egypt	Morocco
Iraq	Saudi Arabia
Jordan	Sudan
Kuwait	Syria
Lebanon	Tunisia
	Yemen

Religious differences

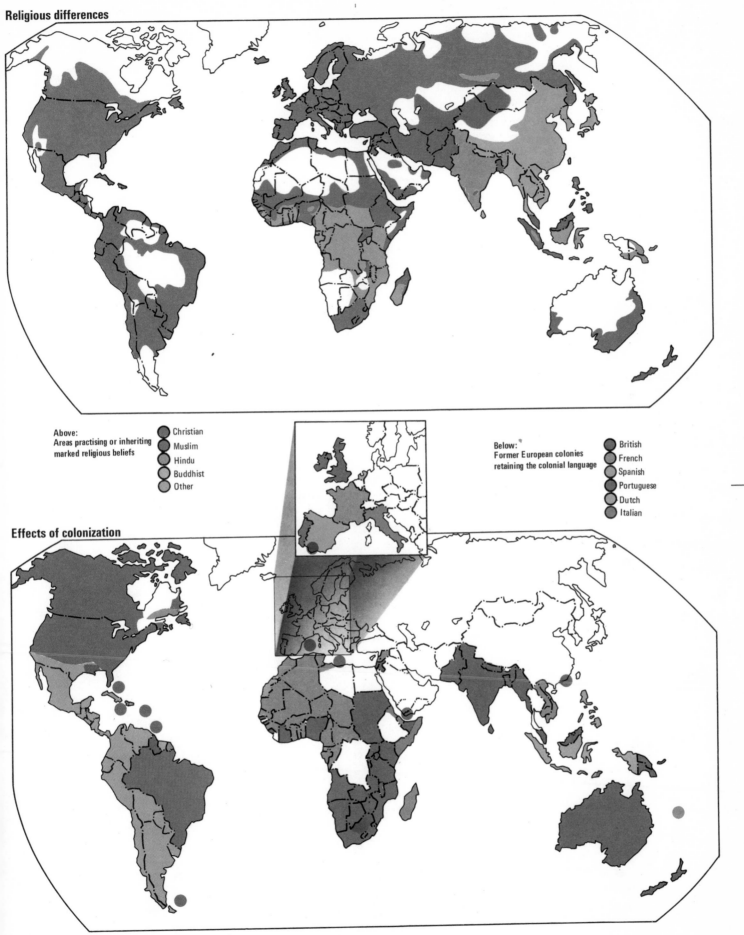

Above:
Areas practising or inheriting marked religious beliefs

- Christian
- Muslim
- Hindu
- Buddhist
- Other

Below:
Former European colonies retaining the colonial language

- British
- French
- Spanish
- Portuguese
- Dutch
- Italian

Effects of colonization

The world **space race**

Spending on space

Since space technology is closely linked with missile development, military considerations also provide an impetus for the space race. When President John F. Kennedy announced in May 1961 that the United States would put a man on the Moon before the end of 1969, it was widely interpreted as a challenge to the Soviet Union.

Russia had acquired an early lead in the space race by the launching of Sputnik I in October 1957. Russia, too, was the first to put a man into orbit—in April 1961.

In the late 1960s, however, the Russians showed signs of having abandoned the Moon race. Soviet scientists emphasized the greater value of exploring the Moon by instruments (an attitude shared by some American scientists). Consequently, it was two Americans who were the first men to land on the lunar surface—on July 20, 1969.

Although neither the Moon nor orbiting space stations appear at present to lend themselves to aggressive military purposes, a "space confrontation" could theoretically develop if one country were to interfere with another's satellites. In addition to scientific and communications purposes, Russian and American "spy" satellites provide a continuous picture of military developments in each country's territory, using optical, radar, and infrared cameras.

Principal space launching sites and rocket ranges

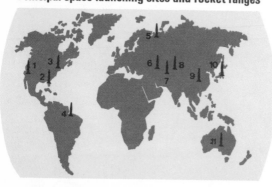

1 Vandenberg, California
2 Cape Kennedy, Florida
3 Wallops Island, Virginia
4 Kourou, French Guiana
5 Plesetsk, USSR
6 Kapustin Yar, USSR
7 Tyuratam, USSR
8 Baykonur, USSR
9 Lop Nor, China
10 Uchinoura, Japan
11 Woomera, Australia

A summary of space launches

	USSR	USA	Others	Outside Earth's orb
Scientific research				
Military (reconnaissance, communications, etc.)				
Civil (communications, meteorological, etc.)				
Manned space launches				

1957
1958
1959
1960
1961
1962
1963
1964
1965
1966
1967
1968
1969

Achievements in space

Sputnik 1 — Sputnik 2 — Explorer 1 — Vanguard 1

Sputnik 3 — Score — Luna 1 — Discoverer 2 — Explorer 6

Luna 2 — Luna 3 — Pioneer 5 — Tiros 1 — Transit 1B

Transit 2A Greb 1 — Echo 1 — Sputnik 5 — Venus 1

Explorer 9 — Vostok 1 — Mercury 6 — OSO 1 — Cosmos 1

Ariel 1 — Telstar 1 — Vostok 3 and 4 — Anna 1B

Syncom 1 — Vostok 6 — Vela 1 — Echo 2 — Ariel 2

Ranger 7 — Syncom 3 — Nimbus 1 — Voskhod 1

Mariner 4 — Pegasus 1 — Voskhod 2 — Gemini 3

Early Bird — Molniya 1A — Proton 1 — Asterix 1

Gemini 7 — Luna 9 — Luna 10 — Surveyor 1 — Lunar Orbiter 1

ATS 1 — Soyuz 1 — Venus 4 — Mariner 5

Cosmos 186 and 188 — Iris — Zond 5

Zond 6 — Apollo 8 — Soyuz 4 and 5 — Apollo 10

Apollo 11 — Apollo 13 — First Chinese satellite (Actual shape unknown) — Soyuz 9

The world **military technology**

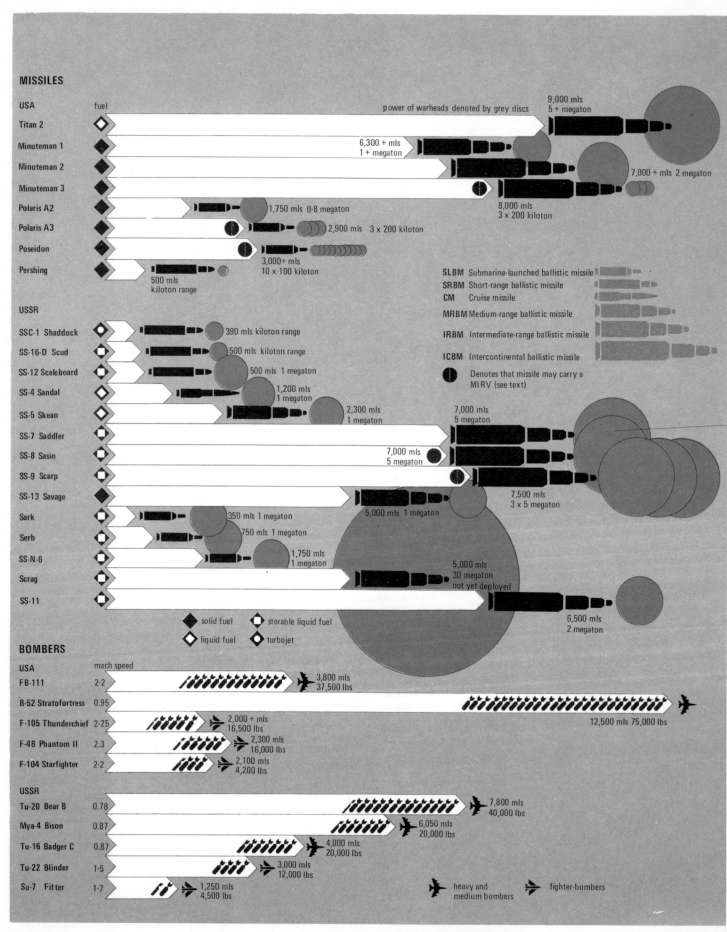

MISSILES

USA

	fuel		power of warheads denoted by grey discs

Titan 2 — 9,000 mls 5 + megaton

Minuteman 1 — 6,300 + mls 1 + megaton

Minuteman 2 — 7,000 + mls 2 megaton

Minuteman 3 — 8,000 mls 3 x 200 kiloton

Polaris A2 — 1,750 mls 0·8 megaton

Polaris A3 — 2,900 mls 3 x 200 kiloton

Poseidon — 3,000+ mls 10 x 100 kiloton

Pershing — 500 mls kiloton range

USSR

SSC-1 Shaddock — 390 mls kiloton range

SS-16-D Scud — 500 mls kiloton range

SS-12 Scaleboard — 500 mls 1 megaton

SS-4 Sandal — 1,200 mls 1 megaton

SS-5 Skean — 2,300 mls 1 megaton

SS-7 Saddler — 7,000 mls 5 megaton

SS-8 Sasin — 7,000 mls 5 megaton

SS-9 Scarp — 7,500 mls 3 x 5 megaton

SS-13 Savage — 5,000 mls 1 megaton

Sark — 350 mls 1 megaton

Serb — 750 mls 1 megaton

SS-N-6 — 1,750 mls 1 megaton

Scrag — 5,000 mls 30 megaton not yet deployed

SS-11 — 6,500 mls 2 megaton

SLBM Submarine-launched ballistic missile
SRBM Short-range ballistic missile
CM Cruise missile
MRBM Medium-range ballistic missile
IRBM Intermediate-range ballistic missile
ICBM Intercontinental ballistic missile

Denotes that missile may carry a MIRV (see text)

◆ solid fuel   ◈ storable liquid fuel
◇ liquid fuel   ◈ turbojet

BOMBERS

USA

	mach speed		

FB-111 — 2·2 — 3,800 mls 37,500 lbs

B-52 Stratofortress — 0·95 — 12,500 mls 75,000 lbs

F-105 Thunderchief — 2·25 — 2,000 + mls 16,500 lbs

F-4B Phantom II — 2·3 — 2,300 mls 16,000 lbs

F-104 Starfighter — 2·2 — 2,100 mls 4,200 lbs

USSR

Tu-20 Bear B — 0·78 — 7,800 mls 40,000 lbs

Mya-4 Bison — 0·87 — 6,050 mls 20,000 lbs

Tu-16 Badger C — 0·87 — 4,000 mls 20,000 lbs

Tu-22 Blinder — 1·5 — 3,000 mls 12,000 lbs

Su-7 Fitter — 1·7 — 1,250 mls 4,500 lbs

heavy and medium bombers   fighter-bombers

Spending on "overkill"

Both the Soviet Union and the United States possess sufficient nuclear destructive power to destroy each other many times over—sometimes called an "overkill" capacity. But the situation, in strategic terms, is not as nonsensical as it may seem. The large number of weapons on each side is dictated by the policy of maintaining enough to survive an attack by the other party and to retaliate. In theory nuclear weapons do not have to be used to achieve their effect; the *threat* to use them should be sufficient. But where both sides know that a nuclear exchange means mutual annihilation, the tendency is to reopen the possibility of "conventional" war, or to encourage aggression at a lower level, that of subversion, against which nuclear weapons offer no defence.

Between 1962 and 1967 world expenditure on arms and military services increased by 50 per cent, from $120,000 million to $182,000 million. More money is now being spent on weapons than at any time except during World War II. According to the *Unesco Courier*, this represents seven per cent of the world's gross product, a sum equal to the combined incomes of all the 1000 million people who live in Latin America, South Asia, and the Near East. Figures show that between 1964 and 1967, for instance, the developed countries were spending an average of $170 per capita, against an average of only $8 per capita in the developing countries. But since the latter contain nearly three quarters of the world's population, that burden is extremely heavy.

The nuclear weapons systems available to the Soviet Union and to the United States comprise three main components: the warhead, the delivery vehicle (missile or bomber), and the guidance system. Warheads come in many different sizes, partly reflecting the purpose for which they are intended. Nearly all strategic warheads today carry hydrogen (fusion) bombs. They range from about 1 megaton—equivalent to 1 million tons of TNT—to a possible 30 megatons. (The first atomic bomb, dropped on Hiroshima (1945), had an explosive power equal to 20,000 tons of TNT.) The damage and casualties they can cause depend partly on the height at which they are exploded. A high-level burst causes the most widespread damage; a low-level or ground burst has a more concentrated effect and would be used, for example, against an opponent's underground launching sites. In general a number of smaller warheads would do more damage than a single warhead of equivalent megatonnage, because much of the force of a large explosion is wasted. This has led to the development of the system known as MIRVs (Multiple Individually Targetable Re-entry Vehicles), which can be electronically guided to individual targets after separation. MIRVs can be fitted to the American Poseidon (sea-based) and Minuteman 3 (land-based) missiles, as well as to the land-based Soviet SS-9. The MIRV offers a means of confusing and saturating anti-missile defences, although it was actually thought of before the anti-ballistic missile (ABM) system.

Nuclear weapons are frequently classified as "strategic" or "tactical". Usually strategic weapons mean inter-continental ballistic missile (ICBM) or bomber delivery systems with ranges of 6000–8000 miles; or submarine-launched intermediate-range missiles with ranges of about 3000 miles. They have the capacity to destroy an opponent's cities or his strategic weapons.

Tactical weapons generally mean battlefield weapons. They are usually of the fission, or A-bomb, type, and may have a deliberately restricted radius of damage. But the idea that a war might be confined to the use of tactical nuclear weapons has been generally discarded.

The Soviet Union possesses a number of strategic medium-range missiles (MRBMs), with a range of about 2000 miles, which are directed on targets in Western Europe and, reportedly, in China.

(The relative strengths of the United States and the USSR in nuclear missiles are set out on p. 22.)

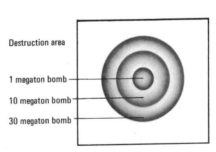

Destruction area

1 megaton bomb

10 megaton bomb

30 megaton bomb

Diagram (**left**) lists the principal American and Russian missiles and bombers, together with their maximum ranges, capable of carrying nuclear warheads. Soviet missiles and aircraft are designated by their NATO code names.

City targets

London

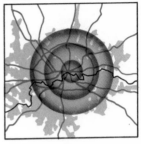

Washington

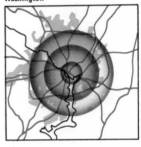

Detroit

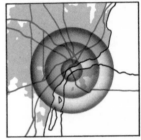

Los Angeles

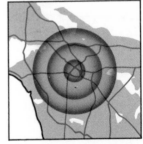

Moscow

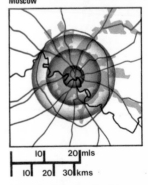

Five major cities, showing the maximum area of destruction likely to be caused by a one-megaton, a 10-megaton, and a 30-megaton warhead.

The world nuclear balance

Missile strengths

Apart from the Soviet Union and the United States, three other countries—Britain, France, and China—now possess nuclear weapons. And probably eight other countries could find the skills and resources needed to develop their own nuclear capability at short notice. These are Canada, India, Israel, Italy, Japan, Poland, Sweden, and West Germany.

The symbols set out on this page indicate the relative strengths of the United States and the Soviet Union in nuclear missiles. (It may be useful to compare this information with that relating to military technology, which was set out on pages 20 and 21.) But not all the factors that make up the strategic "balance" can be depicted graphically. Soviet missiles, for example, are often designed to carry much larger warheads. The Russian SS-9 missile can carry a warhead of up to 25 megatons, whereas the largest of America's present missiles, the Titan 2, has a warhead of only a little over 5 megatons.

Ever since the late 1950s—when the Soviet Union and the United States first reached the position of being able to threaten each other with near total destruction—each side has aimed at having enough nuclear forces to survive an initial attack and still be able to deliver an "unacceptable" counter-blow.

But as stockpiles grow and offensive missiles become more accurate, the situation could arise in which one side might be tempted to launch a devastating first strike, destroying its opponent's forces completely.

Current developments of multiple warheads and of bomber-launched air-to-surface missiles could give America a total of 11,000 nuclear warheads by 1975, compared with its 1970 total of 4200. The Soviet Union, which is also developing MIRVs (p. 21), is capable of achieving a similar percentage increase on its current strength of 1800 warheads.

Nuclear weapons are not the only means of mass destruction available to a determined or unscrupulous nation. There now exists various kinds of deadly bacteria that can, even in absurdly small concentrations, wipe out whole populations. One pound of a bacteriological agent, botulinum toxin (Type A), would kill everyone in the world, if suitably distributed. So would 30 tons of a nerve gas called tabun.

Except for gas in World War I, lethal chemical agents have not yet been used on a large scale. But big stocks are held by the major military powers.

Diagram (top) sets out the number of missiles and bombers held by the five powers that now possess nuclear weapons. The other diagram shows how rapidly the number of ICBMs (intercontinental ballistic missiles) and submarine-launched missiles held by the United States and the Soviet Union has grown in the past decade.

Missiles and bombers: the strategic balance

Each symbol equals 20

	Land-based ICBMs	Submarine-launched missiles	Long-range heavy bombers	Medium-range bombers
USA	1,054	656	450	60
UK		48		50
France				a few
China				a few
USSR	1,050	160	200	1,050

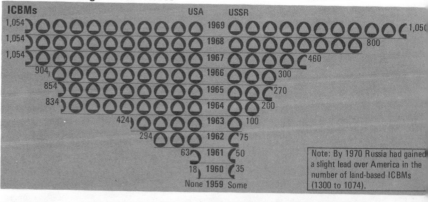

Growth of strategic missile forces

ICBMs

	USA		USSR	
1,054		1969		1,050
1,054		1968		800
1,054		1967		460
904		1966		300
854		1965		270
834		1964		200
424		1963		100
294		1962		75
63		1961		50
18		1960		35
None		1959		Some

Note: By 1970 Russia had gained a slight lead over America in the number of land-based ICBMs (1300 to 1074).

Submarine-launched missiles

	USA		USSR	
656		1969		160
656		1968		130
656		1967		130
592		1966		125
496		1965		120
416		1964		120
224		1963		100
144		1962		Some
96		1961		Some
32		1960		None
None		1959		None

Polar confrontation

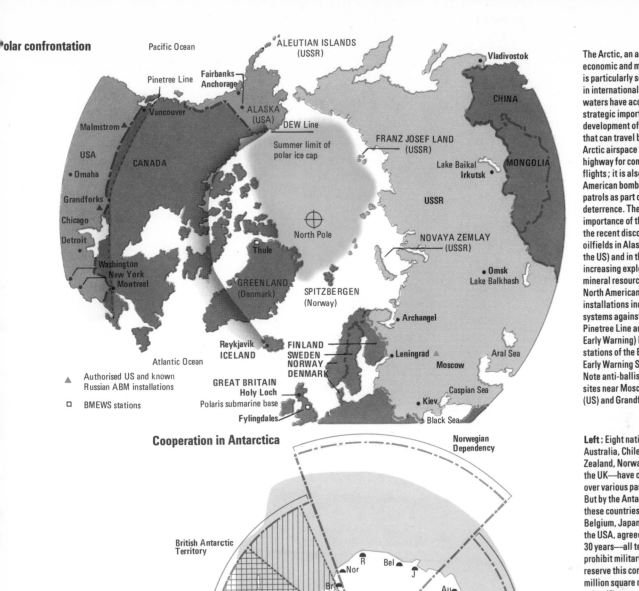

Pacific Ocean

ALEUTIAN ISLANDS (USSR)

Vladivostok

CHINA

Pinetree Line

Fairbanks
Anchorage

Vancouver

Malmstrom ▲

ALASKA (USA)

DEW Line

FRANZ JOSEF LAND (USSR)

Lake Baikal
Irkutsk

MONGOLIA

USA

CANADA

Summer limit of polar ice cap

USSR

Omaha

Grandforks ▲

Chicago

Detroit

North Pole ⊕

NOVAYA ZEMLAY (USSR)

Thule

Omsk
Lake Balkhash

Washington
New York
Montreal

GREENLAND (Denmark)

SPITZBERGEN (Norway)

Archangel

Reykjavik
ICELAND

Atlantic Ocean

FINLAND
SWEDEN
NORWAY
DENMARK

Leningrad ▲

Moscow

Aral Sea

▲ Authorised US and known
Russian ABM installations

GREAT BRITAIN
Holy Loch

Caspian Sea

□ BMEWS stations

Polaris submarine base

Kiev

Fylingdales

Black Sea

The Arctic, an area of growing economic and military significance, is particularly sensitive to changes in international tension. Arctic waters have acquired a new strategic importance with the development of nuclear submarines that can travel beneath the ice cap. Arctic airspace has become a highway for commercial transpolar flights; it is also used by American bombers flying nuclear patrols as part of the system of deterrence. The growing economic importance of the region is seen in the recent discovery of large oilfields in Alaska (the 49th state of the US) and in the Soviet Union's increasing exploitation of the mineral resources of Siberia. North American defence installations include two radar systems against bombers—the Pinetree Line and DEW (Distant Early Warning) Line—and radar stations of the Ballistic Missile Early Warning System (BMEWS). Note anti-ballistic missile (ABM) sites near Moscow, Malmstrom (US) and Grandforks.

Cooperation in Antarctica

Norwegian Dependency

British Antarctic Territory

Nor

Bel

J

Br

Au

Arg

US

Au

South Pole(US) ⊕

R

Australian Dependency

R

R

Limit of Polar ice

R

0   400 mls
0   800 kms

US

NZ

Au

⬤ Scientific bases

US

Arg   Argentina
Au   Australia
Bel   Belgium
Fr   France
J   Japan
NZ   New Zealand
R   USSR
US   United States

US/NZ

Fr

French Dependency

Australian Dependency

|||| Claimed by Argentina

— Claimed by Chile

New Zealand Dependency

Left: Eight nations—Argentina, Australia, Chile, France, New Zealand, Norway, the USSR, and the UK—have claimed sovereignty over various parts of Antarctica. But by the Antarctica Treaty (1961), these countries, together with Belgium, Japan, South Africa, and the USA, agreed to suspend—for 30 years—all territorial claims, to prohibit military activities, and to reserve this continent of five million square miles for joint scientific research. Since 1961 Poland, the Netherlands, Denmark, and Czechoslovakia have also signed the treaty.

Below: Since 1945, when the US carried out its first atomic bomb test, the number of countries with nuclear weapons has increased at the rate of about one every five years. Progress from the A-bomb to the H-bomb has generally taken four to six years. China's progress was particularly fast.

The nuclear race: time taken to acquire the H-bomb

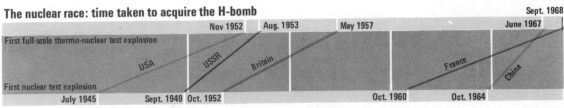

Sept. 1968

Nov 1952   Aug. 1953   May 1957   June 1967

First full-scale thermo-nuclear test explosion

USA   USSR   Britain   France   China

First nuclear test explosion

July 1945   Sept. 1949   Oct. 1952   Oct. 1960   Oct. 1964

1900-50

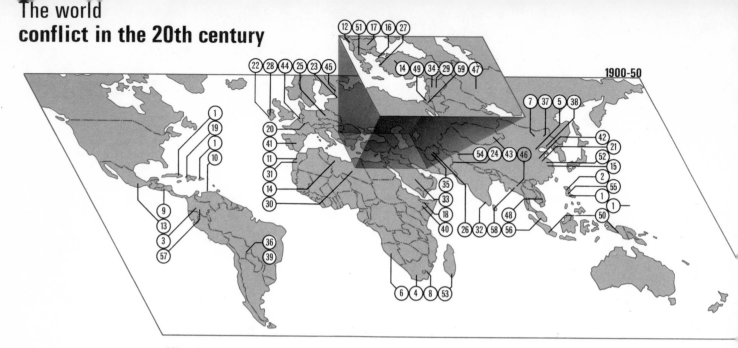

War, insurrection, and use of force

As this century has progressed, conflict between states, and between governments and insurgent forces, has become more frequent—though this partly reflects the increase in the number of new states in the post-colonial era.

In general, wars have become smaller in scale, and since World War II the major powers have shown a reluctance to become involved in set-piece military confrontations between lesser states—except in Korea and Vietnam.

The existence of nuclear weapons may have made the developed countries more reluctant to engage in major war, but it has not prevented poorer countries from frequent recourse to arms. The list below is based on the definition of conflict adopted by David Wood in his paper "Conflict in the Twentieth Century" published by the Institute for Strategic Studies in 1968.

That is to say, the conflicts indicated have involved the use of regular forces on at least one side and the use of weapons of war with intent to kill or wound over a period of at least one hour.

1 Spanish-American War: 1898
2 Philippine Insurrection: 1899–1902
3 Colombian Civil War: 1899–1902
4 Boer War (South Africa): 1899–1902
5 Boxer Expedition (China): 1900–01
6 Herero Revolt (German SW Africa): 1903–08
7 Russo-Japanese War: 1904–05
8 Zulu Revolt (Natal): 1906
9 Central American War (Guatemala, Honduras, Nicaragua, Salvador): 1906–07
10 Dutch-Venezuelan Naval Action: 1908
11 Spanish-Moroccan War: 1909–10
12 Albanian Revolt against Turkey: 1910
13 Mexican Civil War: 1910–20
14 Italo-Turkish War: 1911–12
15 Revolt against Manchus (China): 1911–12
16 First Balkan War (Bulgaria, Greece, Montenegro, Serbia, Turkey): 1912–13
17 Second Balkan War (Bulgaria, Greece, Rumania, Serbia, Turkey): 1913
18 British Somaliland Insurgency: 1913–20
19 US Invasion of Haiti: 1914
20 World War 1: 1914–18
21 Chinese Civil Wars: 1916–36

22 Irish Rebellion: 1916
23 Russian Revolution and Civil War: 1917–20
24 Amritsar Incident (India): 1919
25 Russo-Polish War: 1919–21
26 Third Afghan War (Britain-Afghanistan): 1919
27 Graeco-Turkish War: 1919–24
28 Irish Civil War: 1920–22
29 French Annexation of Syria: 1920
30 Italian Conquest of Libya: 1920–32
31 Rif War (France, Spain, Moroccan nationalists): 1921–25
32 Moplah Rebellion (India): 1921–22
33 Saudi Conquest of Arabia: 1924–25
34 Syrian Revolt: 1925–26
35 Afghan Civil War: 1928–29
36 Chaco War (Bolivia-Paraguay): 1928–35
37 Soviet Operations in Manchuria: 1929
38 Manchurian Hostilities (China-Japan): 1931–33
39 Brazil Civil Disturbances: 1932
40 Abyssinian War: 1935–36
41 Spanish Civil War: 1936–39
42 Sino-Japanese War: 1937–41
43 Soviet-Japanese Border Fighting: 1938–39
44 World War II (Europe): 1939–45
45 Russo-Finnish War: 1939–40
46 World War II (Asia): 1941–45
47 Soviet-supported Insurgency in Iran: 1941–45
48 First Indo-China War: 1945–48
49 Palestine Troubles: 1945–48
50 Indonesia War of Independence: 1945–49
51 Greek Civil War: 1946–49
52 Chinese Civil War: 1946–49
53 Madagascar Uprising: 1947
54 Kashmir Hostilities: 1947–49
55 Hukbalahap Rebellion (Philippines): 1948–54
56 Malayan Emergency: 1948–60
57 Colombian Civil War: 1948–53
58 Burmese Civil War: 1948–54
59 First Arab-Israeli War: 1948–49

Diagram (opposite) lists the number of people – military and civilian – who have been killed in the four major wars of the 20th century. (No reliable figure is available for the hundreds of thousands of civilians who have died on both sides in the Vietnam War.) Since World War II there has not been a formal declaration of war anywhere.

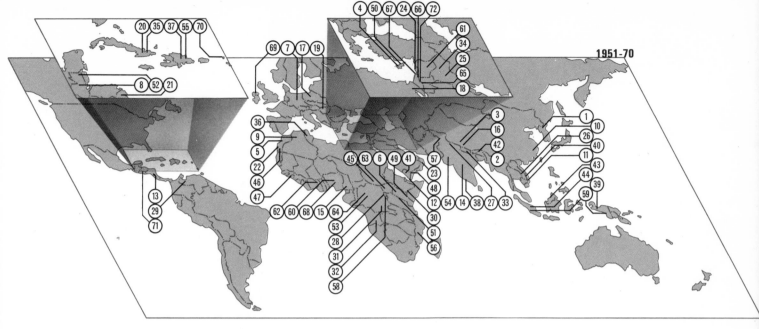

1 Korean War: 1950–53	**37** Dominican Republic Crisis: 1961–62
2 Burmese Border Troubles: 1950–54	**38** Indian Invasion of Goa: 1961
3 Chinese Invasion of Tibet: 1950–51	**39** West Irian Campaign (Indonesia): 1962
4 Cyprus Emergency: 1952–59	**40** Third Indo-China War (US-North Vietnam): 1962
5 Moroccan Revolt: 1952–56	**41** Yemen Civil War: 1962
6 Mau-Mau Revolt (Kenya): 1952–57	**42** Chinese Invasion of India: 1962
7 East German Rising: 1953	**43** Brunei Revolt (Borneo): 1962
8 American Intervention in Guatemala: 1954	**44** Indonesia-Malaysia Confrontation: 1963–66
9 Algerian Revolutionary War: 1954–62	**45** Sudan Civil War: 1963
10 Quemoy-Matsu Bombardments: 1954–58	**46** Algerian-Moroccan Border Fighting: 1963
11 Second Indo-China War (South Vietnam-Vietcong insurgents): 1954–62	**47** Portuguese Guinea Insurgency: 1963–66, 1967–68
12 Aden-Yemen Border Troubles: 1955–59	**48** Aden Troubles: 1963–67
13 Nicaragua-Costa Rica Dispute: 1955	**49** Kenya-Somalia Border Fighting: 1963–67
14 Naga Revolt (India): 1955–62 and 1968	**50** Cyprus Troubles: 1963–64
15 Cameroon Civil War: 1955–61	**51** East African Mutinies: 1964
16 Tibetan Revolt: 1955–59	**52** Guatemala Insurgency: 1964
17 Poznan Riots (Poland): 1956	**53** Congo Rebellion: 1964
18 Second Arab-Israeli War: 1956	**54** Rann of Kutch Incident (India): 1965
19 Hungarian Uprising: 1956	**55** Dominican Civil War: 1965
20 Cuban Civil War: 1956–58	**56** Mozambique Insurgency: 1965
21 Honduras-Nicaragua Dispute: 1957	**57** India-Pakistan War: 1965
22 Spanish Morocco Border Fighting (Morocco-Spain): 1957–58	**58** Burundi Revolt (Central Africa): 1965
23 Muscat-Oman Revolt: 1957	**59** Indonesia Internal Troubles: 1965–66
24 Lebanese Civil War: 1958	**60** Nigerian Coup d'etat: 1966
25 Mosul Revolt (Iraq): 1959	**61** Syrian Coup d'etat: 1966
26 Laos Civil War: 1959	**62** Ghana Coup d'etat: 1966
27 Longju and Ladakh Incidents (China-India): 1959	**63** Ugandan Coup d'etat: 1966
28 Ruanda-Urundi Tribal Warfare: 1959	**64** Kisangani Mutiny (Congo): 1966
29 Venezuelan Insurgency: 1960–66	**65** Es-Samu Incident (Israel-Jordan): 1966
30 Somalia-Ethiopia Border Troubles: 1960–64	**66** Lake Tiberias Incident (Syria-Israel): 1967
31 Congo Civil War: 1960–64	**67** Third Arab-Israeli War: 1967
32 Angolan Insurgency: 1960	**68** Nigerian Civil War: 1967–70
33 Nepal Civil War: 1961	**69** Ulster: 1969
34 Kurdish Civil War (Iraq): 1961–67	**70** Anguilla Revolt: 1969
35 Bay of Pigs Invasion: 1961	**71** El Salvador-Honduras War: 1969
36 French Occupation of Bizerta: 1961	**72** Jordan Fighting (Palestinians-Royal forces): 1970

ead (military and civilian)

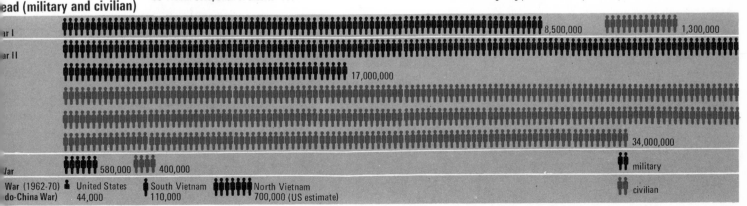

War I   8,500,000   1,300,000

War II

17,000,000

34,000,000

/ar   580,000   400,000   military

War (1962-70)   United States   South Vietnam   North Vietnam   civilian
do-China War)   44,000   110,000   700,000 (US estimate)

50 0 50 100 150 200 250 300 miles
50 0 50 100 150 200 250 300 350 400 450 km

GULF OF MEXICO

ATLANTIC OCEAN

CANADA

QUEBEC

ONTARIO

MAINE

NEW BRUNSWICK

MINNESOTA

WISCONSIN

MICHIGAN

IOWA

MISSOURI

ILLINOIS

INDIANA

OHIO

KENTUCKY

TENNESSEE

ARKANSAS

LOUISIANA

MISSISSIPPI

ALABAMA

GEORGIA

FLORIDA

SOUTH CAROLINA

NORTH CAROLINA

VIRGINIA

WEST VIRGINIA

PENNSYLVANIA

NEW YORK

NEW JERSEY

MARYLAND

DELAWARE

VERMONT

NEW HAMPSHIRE

MASS.

CONN.

Lake Superior

Lake Michigan

Lake Huron

Lake Erie

Lake Ontario

Georgian Bay

Lake Winnipeg

MONTREAL
Ottawa
Quebec
TORONTO
Hamilton
Buffalo
Rochester
Syracuse
Albany
Boston
NEW YORK
PHILADELPHIA
Baltimore
WASHINGTON D.C.
Pittsburgh
Cleveland
DETROIT
CHICAGO
Milwaukee
Minneapolis
St. Paul
Duluth
Des Moines
Kansas City
St. Louis
Cincinnati
Indianapolis
Columbus
Dayton
Louisville
Nashville
Memphis
Little Rock
Atlanta
Birmingham
Montgomery
Mobile
New Orleans
Baton Rouge
Shreveport
Jackson
Savannah
Charleston
Columbia
Charlotte
Chattanooga
Knoxville
Richmond
Norfolk
Raleigh
Jacksonville
Tampa
St. Petersburg
Orlando
Miami
Tallahassee
Houston
Galveston
Beaumont
Port Arthur
Tulsa

Bahama Islands (Br.)
Eleuthera I.
New Providence
Andros
Nassau
Exuma Sound
Gt. Abaco
Grand Bahama I.
N.E. Providence Channel
N.W. Providence Chan.

Delta of the Mississippi
Florida Keys
Key West
Florida Bay
C. Sable
C. Canaveral
C. Kennedy
Lake Okeechobee
Everglades

Tensions within the US

The United States, with a population of 204 million (1970), and armed forces equalled only by those of the Soviet Union, dominates not only the American continent but much of the non-communist world. Its commercial and technological resources dwarf those of any other Western state—though they could be matched, in time, by a united Europe. But although United States history has repeatedly exhibited the pioneering spirit of the first settlers, it is only since World War II that the country has emerged as a "super-power". The idealism behind a global policy, which many have seen in a less favourable light, was well-expressed in the words of President Kennedy's inaugural speech in January 1961. He announced that the United States was willing "to pay any price, bear any burden . . . to assure the survival and success of liberty".

America's preoccupation with foreign affairs during the 1960s was rudely interrupted by the growth of Negro militancy at home and by the alienation of a large section of the student population in whose hands the future of the country would lie. The United States and the Soviet Union had in fact each diverted substantial resources into education in order to secure a technological advantage over the other; but in America many students began to feel oppressed by the bureaucratic "multiversities" in which they found themselves. Explosion point was reached when the student generation found (from 1965 on) that it was also expected to participate in the Vietnam war.

A combination of the draft and the realization that much university research was closely linked to government and business interests drove a significant minority of students to move into open hostility to the government—even to the extent of desiring and planning its violent downfall.

More serious, in the sense of being more threatening to the internal stability of the United States, has been the upsurge of urban violence, particularly racial violence. There are 22·7 million Negroes in the United States, about 11 per cent of the population. Today the most militant organized groups of Negroes are to be found in the growing Black Power movement. The Negroes were originally based in the slave states of the South, but the virtual denial of human rights and the lack of economic opportunity there has led to their steady migration to the North. Today barely half live in the South and (as the accompanying diagram shows) there are large Negro communities, including many militants, in Chicago, Detroit, and other northern industrial cities.

The growth of violence in American political life was symbolized by the murders of President Kennedy (November 1963), the moderate Civil Rights leader Martin Luther King (April 1968), and Senator Robert Kennedy (June 1968). These tragedies, coupled with frequent scenes of political violence seen by the greater part of the population on television, have undermined the self-confidence that marked American life and policies up to the end of the 1950s.

The struggle of black Americans to achieve justice, equality and a greater share of material wealth poses an issue crucial to US survival. Negroes must overcome disadvantages in such fields as education (only 7 per cent of US undergraduates are black); unemployment (usually twice as high among blacks as among whites); and life expectancy (64 years for a Negro, 71 years for a white man).

The Negro minority

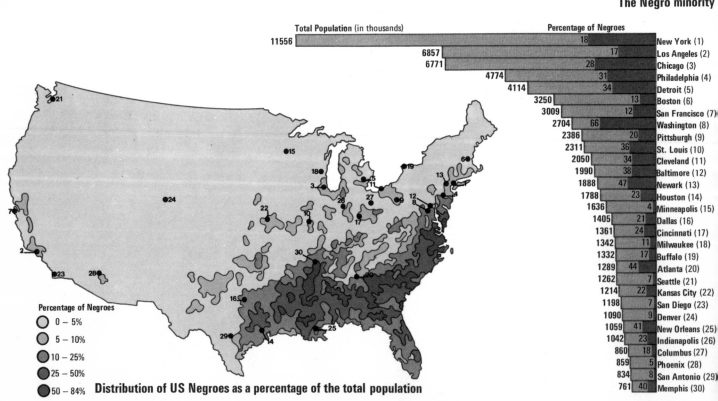

Total Population (in thousands)	Percentage of Negroes	
11556	18	New York (1)
6857	17	Los Angeles (2)
6771	28	Chicago (3)
4774	31	Philadelphia (4)
4114	34	Detroit (5)
3250	13	Boston (6)
3009	12	San Francisco (7)
2704	66	Washington (8)
2386	20	Pittsburgh (9)
2311	36	St. Louis (10)
2050	34	Cleveland (11)
1990	38	Baltimore (12)
1888	47	Newark (13)
1788	23	Houston (14)
1636	4	Minneapolis (15)
1405	21	Dallas (16)
1361	24	Cincinnati (17)
1342	11	Milwaukee (18)
1332	17	Buffalo (19)
1289	44	Atlanta (20)
1262	7	Seattle (21)
1214	22	Kansas City (22)
1198	7	San Diego (23)
1090	9	Denver (24)
1059	41	New Orleans (25)
1042	23	Indianapolis (26)
860	18	Columbus (27)
859	5	Phoenix (28)
834	8	San Antonio (29)
761	40	Memphis (30)

Percentage of Negroes
- 0 – 5%
- 5 – 10%
- 10 – 25%
- 25 – 50%
- 50 – 84%

Distribution of US Negroes as a percentage of the total population

Separatism in Canada

Canada, the second largest country in the world (after the Soviet Union), is in a period of rapid economic expansion and social change.

Nine out of every 10 Canadians live within 200 miles of the 5500-mile long frontier with the United States, most of them in Ontario and Quebec, the two richest provinces, containing the St Lawrence valley and the shores of the Great Lakes.

Canadians of British origin still form the nation's largest ethnic group—about 40 per cent of the population; Canadians of French extraction account for another 30 per cent. The rest of the population consists of those who have no ethnic ties with Britain or France—an element that is steadily increasing as the government encourages a flow of immigrants equivalent to about one per cent of the population annually.

Continued population growth could help to solve Canada's most difficult socio-political problem—that of French separatism. Most French Canadians live in Quebec Province, where they make up more than 60 per cent of the population (see diagram, right). The province has a vigorous separatist party—the Parti Québecois, which campaigns for separate statehood for Quebec.

The demand for separatism has been strongly opposed by Mr Pierre Trudeau, the French Canadian elected to the premiership in 1968. Mr Trudeau and his Liberal Party argue that the best way to preserve French minority culture is to modernize parliamentary procedure and so make federalism more effective.

In 1967 Anglo-French relations were momentarily disturbed by the encouragement of French Canadian separatists in a speech by General de Gaulle while visiting Quebec. In 1970 a more ugly development was the murder of a Quebec provincial minister, Mr Pierre Laporte, by a separatist extremist group, the Front for the Liberation of Quebec.

The second problem confronting Canadians is how to develop a stable and prosperous economy without becoming economically subservient to the United States. Many Canadians believe that America casts covetous eyes on Canada's water and mineral resources; and it was partly this fear that in 1970 caused the Canadian government to institute a 100-mile pollution control area covering Canada's northern waters. The issue arose after an American proposal to start an all-the-year service of ice-breaking supertankers bringing oil from the new Alaska oilfields to the US eastern seaboard. The Canadian measure effectively establishes Ottawa's control over all shipping through the Northwest Passage, and has drawn a strong protest from the American government.

Canada has always lacked the enormous capital resources needed to develop its major industries. The necessary investment has had to come from abroad, particularly from the United States, and this dependence on America will increase as economic development gets under way. Already three quarters of the country's petroleum and natural gas industry, and more than half of its mining and smelting industries are controlled by foreign firms. To counter United States pressure, a succession of laws have been enacted restricting foreign ownership of key industries.

The United States remains the principal source of foreign capital—its current investment of $24,000 million is already rather more than four times the total for 1945. British investment, on the other hand, accounts for less than 15 per cent, about half of what it was in 1945. Since World War II, Canada has played an important part in the work of the United Nations and its international agencies, providing troops and other personnel for UN forces or missions in various parts of the world. But since Mr Trudeau's election there has been an intensive reassessment of Canada's world role. Defence spending has been fixed at $1800 million a year for three years, and Canada's land and naval contribution to NATO has been cut. These reductions are associated with a growing belief that Europe has attracted too much of Canada's attentions, and that the country should pay more regard to developing relations across the Pacific—with Australia, Japan, and China.

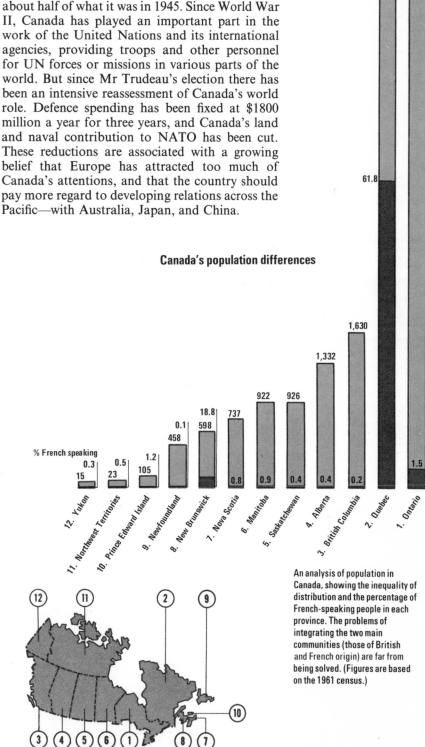

Canada's population differences

An analysis of population in Canada, showing the inequality of distribution and the percentage of French-speaking people in each province. The problems of integrating the two main communities (those of British and French origin) are far from being solved. (Figures are based on the 1961 census.)

The Americas US global power

Deployment of US forces, 1969-70

1 North America
2 armoured divisions, 2 brigades of
1 mechanized division (for reinforcing
Seventh Army in Europe), 1 airborne
division, 4 infantry divisions,
1 armoured brigade, 1 armoured
cavalry regiment. 2 marine divisions or
equivalent, 1 training division
(for forces in Vietnam)
Tactical Air Command (1000 aircraft)
Strategic Air Command: 510 aircraft
(plus 560 tankers)
1054 inter-continental missiles
North American Air Defence
Command: 750 aircraft including
Canadian units, plus 186
long-range air defence missiles in
NE United States and Canada

2 Atlantic
Second Fleet

3 Panama Canal Zone
1 Infantry brigade

4 East Pacific
First Fleet

5 Pacific
7 Polaris submarines

6 Europe
US Air Force Europe, 450 tactical
aircraft
Third Air Force UK
Sixteenth Air Force Spain
Seventeenth Air Force Germany

7 Arctic-North Atlantic-Mediterranean
25 Polaris submarines

8 Germany
Seventh Army (200,000 men)
5th Corps:
1 armoured division
1 mechanized division
1 armoured cavalry regiment
7th Corps:
1 armoured division
1 mechanized division
(less 2 brigades in US)
Berlin: 1 infantry brigade

9 Iceland
1 squadron interceptors

10 Mediterranean
Sixth Fleet

11 Italy
South European Task Force
(HQ elements only)

12 Pacific
Pacific Air Forces, HQ Hawaii
(1000 tactical aircraft)
Fifth Air Force:
Japan
Korea
Okinawa
Thirteenth Air Force:
Philippines
Seventh Air Force:
Vietnam

13 South Korea
2 Infantry divisions, Missile Command

14 Hawaii/Okinawa
Special Forces Group

15 West Pacific
Seventh Fleet

16 South Vietnam
(400,000 men – decreasing)
5 infantry divisions (less redeployed
brigades),2 airmobile divisions,3 Marine
divisions (less redeployed regimental
combat teams), 1 light infantry brigade,
1 airborne brigade, 1 armoured cavalry
regiment, Special Forces Group

Footnote: In addition Military Airlift
Command is deployed worldwide,
with about 350 heavy transports.

Leader of the Western world

After World War II, when the United States—
armed with the atom bomb—took on the leadership of the Western world, there were few to
challenge its role. The isolationism of prewar days
was gone, and the twin policy of rebuilding a
shattered Europe and holding off what was widely
thought to be a communist threat met with general
support.

To put Europe on its feet again, the Americans
sponsored the Marshall Plan, which in four years
(1948–51) gave $13,280 million worth of aid to
16 countries.

The United States also played a leading role in
establishing the North Atlantic Treaty Organization (NATO) in 1949, an organization that was
designed to coordinate the defence of Western
Europe against a possible Soviet attack (p. 41).

Later, after the success of the communist revolution in China in 1949, the administrations of
President Dwight D. Eisenhower (1952–60) set
out to "contain" the spread of communist influence
in Asia. In 1954, after the victory of the communist
(Vietminh) forces over the French in Vietnam, the
Southeast Asia Treaty Organization (SEATO)
was set up, with headquarters at Bangkok (p. 97).
A system of bilateral treaties already in operation
in the area was thus consolidated.

The United States has made many other moves
to assert its leadership of the Western world. In
1947, together with most of the Latin American
nations, it signed the Inter-American Treaty of
Reciprocal Assistance known as the Rio Treaty.
The Organization of American States (OAS) was
set up the following year. In 1957 the US became
associated with the Baghdad Pact (renamed
CENTO in 1959), a defence organization in the
Middle East (p. 64).

Other bilateral defence and aid treaties were
concluded during this period, and substantial
sums were devoted to overseas aid programmes.

So long as the cold war persisted, the problems
of the United States were relatively straight-
forward. But with the passage of time, it began to
dawn both on the US and the Soviet Union that
their enormous power gave them certain interests
in common. The evident dangers in unchecked
nuclear testing, and the increasing burden of
military spending, particularly on a fresh generation of nuclear weapons systems, stimulated
United States interest in exploring, together with
the Russians, the possibility of scaling down the
arms race.

In 1963 the two super-powers finally signed the
Moscow Test Ban Treaty, whereby they agreed to
stop the atmospheric testing of nuclear weapons.
In 1967 they signed a treaty prohibiting weapons
of mass destruction in outer space, and in 1968
concluded the Nuclear Non-Proliferation Treaty
to inhibit the spread of nuclear weapons to states
not already possessing them. In November 1969
they started Strategic Arms Limitation Talks
(SALT), holding their meetings alternately in
Helsinki and Vienna.

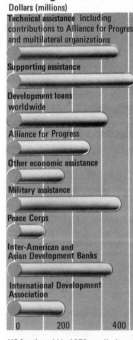

US foreign aid, 1970

Dollars (millions)

US foreign aid in 1970 totalled
around $2000 million, allocated as
shown in diagram above.

The US quest for security

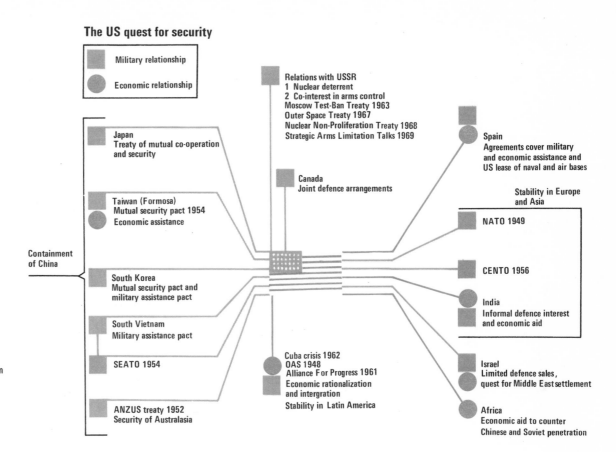

■ Military relationship

● Economic relationship

Relations with USSR
1 Nuclear deterrent
2 Co-interest in arms control
Moscow Test-Ban Treaty 1963
Outer Space Treaty 1967
Nuclear Non-Proliferation Treaty 1968
Strategic Arms Limitation Talks 1969

Canada
Joint defence arrangements

Japan
Treaty of mutual co-operation
and security

Taiwan (Formosa)
Mutual security pact 1954
Economic assistance

Containment
of China

South Korea
Mutual security pact and
military assistance pact

South Vietnam
Military assistance pact

SEATO 1954

ANZUS treaty 1952
Security of Australasia

Cuba crisis 1962
OAS 1948
Alliance For Progress 1961
Economic rationalization
and intergration
Stability in Latin America

Spain
Agreements cover military
and economic assistance and
US lease of naval and air bases

**Stability in Europe
and Asia**

NATO 1949

CENTO 1956

India
Informal defence interest
and economic aid

Israel
Limited defence sales,
quest for Middle East settlement

Africa
Economic aid to counter
Chinese and Soviet penetration

Both military and economic
relationships have been used to
bolster the security of the US and
its overseas interests. The diagram
shows the pattern and purpose of
America's principal alliances and
treaties, including those with the
USSR.

Decline in foreign aid

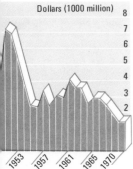

Dollars (1000 million)

1953 1957 1961 1965 1970

In 1948, when the Marshall Plan
began, American economic aid to
poorer nations amounted to 2.79
per cent of the US gross national
product, and 11.5 per cent of the
federal budget. In 1970 such aid
programmes constituted less than
0.3 per cent of GNP and less than
1 per cent of the budget.

This rapprochement with the Soviet Union had inevitable repercussions on America's allies all over the world. As the prospect of direct Soviet aggression receded, the European countries grew restive at their defence burden, even though the largest share of Europe's defence bill had been borne by the United States. European countries began to demand a greater voice in NATO planning decisions, especially with regard to nuclear weapons.

At the same time, many people in Western Europe began to distrust the increasing economic power wielded in Europe by the United States. Their concern was in fact much exaggerated; but it may have contributed to the growth of anti-American feeling, particularly in France, which has been a persistent critic of US policy towards Southeast Asia and which withdrew in 1966 from the military side of NATO. Even by 1970, however, the American economic stake amounted to no more than a few per cent of the total business of any one country. Activities where US investment is heaviest in Europe include computers, oil, motor vehicles, and rubber.

In Asia too, the hitherto uncontested strategy of "containment" was greatly discredited when— even with vast American assistance and the unparalleled use of air power—the South Vietnamese government proved unable to counter a communist-inspired rebellion (p. 95).

In Latin America, where the United States had managed to isolate Castro's Cuba from its neighbours, a new generation of military rulers who had successfully crushed rural guerrilla rebellions began to see US economic power as a greater threat to their national interest than the ideology broadcast from Havana.

Between 1969 and 1970 the United States began to respond to these manifold pressures, both in its nuclear capability vis-à-vis the Soviet Union and in its worldwide military posture. It began to reduce its forces in Vietnam; and domestic, political, and economic groups in America continued to press for troop withdrawals from Europe.

President Richard Nixon, who took office in 1969, reaffirmed his intention of maintaining the forces necessary to back up overseas commitments, provided that America's allies assumed a fair share of the defence burden. Thus whatever the outcome of the mainland war in Indochina, the US government clearly intended that the Seventh Fleet should remain in the eastern Pacific, protecting bases off the Asian mainland in Taiwan, the Philippines, and (subject to Japanese agreement) Okinawa.

The Sixth Fleet continued to cover NATO's southern flank in the Mediterranean, and had to meet an unprecedently large Soviet naval presence in the area (p. 60). The presence of the Seventh Army in Germany remained a guarantee of America's involvement in any war resulting from aggression against Western Europe. A strategic reserve, backed by a huge airlift capability, was also available to act anywhere in the world in defence of vital United States interests.

Nuclear crisis

Western defence planners never foresaw that the world's most dangerous nuclear crisis would actually occur on America's own doorstep.

On September 22, 1962 President Kennedy announced that reconnaissance aircraft had detected the installation of Soviet medium-range nuclear missiles in Cuba. The missiles, with ranges of up to 2000 miles, could have reached targets throughout the United States—and in much of Latin America. Unwilling to contemplate possible nuclear blackmail by Cuba, the American government called on the Soviet Union to remove the missiles. When it declined to do so, President Kennedy's specially formed "executive committee" examined the various possibilities of military action open to the US—air strikes, a full-scale invasion of the island, or a naval blockade to prevent more Russian equipment and technicians reaching Cuba.

All three courses entailed the danger of nuclear retaliation, but most of the executive committee voted in favour of the third because it gave the Russians a chance to back down. The blockade was instituted on October 24, and for several days the world sweated it out, wondering if Soviet ships would try to force the blockade. On October 26 the Soviet premier, Nikita Khrushchev, offered to withdraw the missiles if American medium missiles were removed from Turkey. President Kennedy refused.

Khrushchev finally changed his mind. Russian ships carrying further equipment turned back. Some weeks later, on November 22, President Kennedy was able to announce that the Russians had started to dismantle the Cuban missiles. The successful outcome to the world's first nuclear crisis was, ironically, largely due to the American ability to deploy an overwhelming superiority of *conventional* force in the Caribbean area.

Russia's motive in sending missiles to Cuba remains a matter of debate. It was thought at the time that Khrushchev, under-estimating the determination of the new president, was hoping to effect a radical alteration in the strategic balance. But in practice, missiles in Cuba were only marginally more threatening to American security than missiles aimed from the Soviet Union.

Khrushchev may also have hoped to prevent a second invasion of Cuba. In 1961 President Kennedy had allowed anti-Castro Cuban exiles (backed by the Central Intelligence Agency) to launch an invasion of Cuba at the Bay of Pigs. The CIA proved to have been completely misinformed about the prospects of local support, and the invasion group was destroyed by the Cuban army and air force within 36 hours.

As a result of the October missile crisis, Cuba secured a tacit American promise that there would be no further invasions. But the Americans felt free to exercise every kind of other pressure to dislodge Castro, including an embargo on all American trade with Cuba. Similar measures, including the severance of diplomatic relations, were applied by all members of the Organization of American States, with the exception of Mexico.

The Dominican Republic

A further crisis occurred in the Caribbean in 1965 when the United States landed 20,000 marines in the Dominican Republic. Although Washington claimed the troops had been sent to rescue American nationals who were liable to become victims of the civil war that had broken out in April 1965, it was later admitted that United States intervention was designed to ensure that left-wing elements in the island did not gain the upper hand. (There had been earlier US intervention in 1954.) The Americans regularized their military presence on the island by incorporating it into an Inter-American Peace Force, hastily set up for the occasion by the OAS with a number of token Latin American troops. Suffocated by this military force, the civil war—or rebellion—ran out of steam. The troops were eventually able to withdraw and elections were held in June 1966. Juan Bosch, the more radical candidate, was defeated by Joaquín Balaguer, who had been the vice-president of the dictator Rafael Trujillo, assassinated in 1961.

Below: Cuba, the largest island in the Caribbean, lies within 90 miles of the United States. Map **(left)** pinpoints the site of the abortive Bay of Pigs invasion (1961) by Cuban exiles under control of the US Central Intelligence Agency; the location sites of Soviet missile installations (1962), and the port of Cienfuegos, where in late 1970 the US alleged Russia was building a base capable of handling missile-carrying submarines. Other map shows areas of US threatened by missiles in 1962. The missiles had a range of up to 2000 miles.

Cuba and its neighbours

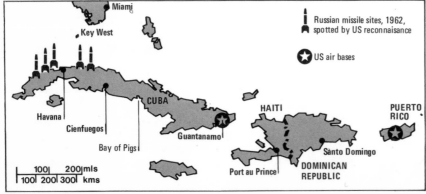

Russian missile sites, 1962, spotted by US reconnaisance

US air bases

Miami
Key West
Havana
Cienfuegos
Bay of Pigs
CUBA
Guantanamo
HAITI
Port au Prince
Santo Domingo
DOMINICAN REPUBLIC
PUERTO RICO

100 200 mls
100 200 300 kms

Cuban missile threat, 1962

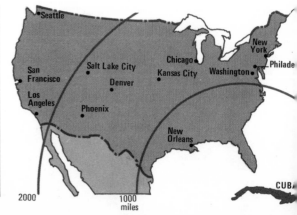

Seattle
San Francisco
Los Angeles
Salt Lake City
Denver
Phoenix
Chicago
Kansas City
New York
Washington
Philade
New Orleans
2000
1000 miles
CUBA

El Salvador-Honduras War

El Salvador, with 372 people per square mile, is the smallest but most densely populated republic in Central America. Honduras, its neighbour to the northeast, is five times as large but has an average of only 57 people per square mile. There has therefore been a considerable flow of trans-migration into Honduras; in 1969, for instance, 300,000 Salvadorans moved there in search of work. But Honduras, the poorest country in Central America, is in no position to absorb surplus numbers, and the presence there of so many foreigners—more than 10 per cent of the population—caused much resentment.

In July 1969, after a number of frontier incidents and a controversial football match in Mexico City between the two countries, the situation exploded into violence, and El Salvador invaded Honduras.

The war ended in three weeks, after diplomatic intervention by the Organization of American States. But the underlying causes of tension remain, and the precarious economies of the two republics have been further weakened.

Atlantic trade

Towards the end of the 1960s discussion began about the possibility of creating a North Atlantic Free Trade Area (NAFTA). The proposal is not new, and was first mooted in the 1940s. Enthusiasm for the idea has come mainly from the west side of the Atlantic, especially from Canada, the most important industrial country not yet integrated with a major economic grouping. Though US participation in such a free trade area at present seems unlikely, the Americans themselves do not rule out the possibility. The objective would be to eliminate tariffs on industrial materials and manu-factured goods. Apart from an initial nucleus that would include the US, Canada, and the European Free Trade Association (EFTA) countries (p. 52), the plan would be for the developed countries of Asia to join in—Japan, Australia, and New Zealand—and eventually the six countries of the European Common Market.

Diagram (far right) shows the extent to which the United States has increased its dependence on overseas countries for supplies of metallic minerals—a development that has influenced American foreign policy and the disbursement of foreign aid.

Four alternative routes (right) for a new, sea-level canal to replace the Panama Canal, which is no longer adequate for modern shipping needs. The present waterway, 85 feet above sea level, cannot handle ships bigger than 65,000 tons. Another proposal is for a $3000 million waterway inside the US-leased Panama Canal Zone or just outside the zone in territory of the Republic of Panama.

Panama Canal : alternative routes

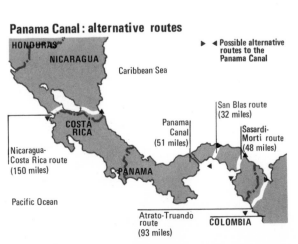

US mineral imports

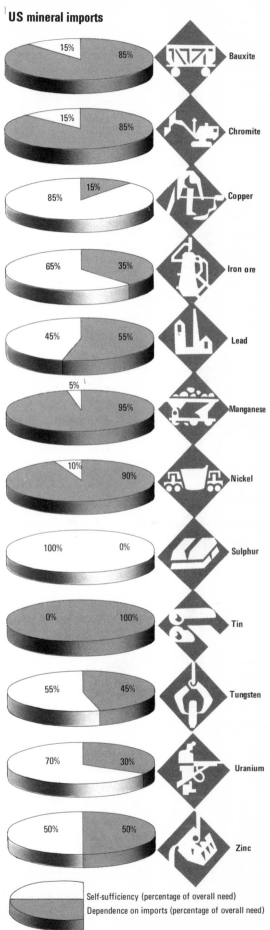

The Americas West Indies

ft Land m
Approximate
6000   4000   3000   2000   1500   1000   400   200   0
18,000   12,000   9000   6000   4500   3000   1200   600   0
ft
m
Sea
0   200   600   3000   6000   12,000   18,000   24,000 ft
0   600   1800   3600   5400   7200 m

WINDWARD ISLANDS 1:8,000,000

Martinique Passage
Ste. Marie
Mt. Pelée 4800
Fort de France
MARTINIQUE (Fr.)
Rivière Pilote
Soufrière
St. Lucia Channel
Castries
St. Lucia
St. Vincent Passage
Southeast
St. Vincent
Bequia
Kingstown
Port Elizabeth
Mustique
The Grenadines
Canouan
Union I.
Carriacou
Grenville
Grenada
Ronde I.
St. 2749
St. George's
Pointe Saline
BARBADOS
Speightstown
Bridgetown

TRINIDAD & TOBAGO 1:8,000,000

Tobago
TRINIDAD
Gulf of Paria
Port of Spain
Chaguaramas
Arima
San Fernando
Pointe Fortin

LEEWARD ISLANDS 1:8,000,000

Anguilla
Marigot
St. Martin (Fr.)
St. Maarten (Neth.)
Saba (Neth.)
St. Eustatius (Neth.)
St. Barthélemy (Fr.)
Barbuda
St. Christopher (St. Kitts)
Nevis
Codrington
Redonda
St. John's
Antigua (Br.)
Falmouth
Montserrat
Plymouth
Basse Terre
GUADELOUPE
La Désirade
Grande Terre
Pointe-à-Pitre
Marie Galante (Fr.)
Grand Bourg
Basse Terre
Les Saintes
Marie Dalhesan 4747
Roseau
Dominica (Br.)
Portsmouth
(Port of Windward Is.)

JAMAICA 1:8,000,000

KINGSTON
Spanish Town
Montego Bay
St. Ann's Bay
Port Antonio
Port Morant
Portland Point
Savanna la Mar
West Pt.

BERMUDA 1:1,000,000

St. George's
St. George I.
St. David's I.
Castle Harb.
Tuckers Town
Ireland I.
North Village Town
Hamilton
The Spanish Flatts
Somerset I.

ATLANTIC OCEAN

CARIBBEAN SEA

GREATER ANTILLES

LESSER ANTILLES

WINDWARD ISLANDS

LEEWARD ISLANDS

HISPANIOLA

VENEZUELA

COLOMBIA

NICARAGUA

HONDURAS

COSTA RICA

PANAMA

CANAL ZONE

MEXICO

GULF OF MEXICO

PACIFIC OCEAN

GUIANA

BAHAMA ISLANDS (United Kingdom)
GREAT BAHAMA BANK
Nassau
New Providence
Freeport
Grand Bahama I.
Little Abaco I.
Great Abaco I.
Eleuthera I.
Cat I.
San Salvador or Watlings I.
Rum Cay
Long I.
Crooked I.
Acklins I.
Mayaguana I.
Great Inagua I.
Little Inagua I.
Turks Is. (Br.)
Caicos Islands

CUBA
HAVANA
Pinar del Río
Matanzas
Santa Clara
Cienfuegos
Sancti Spíritus
Ciego de Ávila
Camagüey
Holguín
Bayamo
Santiago de Cuba
Guantánamo

HAITI
Port-au-Prince
Cap-Haïtien

DOMINICAN REP.
Santo Domingo
Santiago

JAMAICA
Kingston

PUERTO RICO (U.S.A.)
San Juan
Ponce
Mayagüez

Cayman Islands (Br.)
Grand Cayman

Virgin Is. (U.S.A.)
Virgin Gorda (Br.)

Aruba (Neth.)
Curaçao (Neth.)
Bonaire (Neth.)

Margarita I. (Ven.)
Tortuga I.
La Asunción
Trinidad
Port of Spain

MARACAIBO
Lake Maracaibo
BARRANQUILLA
Cartagena
CARACAS
Valencia
Barquisimeto
San Cristóbal
Bucaramanga
Cúcuta
Maturín
Ciudad Bolívar

TRINIDAD
Delta of the Orinoco

FLORIDA
MIAMI
Fort Lauderdale
Palm Beach
West Palm Beach
Fort Pierce
Fort Myers
Key West
Florida Keys

Projection: Bi-polar oblique Conical Orthomorphic

West from Greenwich

COPYRIGHT GEORGE PHILIP & SON, LTD.

The Americas Latin America

Reform and revolution

Latin America, more than any other continent, is characterized by the marked division between rich and poor. In cities such as Buenos Aires, Rio de Janeiro, Lima, and Mexico City the rich enjoy an immensely high standard of living, while the shanty-towns that mushroom around the cities are often packed with millions of people living in conditions of great poverty and degradation.

After the Cuban Revolution (January 1959), when the skill of Fidel Castro allowed a small guerrilla army rather rapidly to take power, many people believed that the whole of Latin America was about to explode. Soviet and Chinese support of the Castro regime seemed to threaten the 19th-century Monroe Doctrine that established Latin America as a US foreign policy preserve and effectively warned other powers against interfering there. The United States acted swiftly. With one hand it sought to isolate Cuba from the mainland (p. 32), and with the other it tried to build up the economies of Latin America. Out of the crisis posed by the Cuban Revolution was born President Kennedy's Alliance for Progress (Charter of Punta del Este, signed August 1961). It was designed to be a vast cooperative effort of all the Latin American nations (except Cuba) to satisfy the needs of the people for houses, work, land, health, and schools. Its goals were ambitious—a growth rate of 2·5 per cent per capita per year, tax and land reform, and "by 1970 to ensure access to at least six years of primary education for each school-age child".

In practice the Alliance never got off the ground. Land-reform laws were passed in nearly every country, but only in Chile did the reform begin to bite at all. Elsewhere the landed élite retained its power and prestige without difficulty. In some countries, like Colombia, the conditions of certain sections of the population actually declined during the years of the Alliance for Progress, in spite of the massive inflow of United States aid (see diagram, p. 37).

But if the Alliance had little success, neither did the guerrilla fighters who tried to follow in Castro's footsteps. There were guerrilla movements in the 1960s in Guatemala, Venezuela, Colombia, Peru, Argentina, Brazil, and Bolivia, all of which met with varying degrees of failure. In 1967 Ernesto Che Guevara, an Argentine doctor who had helped Castro take power and who subsequently enjoyed an important Cabinet position in Cuba (Minister of Industries), launched a guerrilla campaign in Bolivia. But with his death later in the year at the hands of the Bolivian military, it seemed as though an era had ended. Revolutionaries began to switch their attention from the country to the cities—where nearly half the continent's population now lives. Their tactics included the kidnapping of foreign diplomats, and the frequent hi-jacking of aircraft.

To help the Latin American armies counter the guerrilla threat, the United States gave military aid and training. But by the end of the 1960s this

Territorial and boundary disputes

1 Guatemala X Honduras
2 Honduras X Nicaragua
3 Costa Rica X Panama
4 Ecuador X Peru
5 Venezuela X Guyana
6 Argentina X Bolivia
7 Argentina X Chile
8 Argentina X Falkland Islands (UK)

American aid was beginning to provoke a nationalist reaction within the Latin American armed forces. Military coups in Peru (1968) and Bolivia (1969) produced a new kind of military dictatorship that proved to be hostile to certain entrenched economic interests of the United States. Both countries nationalized American oil companies and set about programmes of internal reforms that excited interest throughout Latin America.

Map shows location of various territories and boundaries in Latin America that have been the subject of dispute in recent years.

Economic problems

Much of the rural and urban violence that seems characteristic of Latin America is rooted in the economic situation, with its appalling extremes of wealth and poverty. Between 1961 and 1969 the per capita income of Latin America increased by a mere 1·6 per cent, compared with 3·2 per cent in Western Europe and 3·9 per cent in the United States. In Uruguay, for example, the per capita GNP (Gross National Product) rose by only 0·3 per cent annually; in the Caribbean state of Haiti individual incomes actually went down by 2·3 per cent a year.

Although on the face of it Latin America's trade balance was in credit throughout this period, by amounts ranging from $923 million in 1961 to $2445 million in 1965, interest on debts and remission of profits (mainly on United States investments) put the current account into heavy deficit in each of the eight years. These deficits ranged from $433 million in 1963 to $1568 million in 1967.

Payments on service accounts already swallow up about one third of Latin America's entire export revenue, and continue to rise much faster than the growth in export earnings.

Plans for improvement

The Economic Commission for Latin America, an organ of the United Nations, with its headquarters in Santiago, Chile, helped to set up the Central American Common Market in 1960, and the Latin American Free Trade Association in 1961. Neither has fulfilled the hope placed in it. For the poorer Latin American countries, however, the best long-term hopes of economic improvement lie in the revival in 1969 of the continent-wide Special Coordination Committee for Latin America. This committee aims to coordinate the views of individual Latin American countries, and to present specific requests to the developed world for such matters as tariff reductions, the freer flow of capital, reduction of transport costs, and an increased flow of technical knowledge. Approaches have been made to the United States and West European countries. The committee differs from most other Pan-American organizations in that it can deliberate without the presence of a US delegation. It has no fixed headquarters. In 1969 another Latin American organization, the Andean Economic Integration Association, was set up. It consists of Colombia, Ecuador, Peru, Bolivia, and Chile. Between them these five smaller countries (which may be joined by Venezuela) control a large part of the world's tin and copper supplies. They have agreed to introduce full free trade by 1980 and to integrate industries for the benefit of the area as a whole.

Argentina and Brazil have better individual prospects than the smaller countries, so they are less interested in joining economic groupings. But in 1969 they helped Uruguay, Paraguay, and Bolivia form the River Plate Basin Treaty, which

has been set up to initiate joint development schemes in the large area drained by the rivers that flow into the River Plate estuary.

European interests

Europe, which once played the dominanting economic and financial role in Latin America that is currently played by the United States, now has only minor headaches to deal with in the region. Surinam, formerly Dutch Guiana, gained virtual independence from the Netherlands in 1954; but with the Dutch Antilles (six Caribbean islands, which include Curaçao and Aruba) it chose to remain associated with Holland. French Guiana is an overseas department of France and sends deputies to the French parliament in Paris.

Guyana, formerly British Guiana, became independent in 1966, and the UK has been involved in supporting it against territorial claims by neighbouring Venezuela. British Honduras, a colony with a population of 115,000, is scheduled for independence in 1971. It is not self-supporting and is claimed in its entirety by neighbouring Guatemala. The Falkland Islands in the South Atlantic support 2000 British sheepfarmers. The islands have been claimed by the Agentinians, who call them Las Malvinas; and the British government, which sees no economic prospects for the islands, has been putting pressure on the islanders during the late 1960s to think very seriously about their future.

US investment

During the 1960s in Latin America, as the diagram on page 37 indicates, there was a substantial decline in United States investment in petroleum and a small, though noticeable, decline in investment in mining. The most significant increase has been in manufacturing. United States businesses in Latin America supply one tenth of production, pay one fifth of all taxes, and account for one third of all export earnings. There are one and a half million Latin Americans employed in United States businesses—only two per cent of all their employees are US citizens.

Urban guerrilla movements

At the end of the 1960s Latin America saw the development of a new form of guerrilla activity—that of the urban guerrilla who uses kidnap and other forms of terrorism to extort political concessions. Between 1968 and 1970 more than 15 foreign diplomats and businessmen were abducted by left-wing revolutionary groups. West Germany, the United States, and Japan (the largest foreign investors in Latin America) suffered the worst: in Guatemala the German and American ambassadors were shot dead; in Brazil they were freed by the kidnappers only after the government had released a number of political prisoners. In January 1971 Uruguayan Tupamaros kidnapped the British ambassador in the Uruguayan capital, Montevideo. The most spectacular urban guerrilla movement, the Tupamaros, operates in Uruguay, the smallest

Economic groupings

OAS	LAFTA	CACM	
			1. Argentina
			2. Barbados
			3. Bolivia
			4. Brazil
			5. Chile
			6. Colombia
			7. Costa Rica
			8. Dominican
			9. Ecuador
			10. El Salvador
			11. Guatemala
			12. Haiti
			13. Honduras
			14. Mexico
			15. Nicaragua
			16. Panama
			17. Paraguay
			18. Peru
			19. Trinidad an
			20. USA
			21. Uruguay
			22. Venezuela
✱			23. Cuba

✱ (expelled 1962)

OAS Organization of American States

LAFTA Latin American Free Trade Association

CACM Central American Common Ma

South American state (just over 72,000 square miles). There is also an effective group in Argentina. But although they are a threat to law and order, the urban guerrillas have little chance of taking over power. They have been forced to operate in the cities by the success of counter-guerrilla activity in the countryside and the guerrillas' failure to win support among Amerindian peasants.

In September 1970 the election of Dr Salvador Allende, the marxist socialist candidate, as the new president of Chile came as a surprise to most people, for Allende had always been a great advocate of guerrilla movements in countries other than his own.

Chile has a markedly more peaceful political history than that of its neighbours, and is something of an exception in the continent. There seemed little prospect of other countries following in the same direction, if only because few countries share Chile's tradition of regularly holding free elections. The United States could hardly be expected to express enthusiasm at the election of Allende—with its implication that a second socialist state would soon be planted in the Americas. But the end of the isolation of Cuba, following the re-establishment of diplomatic relations between Cuba and Chile, was seen by many as a positive factor.

US investment in industry

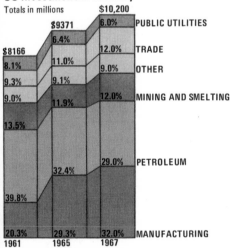

Totals in millions

	$8166 (1961)	$9371 (1965)	$10,200 (1967)	
PUBLIC UTILITIES		6.4%	6.0%	
TRADE	8.1%	11.0%	12.0%	
OTHER	9.3%	9.1%	9.0%	
MINING AND SMELTING	9.0%	11.9%	12.0%	
	13.5%			
PETROLEUM	39.8%	32.4%	29.0%	
MANUFACTURING	20.3%	29.3%	32.0%	
	1961	1965	1967	

Above: Analysis of investment in selected industries in Latin American states. The most marked changes—the increase in the manufacturing figure and the decline of the petroleum figure—reflect the general trend of US foreign investment over the period.

US direct investment

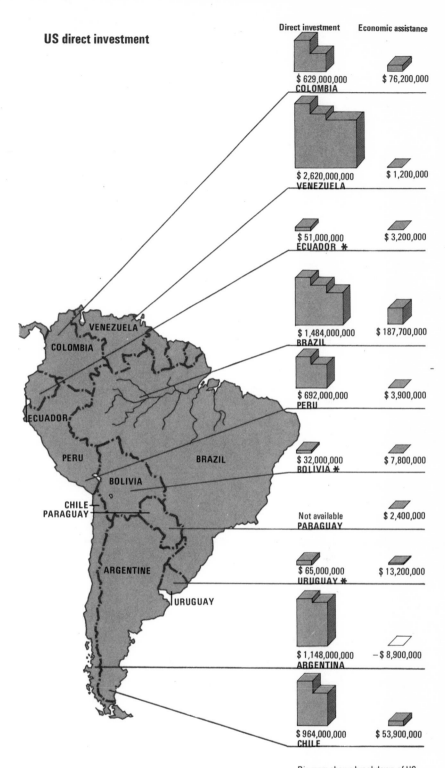

	Direct investment	Economic assistance
COLOMBIA	$ 629,000,000	$ 76,200,000
VENEZUELA	$ 2,620,000,000	$ 1,200,000
ECUADOR *	$ 51,000,000	$ 3,200,000
BRAZIL	$ 1,484,000,000	$ 187,700,000
PERU	$ 692,000,000	$ 3,900,000
BOLIVIA *	$ 32,000,000	$ 7,800,000
PARAGUAY	Not available	$ 2,400,000
URUGUAY *	$ 65,000,000	$ 13,200,000
ARGENTINA	$ 1,148,000,000	− $ 8,900,000
CHILE	$ 964,000,000	$ 53,900,000

Diagram shows breakdown of US direct investment—expenditure on factories, machinery, and other equipment—in Latin America, with US commitments for economic assistance to individual states. Figures are for 1968 (the latest available) unless marked*. Negative figure for Argentina indicates that repayment of interest on previous aid is now greater than the current rate of aid. As with all US foreign aid, 90 per cent of the money must be spent on American products.

ft
m
Sea

18,000

12,000 9,000 6,000 4,500 3,000 1,500 1,200 600 0 0 2000 4000 5000 6000 8000 10000

4000 3000 2000 1500 1000 400 200 0 -200 -600 6000 12,000 15,000 18,000 24,000

Direction of Currents

COPYRIGHT GEORGE PHILIP & SON LTD.

ANGOLA
SOUTH WEST AFRICA
SOUTH AFRICA

Ponte Noire
Banana
Congo
Cabinda
Luanda
Benguela
Mossâmedes
Pte. Marca
Cunene
Swakopmund
Walvis Bay
Windhoek
Lüderitz
Orange
Port Nolloth
Walvis Bank
Cape Town
C. of Good Hope
C. Frio
C. Cirio

BENGUELA COLD CURRENT

Angola Basin
·18,707

St. Helena
·19,849

Ascension

Madeira to Cape Town 4677

SOUTH ATLANTIC OCEAN

Mid-Atlantic Ridge

Tropic of Capricorn

Trinidad
·19,774

Brazil Basin

·18,882

BRAZIL

Fortaleza
Recife
Salvador
Belo Horizonte
Brasília
São Paulo
Rio de Janeiro
Santos
Porto Alegre
Goiânia
Goiandio

Mato Grosso
Araguaia
Tapajós
Xingu
Tocantins
Madeira
Aripuana
Iquitos
Ucayali
Marañón
Leticia
Pta. Parinas
1340
20,577

PERU
Lima
Callao
Arequipa ·21,490
Nimo
La Paz
L. Titicaca
Arica
Iquique
Antofagasta 26,173
Ojos del Salado
Deep
20,886

BOLIVIA
PARAGUAY
Asunción
Pilcomayo
Paraguay
Paraná

ARGENTINA
Córdoba
Tucumán ·21,146
Aconcagua 22,835
Santiago
Valparaíso
Concepción
Chile
Juan Fernández Is.

CHILE

Salvador ·22,590

Grande
Iguassu
Rio Grande
Montevideo
URUGUAY
L. Mirim
Rio de la Plata
Rosario
Santa Fé
Salado
Buenos Aires
Pampas
Bahía Blanca
Colorado
Chubut
G. de San Matías
Valdés Pen.
G. de S. Jorge

Patagonia
Puerto Montt
Chonos Arch.
Taitao Pen.
G. of Penas 1187
Sta. Inés I.
Magellan's Str.
Tierra del Fuego
C. Horn

17,903
·17,356

PACIFIC OCEAN
South East Pacific Basin

Antarctic (Southern Pacific) Basin

PERUVIAN COLD CURRENT
2613

Chile Rise 8999

S. Ambrosio

·9226

718.

33047

·10,290

21,59
Bromley Plateau

·18,940
Bouvet I.

3778

Walvis Ridge

Cape Basin

Tristan da Cunha
Gough I. ·1348

Agulhas Basin

Southern

WEST WIND DRIFT

Atlantic Indian Ridge

Equatorial Limit of Icebergs

Argentine Basin
·20,380

1070

South Georgia
Shag Rocks
South Sandwich Is.
27,108 Trench
South Orkney Is.
South Shetland
Scotia Sea
South Rocks

FALKLAND IS.
DEPENDENCIES
Falkland Is. (Islas Malvinas)
1355

Burdwood Bank
95 Bank
CAPE HORN COLD CURRENT

Magellan's Str.
550
660

SOUTHERN OCEAN

Weddell Sea

BRITISH ANTARCTIC TERRITORY

Antarctic Peninsula
Graham Land
Palmer Land
Charcot I.
Peter I st I.
Antarctic Circle

Queen Maud Land
Coats Land
Enderby Land

Antarctic Basin

Ellsworth Land

Ross Sea

Byrd Land

Principal Shipping Routes
(Distances in Nautical Miles)
3778

Projection: Mollweide

Europe military confrontation

	Army — Each symbol represents 20,000 men	Air Force — Each symbol represents 200 combat aircraft	Navy — Each symbol represents 20,000 men
NATO FORCES			
USA	1,522,000	7,000	761,000
Belgium	80,000	200	4,400
Britain	200,000	750	92,000
Canada	40,000	300	18,300
Denmark	30,000	100	7,000
France	330,000	475	70,000
German Federal Republic	330,000	600	36,000
Greece	120,000	200	18,000
Italy	310,000	450	42,400
Netherlands	80,000	150	20,000
Norway	20,000	125	8,000
Portugal	150,000	100	16,500
Turkey	400,000	500	40,000
THE WARSAW PACT			
USSR	2,000,000	9,800	465,000
Bulgaria	125,000	250	7,000
Czechoslovakia	175,000	600	Nil
German Democratic Republic	90,000	270	16,000
Hungary	90,000	140	Nil
Poland	185,000	750	20,000
Rumania	170,000	240	Nil

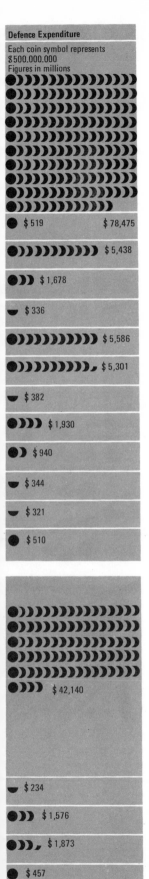

Defence Expenditure

Each coin symbol represents
$500,000,000
Figures in millions

$ 519 $ 78,475

$ 5,438

$ 1,678

$ 336

$ 5,586

$ 5,301

$ 382

$ 1,930

$ 940

$ 344

$ 321

$ 510

$ 42,140

$ 234

$ 1,576

$ 1,873

$ 457

$ 2,080

$ 574

The power balance

In 1939 there were seven major powers in the world: Germany, France, Italy, Britain, Russia, the United States, and Japan. The first four were in Europe. By 1945 the power of Europe had been exhausted. Only the two non-European states emerged as super-powers: the United States and the Soviet Union. Today these two states confront each other in central Europe, where an enormous concentration of firepower is assembled.

The information set out on the left shows the quantitative strength of the conventional military forces in Europe's opposing alliances. But it must be read in conjunction with other factors—geography, training, equipment, and the morale and reliability of different countries' troops.

The map of central Europe (pp. 54–55) shows both the space available for dispersing forces in the Warsaw Pact area and the paucity of natural defences in the North German Plain. Another geographical factor to remember is that the Soviet Union is very much closer to central Europe than is the United States. In an emergency, it would take several days or even weeks to bring United States forces up to full combat strength by means of a transatlantic airlift. The motivation of the troops that make up the opposing armies is more difficult to assess. Some members of both alliances have been historically less warlike than others. In the Warsaw Pact, the Soviet Union must have considerable doubts about the reliability of such allies as the Czechs.

There is not enough evidence to make a complete comparison of training and effectiveness between NATO and Warsaw Pact forces; but NATO air crews probably put in twice as many flying hours a month as do those of the Warsaw Pact countries. On the other hand, Warsaw Pact countries have longer periods of military service (2–3 years) than most NATO countries (1–2 years).

In combat and direct support troops, the Warsaw Pact enjoys a small superiority within Europe—about 1·3 million to NATO's 1·1 million. But in the critical area of northern and central Europe, NATO has only 600,000 men against the Warsaw Pact's 925,000. In southern Europe, NATO's 525,000 combat troops include the large Greek and Turkish contingents defending the exposed southern flank.

Potentially more important, particularly in north Germany, is comparative tank strength. In northern and central Europe, NATO has only 5250 tanks to the Warsaw Pact's 12,500. In southern Europe it has 1800 to the Pact's 4600. But that inequality may be offset by the greater firepower and logistic capability of NATO armoured divisions. The table on the left shows also that the Warsaw Pact has a superiority of tactical aircraft within Europe. But that may be offset by the greater versatility of NATO aircraft, and the larger number of aircraft available to NATO outside the main European theatre.

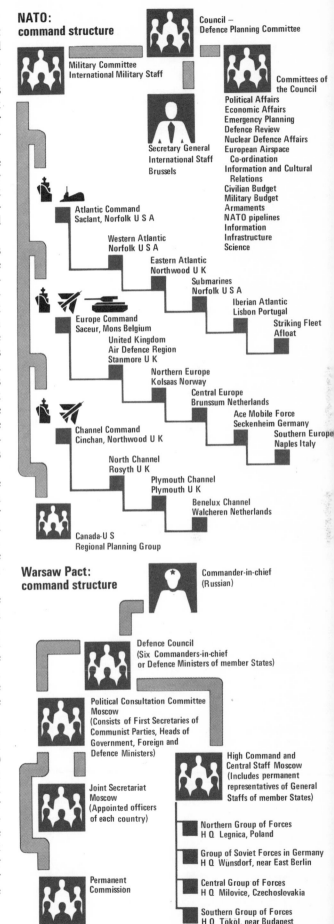

NATO: command structure

Military Committee International Military Staff

Council – Defence Planning Committee

Committees of the Council
Political Affairs
Economic Affairs
Emergency Planning
Defence Review
Nuclear Defence Affairs
European Airspace Co-ordination
Information and Cultural Relations
Civilian Budget
Military Budget
Armaments
NATO pipelines
Information
Infrastructure
Science

Secretary General International Staff Brussels

Atlantic Command Saclant, Norfolk U S A

Western Atlantic Norfolk U S A

Eastern Atlantic Northwood U K

Submarines Norfolk U S A

Iberian Atlantic Lisbon Portugal

Striking Fleet Afloat

Europe Command Saceur, Mons Belgium

United Kingdom Air Defence Region Stanmore U K

Northern Europe Kolsaas Norway

Central Europe Brunssum Netherlands

Ace Mobile Force Seckenheim Germany

Southern Europe Naples Italy

Channel Command Cinchan, Northwood U K

North Channel Rosyth U K

Plymouth Channel Plymouth U K

Benelux Channel Walcheren Netherlands

Canada-U S Regional Planning Group

Warsaw Pact: command structure

Commander-in-chief (Russian)

Defence Council (Six Commanders-in-chief or Defence Ministers of member States)

Political Consultation Committee Moscow (Consists of First Secretaries of Communist Parties, Heads of Government, Foreign and Defence Ministers)

High Command and Central Staff Moscow (Includes permanent representatives of General Staffs of member States)

Joint Secretariat Moscow (Appointed officers of each country)

Northern Group of Forces H.Q. Legnica, Poland

Group of Soviet Forces in Germany H.Q. Wünsdorf, near East Berlin

Central Group of Forces H.Q. Milovice, Czechoslovakia

Permanent Commission

Southern Group of Forces H.Q. Tököl, near Budapest

Europe frontier changes

Europe since 1914

The wars and peace settlements that have affected Europe in the 20th century have changed its political boundaries (as the maps here show) out of all recognition. It has been a harsh century for Europe; some areas on the Russo-Polish frontier have changed hands as many as half a dozen times.

After the German attack on France through Belgium, which marked the start of World War I in 1914, the other European powers (and later the victorious allies) resolved that Germany should never again be able to threaten the rest of Europe. The Treaty of Versailles (1919) contained severe economic clauses, demilitarized the Rhineland, restricted German armaments, confiscated German colonies, and restored France's lost provinces of Alsace and Lorraine.

Equally harsh was the Treaty of Brest Litovsk (1918), forced by Germany on the Russians after the October Revolution and Russia's withdrawal from the war in 1917. The new Soviet state ceded the provinces of Finland, Estonia, Lithuania, Latvia, and a large part of Poland to Germany. After Germany's defeat these Baltic States established their independence. (Estonia, Lithuania, and Latvia lost it again to Russia in 1940, and are now constituent republics of the USSR.)

Poland also regained its ancient sovereignty after World War I and received parts of Silesia and East Prussia. Czechoslovakia and Yugoslavia emerged as new states, being carved out of the old Austro-Hungarian empire, which disappeared from the map.

During the 1920s it was fear of communist Russia rather than of Germany that influenced Western policy-makers, and this fear continued into the 1930s, even after Hitler's rise to power (1933).

In September 1938 Britain and France, unprepared for war, deserted their Czechoslovak allies and, at the Munich conference, allowed Hitler to occupy the Sudetenland, the German-speaking area of Czechoslovakia.

Hitler's occupation of Prague in March 1939 finally convinced Britain and France that war was inevitable if Hitler's territorial ambitions were to be frustrated. Meanwhile the Soviet Union, alarmed by Hitler's "bloodless victories" against the West, and by its own unpreparedness after the military purges of the 1930s, bought time with the Molotov-Ribbentrop Pact (August 1939), which gave the Russians and the Germans a free hand to partition Poland when war broke out two weeks later.

The German attack on Poland, September 1, 1939, led two days later to a declaration of war on Germany by France and Britain in accordance with a guarantee to Poland given after the German invasion of Prague.

In May 1940, after eight months of "phoney war" (and the near-involvement of Britain in Finland's bitter winter war, which repulsed a Soviet invasion), German tanks and mechanized units were launched in a blitzkrieg that took them

Fronts and frontiers, 1914-18

- - - Boundaries 1914
● Germany and her allies
○ Germany's enemies
● Limit of German advance
○ Neutral countries

After World War I, the "peace" boundaries

- - - Boundaries 1924
● Demilitarised Rhineland
Territory lost by:
○ Germany
○ Austria-Hungary
○ Russia

Hitler's Europe

- —— Germany 1937
- -·-· Boundaries Sept. 1939
- ◯ Germany 1942
- ◯ Territory of Hitler's allies
- ◯ Under Axis domination 1942
- ◯ UK and allies
- ◯ Neutral countries

0 100 200mls
0 100 200kms

Pre-1914 Europe **(upper left)** was dominated geographically by three empires, Austria-Hungary, Germany, and Russia. After the war the map was fragmented **(lower left)** into a pattern of smaller successor states that fell easy prey to Hitler. When Hitler's annexations were increased by his World War II conquests, ''Greater Germany'' reached its territorial high water mark in 1942 **(top right)**. After this the territory of the Axis powers, Germany and Italy, was eroded by the Allies. The 1945 division of Europe into Soviet and Western spheres of influence led to Russia's erection of a political ''iron curtain'' **(bottom right)** to prevent Western contacts with the tightly ruled peoples of the East.

After Potsdam, Europe divided

- -·-· Boundaries on eve of war
- ◯ Pre-war USSR
- ◯ Territories annexed by USSR
- ◯ Other communist countries

0 100 200mls
0 100 200kms

through Belgium and France to the English Channel. France was partitioned, and the invasion of Britain was only prevented by RAF fighter defences and by Hitler's subsequent error in invading the Soviet Union on June 22, 1941. The German armies all but took Moscow and Leningrad, and before the turn of the tide in 1942–43 had penetrated to the Caucasus. Russia's terrible war losses, which included 15 million dead, help to explain the fear of Germany that has permeated Soviet policy in the postwar period.

The year 1941 saw the entry of the United States into the war; and with the forging of an alliance between Britain, Russia, and the United States, Hitler's days were numbered. In 1945 Nazi Germany was defeated and its territory divided among the victorious allies, who, at a series of conferences (Teheran, Yalta, Potsdam) redrew the map of Europe.

While Russia was perturbed by the thought of a resurgent Germany, the West European countries became concerned at the possibility of Soviet expansion beyond the sphere of influence assigned to Russia at the Potsdam conference. But although vast sums have been expended on armaments as a result of postwar suspicions, the forcible division of Europe has brought more peace to this violent region than it has known since the 19th century.

West Germany

No nation suffers more from the division of Europe than Germany. The Potsdam Agreement (1945) divided the country into four zones—Soviet, American, British, and French—and put Berlin, the former capital, under four-power control, each power having a separate sector. At the same time all German territory east of the Oder and Neisse rivers was transferred to Poland (except for part of East Prussia, which was taken directly by the Soviet Union) to compensate the country for Russia's acquisition of its eastern borderlands.

In 1948, however, the four-power arrangements that still treated Germany as one country broke down under the stresses of the cold war. The Western zones were amalgamated (by the Basic Law of 1949) in a single economic and political unit—the Federal German Republic. The Russians retaliated by closing the ground routes giving access to Berlin through East German territory. The Western allies sustained Berlin with an airlift, using the three air corridors assigned to them at Potsdam, which remain a vital means of access today. Unwilling to risk war by interfering with the airlift, the Russians abandoned their blockade of Berlin in May 1949.

German rearmament

In 1954, when NATO military strength fell significantly below that of the Warsaw Pact, the Western powers signed the Paris treaties, which provided for a West German contribution to Western defence, under the control of NATO and within the framework of the Western European Union—the defence body originally created by Belgium, France, Great Britain, Luxembourg and the Netherlands in 1948.

In 1955 the Federal Republic was declared a sovereign state. It comprises 11 provinces, or Länder, including West Berlin. The latter, however, is not fully incorporated and is garrisoned exclusively by troops of the three Western powers.

In the Soviet-occupied zone of Germany, the German Democratic Republic was proclaimed in 1949, but it has not been recognized by the Western allies. For many years West Germany refused diplomatic relations with countries recognizing East Germany. This applied particularly to the other communist countries of Eastern Europe, but not to the Soviet Union with whom ambassadors were exchanged in 1956. In 1969 more flexible policies emerged with the coming to power of the Social Democratic coalition government.

In 1958 the Soviet Union provoked a crisis by threatening to sign a separate peace treaty with East Germany, which would have given the latter control over Western access to Berlin. The threat was withdrawn in 1960 after the Western allies had made clear their refusal to accept such control. Another Berlin crisis developed in 1961 when the Communists walled off the Soviet sector to stop the flow of refugees to West Berlin. The Western allies made no attempt to stop the building of the Berlin Wall, but asserted the right of allied officials to enter East Berlin without reference to East German officials at checkpoints.

The wall and the complementary system of the barbed wire separating West Berlin from the surrounding East German countryside, have since been made virtually uncrossable.

Warsaw Pact forces

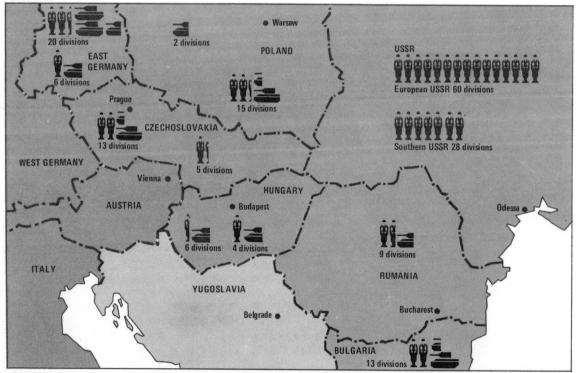

The deployment of Warsaw Pact ground forces, showing the relationship of Soviet and other formations, in Eastern Europe. Soviet formations withdrawn from Czechoslovakia in the 1950s returned after the 1968 uprising.

East Germany

The fifth industrial power in Europe, East Germany now has the highest living standards of any country in Eastern Europe. But only 10 per cent of East German households have a car—compared with 50 per cent in West Germany; and the government admits ruefully that during Hitler's 12-year rule, more houses were built in the eastern part of Germany than in the first 12 years of the German Democratic Republic.

The upward swing in the East German economy dates from 1961, the year of the Berlin Wall (see p. 44). By stopping the outflow of skills to the West, and perhaps, too, by obliging those who remained in the East to look within themselves for economic salvation, the wall ended a period of apathy.

Walter Ulbricht, who has ruled East Germany for 20 years, boasted recently that his country was the most stable in Europe, and there is some truth in the statement, though there have been moments in the last two decades—June 1953, October 1956, and August 1961—when this stability seemed threatened. Most East Germans now seem to tolerate and even accept the régime, though it is noticeable that the Russians still find it necessary to station 20 divisions in East Germany.

In February 1970, the new Social Democrat government, led by Willy Brandt, announced that bilateral talks would begin between the two halves of Germany. But there were signs of uneasiness on the part of the East German government about the development of West German relations with other East European countries—particularly Poland.

Scandinavia

Denmark, Finland, Norway, Sweden, and Iceland form a neutral grouping in international affairs. They cover an area twice the size of France, and with a population of some 20 million, their gross national product—and their standard of living—is higher than that of most West European countries.

After World War II there were discussions among the Scandinavian countries about a possible Nordic defence pact. Sweden, traditionally neutral, hoped to extend the area of neutrality around her. Norway, however, wished to reinforce her security by associating the planned Nordic pact with NATO, an idea that was unacceptable to Sweden. The discussions ended in deadlock: Sweden remained neutral; Norway, Iceland, and Denmark joined NATO; and Finland maintained a kind of institutionalized pro-Russian neutrality. Both Norway and Denmark, however, refused to have foreign military contingents, or nuclear weapons, on their soil. Iceland houses an important United States naval and radar base at Keflavik.

Foiled of their original intention to set up a defence pact, the Nordic countries did eventually come together in the Nordic Council, set up in February 1953 and designed to investigate areas of cooperation other than foreign affairs and defence. In the late 1960s there was renewed discussion about a Nordic economic union.

Germany and Berlin

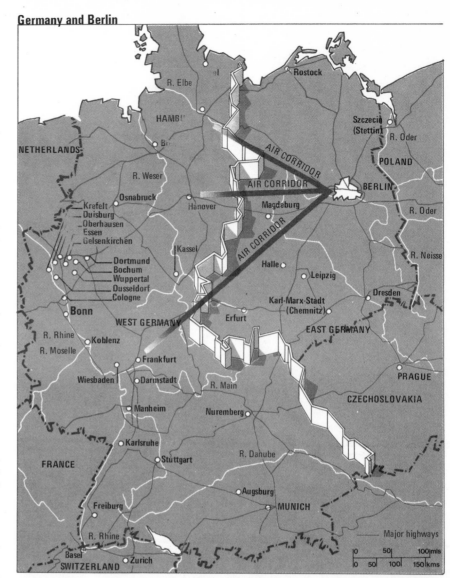

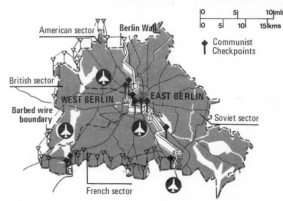

Top map shows interzonal frontier dividing East and West Germany, and the air corridors giving access to West Berlin under the Potsdam agreement. The main overland access route is the autobahn from Hanover **(middle map).** Berlin itself **(right)** is divided into two municipalities—East Berlin, the capital of East Germany, and West Berlin. The whole city, which lies 110 miles inside East Germany, covers 341 square miles.

Europe **Soviet Union**

Projection: Conical Orthomorphic with two standard parallels

East from Greenwich

Europe **Russia as a great power**

Military forces within the USSR

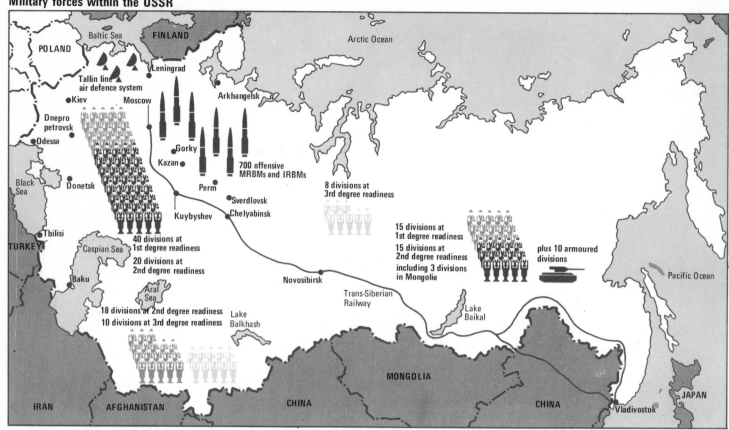

Above: The distribution of military forces inside the Soviet Union. The deployment of Soviet divisions outside the USSR is shown on p. 44, and the strength of Soviet and other Warsaw Pact forces on p. 40. The Soviet army has three degrees of readiness: 1. full combat strength; 2. near combat strength (from which first degree readiness can be quickly reached); 3. low combat strength, requiring major reinforcement if war breaks out. Approximately two thirds of Russia's 157 divisions are in the first two categories.

Problems of national security

During and immediately after World War II, the Soviet Union gained (by treaty or outright annexation) more than 190,000 square miles of territory in Europe, and more than 24 million new subjects. It thus consolidated its political, military, and (later) economic hegemony over Eastern Europe. But when Yugoslavia (in 1948), and Poland and Hungary (in the mid-1950s) began to develop their distinctive national identities, it became clear that the communist world was no monolith. In the 1960s, the Sino-Soviet dispute (p. 88), and other eruptions of national communism, for instance, in Czechoslovakia and Rumania, confirmed these trends.

Unlike the United States, the Soviet Union has not been a great world-trading power. After the 1917 revolution and the civil war that followed it had to put great stress on economic and industrial self-reliance; after 1945 it built up a position of economic dominance in Eastern Europe, co-ordinating and developing its authority through COMECON (p. 52). Only in the late 1960s has it expanded its world economic links, some 15 years after inaugurating a very selective but active aid policy towards some non-communist countries. Today, Russia is one of the world's foremost technological powers.

Problems of national security have been a constant preoccupation of the Soviet state. Early in its history there were those, especially Leon Trotsky, who maintained that security could be found only in permanent revolution: if the Soviet government were left isolated in a counter-revolutionary world, it must eventually fall. However, Joseph Stalin (first secretary of the Communist Party from 1924 until his death in 1953) argued that Russia could be built up and sustained as a socialist country without the revolution necessarily spreading elsewhere. Stalin won, but presided over a régime of increasing cruelty and repression.

Militarily, Russia, like the United States, bases its security on its possession of nuclear weapons (p. 22)—weapons that are sufficiently powerful to deal with an aggressor, even after receiving a nuclear "first strike".

In addition to this nuclear deterrent it maintains large conventional forces in varying degrees of readiness to secure its frontiers, support foreign policy aims, and maintain stability in the Warsaw Pact area.

The Soviet army, two million strong, is organized in 157 divisions of which about two thirds are at—or near—full combat readiness. (Some 40 divisions would need several weeks to be brought to full efficiency.) Soviet divisions are smaller than NATO divisions, but are about equal in artillery strength. Tactical nuclear weapons are a permanent part of them.

The Soviet air force includes long-range bomber forces deployed in western Russia, the central

The Russian quest for security

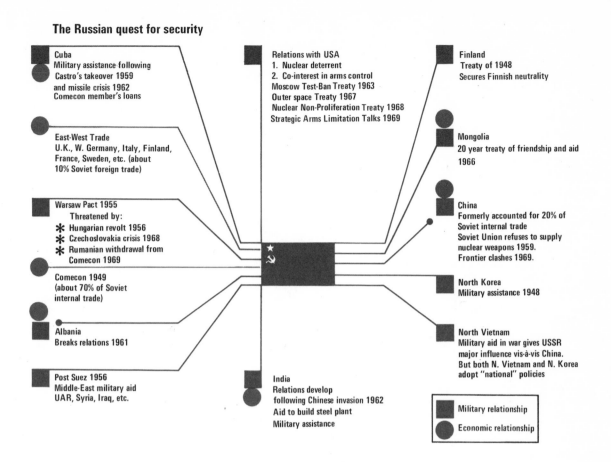

Cuba
Military assistance following
Castro's takeover 1959
and missile crisis 1962
Comecon member's loans

East-West Trade
U.K., W. Germany, Italy, Finland,
France, Sweden, etc. (about
10% Soviet foreign trade)

Warsaw Pact 1955
Threatened by:
✷ Hungarian revolt 1956
✷ Czechoslovakia crisis 1968
✷ Rumanian withdrawal from
   Comecon 1969

Comecon 1949
(about 70% of Soviet
internal trade)

Albania
Breaks relations 1961

Post Suez 1956
Middle-East military aid
UAR, Syria, Iraq, etc.

Relations with USA
1. Nuclear deterrent
2. Co-interest in arms control
Moscow Test-Ban Treaty 1963
Outer space Treaty 1967
Nuclear Non-Proliferation Treaty 1968
Strategic Arms Limitation Talks 1969

India
Relations develop
following Chinese invasion 1962
Aid to build steel plant
Military assistance

Finland
Treaty of 1948
Secures Finnish neutrality

Mongolia
20 year treaty of friendship and aid
1966

China
Formerly accounted for 20% of
Soviet internal trade
Soviet Union refuses to supply
nuclear weapons 1959.
Frontier clashes 1969.

North Korea
Military assistance 1948

North Vietnam
Military aid in war gives USSR
major influence vis-à-vis China.
But both N. Vietnam and N. Korea
adopt "national" policies

■ Military relationship
● Economic relationship

Both military and economic relationships have been used to bolster the security of the USSR and of the communist system in the Soviet-bloc countries. The diagram shows the pattern and purpose of Russia's principal alliances and treaties, including those with the US.

Ukraine, and the Far East. It has fewer intercontinental bombers than the United States Strategic Air Command (about 140 compared with America's 500), but many more medium bombers, which could be used against targets in Europe and China.

The Soviet navy, second only to the United States Navy in tonnage, includes nine guided missile cruisers and 11 older-type cruisers. Its main strength is in submarines, including 80 nuclear-powered and 290 diesel-powered boats. About 150 submarines are normally deployed in the Arctic, 75 in the Baltic, 40 in the Black Sea (or in the Mediterranean), and 105 in the Far East.

Although these forces amount to a powerful offensive capability, all the evidence suggests that Soviet military strategy is cautious and that Soviet planners are fully aware of the dangers of nuclear escalation.

The Warsaw Pact surrounds the Soviet Union with states having similar political institutions, closely linked economies, and an integrated military structure. Only on the northernmost frontier of Norway and the northeastern frontier of Turkey does the Soviet Union directly touch NATO territory. The neutral status of Finland has been secured since World War II by a treaty of neutrality and cooperation.

In the Far East, the Soviet Union has bolstered its position vis-à-vis China by enlarging and strengthening its ties with China's neighbours—

North Korea and North Vietnam. In addition a key role is played by the treaty with the Mongolian Republic, which has entitled the Soviet Union to station large military forces near the Mongolian-Chinese border.

Since the early 1960s, and particularly as a consequence of the Cuban missile crisis, the Soviet Union has paid increasing attention to the development of security understandings with the United States. One of the first was the establishment in 1963 of the "hot line"—a permanent teleprinter link between Washington and Moscow.

Later, out of mutual interest in controlling the arms race as well as under pressure from world opinion, the two countries entered into agreement to stop atmospheric nuclear weapons tests. More recent agreements include adherence to international treaties to prevent the militarization of outer space and the spread of nuclear weapons (p. 30).

This understanding with the United States, which tacitly goes far beyond the signed agreements, has brought the Soviet Union into conflict with its former ally, China. The latter, foreseeing a permanent conflict between East and West, and dismissing the possibility of peaceful coexistence, regards the Soviet Union, no less than the United States, as a threat to its security. The Russians are scarcely less afraid of China, which has a population of over 700 million—more than three times greater than their own.

Europe communist countries

Poland

Squeezed between Russia and Germany, and contained since 1945 within new frontiers, Poland has a particular interest in solving the problem of divided Europe. It has thus been prominent in producing schemes for military "disengagement" by the rival alliances in central Europe.

The present Polish-German frontier, along the Oder and Neisse rivers, was established at the end of World War II by the agreements at Yalta and Potsdam. Many Germans have been reluctant to accept the new frontier, which has yet to be confirmed by a German peace treaty—though West Germany's eastern policy, *Ostpolitik,* has lately produced some improvements in German-Polish relations. The Poles are anxious that the frontier should be guaranteed by an East-West settlement; and the need for Soviet backing in this matter has in the past accounted for the Polish readiness to toe the line within the Warsaw Pact.

There have been several attempts to liberalize the communist régime in Poland; the first and most notable took place in 1956, shortly after Khrushchev had denounced Stalin. But the leaders responsible stopped short of the kind of revolution that led to Soviet intervention in Hungary the same year.

Hungary

In Hungary, a popular revolt against Soviet hegemony led the government under Imre Nagy to try to withdraw from the Warsaw Pact. With its security system threatened, the USSR felt obliged to remove Nagy. Russian tanks moved into Budapest in November 1956, taking advantage of the cover provided by the Anglo-French invasion of Egypt and by the United States elections, which both occurred at that time.

Czechoslovakia

The most serious convulsion within Soviet-controlled Europe occurred in 1968 in Czechoslovakia. At first, the Russians had seemed willing to cooperate with the liberal Czechoslovak régime of Alexander Dubcek, which replaced that of Antonin Novotny early in 1968. But the publication in April of the Czechoslovak Communist Party's proposals to allow a form of parliamentary opposition proved too much. The Russians almost certainly feared that Czechoslovakia might leave the Warsaw Pact. In May, Dubcek was summoned to Moscow, but attempts to secure a compromise failed.

After the Czechs had introduced further democratic reforms, five Warsaw Pact countries—Russia, Poland, Hungary, East Germany, and Bulgaria—decided to hold army exercises in Czechoslovakia. These began on June 20, and provided the Russians with a rehearsal for the later invasion. In July, after the Czechs had refused to participate in a joint conference, the five powers sent a letter to the Czechoslovak Presidium demanding "assurances". When these were not given, the Russians proposed a bilateral meeting with

Poland's shifting frontiers

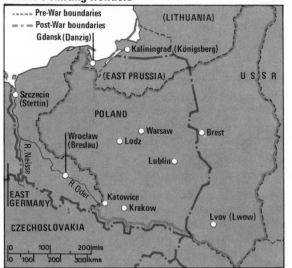

In 1939 Germany and Russia invaded and partitioned Poland (**left**). In 1945 the eastern territories were ceded to Russia, and the western border was extended to the Oder-Neisse Line, previously within Germany. The former German areas of Silesia, Pomerania, and parts of West and East Prussia now contain more than eight million Poles, nearly five million of them born there since 1946.

Invasion of Czechoslovakia, 1968

Map (**above**) shows the direction of entry taken by Warsaw Pact forces when troops from the Soviet Union, Poland, Hungary, East Germany, and Bulgaria invaded Czechoslovakia.

Czech leaders. The Czechs agreed, and the meeting was held at Cierna, on the Soviet-Czechoslovakia border, at the end of July.

For a while it appeared that a settlement had been reached. The Czechs agreed to safeguard the position of the Communist Party in their country; and the Russians repeated assurances that they would not interfere in the affairs of another socialist country. Finally, Soviet troops, which had remained after the army exercise, were withdrawn.

On August 10, however, the Czechoslovak Communist Party published new statutes recognizing the right of minorities to continue to hold dissenting views. That, to the Russians, destroyed any guarantee of the leading role of the Communist Party, and on the night of August 21, 1968, Warsaw Pact forces invaded Czechoslovakia (see map).

The invaders comprised 300,000 Russians, 50,000 Poles, 20,000 Hungarians and East Germans, and not more than 10,000 Bulgarians. Initial landings secured airports, but the main invasion was by road.

The Czechoslovak armed forces offered no opposition. But the widespread civil resistance was brave and dramatic. Students obstructed Soviet tanks and set fire to them. Shopkeepers refused to supply food to the invaders. Press and television transmitted amazing pictures of the invasion to the outside world.

Initially the Russians failed to install a puppet government, and a compromise agreement was reached with Dubcek. Warsaw Pact forces, except for some five Russian divisions, were withdrawn. But the success of the Czechoslovak liberals was very short-lived, and Dubcek was eventually replaced by Gustav Husák, a man more amenable to Moscow.

Rumania

Czechoslovakia was not Russia's only problem in Eastern Europe. The tension between Rumania and its Warsaw Pact partners reached a climax during the 1968 Czechoslovak crisis. It had begun in 1966 when Rumania had tried to establish trade links outside the provisions of COMECON, the trading block of the communist world. (Between 1949 and 1959 about 80 per cent of Rumanian trade had been with communist countries; but by 1966 this had dropped to less than 60 per cent.) Agreements were concluded for joint production schemes with Western companies, and direct links established between Rumanian producers and foreign buyers. At the same time Rumania took an independent stand in the Sino-Soviet ideological quarrel.

During the tense weeks before the Soviet invasion of Czechoslovakia, Soviet-Rumanian differences were emphasized by a popularly acclaimed visit by President Nicolae Ceausescu to Prague. When Warsaw Pact forces invaded Czechoslovakia, Rumania (still a member of the pact, but not taking part in the invasion) started organizing a militia, evidently fearing that it would be the next victim. For several weeks a Soviet invasion of both Rumania and Yugoslavia seemed possible, particularly on September 26, 1968, when *Pravda* enunciated the so-called doctrine of limited sovereignty. By this doctrine, Russia claimed the right to intervene whenever it deemed that socialism, or the interests of other socialist states, was threatened by internal developments in any one country. But the military crisis passed, and Rumania has kept a substantial degree of independence while remaining a member of both COMECON and the Warsaw Pact.

Yugoslavia and Albania

The first move against Soviet leadership in Eastern Europe had come in 1948, when President Tito of Yugoslavia broke with the Soviet bloc coordinating body, the Cominform. When Soviet action against Rumania and Yugoslavia was expected in 1968, there were reports of NATO contingency plans to aid Yugoslav resistance. Such plans were denied by

Industrial resources of communist Europe

Communist Europe's most highly industrialized areas lie in East Germany, Czechoslovakia, and southern Poland. Rumania is the only major oil producer (13.285 million metric tons in 1968), Poland the only major source of hard coal (129 million metric tons in 1968). East Germany is the world's largest producer of lignite (brown coal), now successfully used in making iron and steel. Rumania is the world's fourth largest producer of natural gas.

the Yugoslavs. Invaders could easily occupy the plain around Belgrade, but the mountainous character of the rest of Yugoslavia makes it a difficult land to subjugate—as the Germans found in World War II.

Enmity between Yugoslavia and Albania, dating from 1948, when Albania sided with the majority of the Cominform against Yugoslavia, is now complicated by Albania's alliance with China against Russia. In 1968 a Sino-Albanian military pact led to the appearance of a large Chinese military mission in Tirane, the Albanian capital. But fears that China would set up strategic missile bases in Albania (logistically a difficult operation) proved groundless. While Russia was threatening Rumania and Yugoslavia, China announced that any move by Russia against Albania would be regarded as a declaration of war against Peking.

Europe searching for unity

Rivalry and cooperation

Since the end of World War II, increasing attention has been paid to the question of European unity. Overshadowed by the two continental-sized powers, America and Russia, the individual nations of Western Europe felt that only as a united block could they hope to exercise influence in the world; unification came to be equated with survival and prosperity.

An essential precondition of any attempt at unity was the elimination of the inveterate opposition between Germany and France. In 1948, the two countries became involved in the Organization for European Economic Cooperation—an organization to distribute Marshall Aid (p. 30) to the shattered nations of Europe.

In 1952 the next major step towards unification was taken. The coal and steel production of France, Germany, Italy, Holland, Belgium, and Luxembourg was pooled; supra-national control over these two key industries would, it was hoped, render war between the six members "materially impossible".

The setting up of common bases for economic development was seen as the first step towards the political federation of Europe. In 1957, as a result of the success of the Coal and Steel Community (ECSC), the six countries signed the Treaty of Rome, which arranged for the creation of two new European communities—the European Economic Community (EEC) and the European Atomic Energy Community (Euratom).

The EEC (also known as the European Common Market), Euratom, and ECSC are jointly administered by a Commission of the European Communities and a Council of Members. The latter is the only institution within the Community framework whose six members directly represent their respective governments. Although the Council has the final say in policy decisions, the Commission is in effect more powerful. Its nine members are responsible for implementing the propositions of the Treaty of Rome; as spokesmen for the communities, rather than national governments, they represent a form of European government in embryo.

The greatest difficulties within the Common Market have been encountered over agriculture. The Community aimed at promoting more efficient production, stable market conditions, and "reasonable prices" for farmers and consumers. Common price levels have yet to be realized, although a start has been made in this direction by replacing national protection systems—such as guaranteed prices and government subsidies, operative in Britain—with a Community system, whereby agricultural imports from non-member countries are charged duty to protect the EEC producers. High prices—almost double world market prices—and huge surpluses of dairy produce are two of the major problems confronting EEC members. One serious drawback of membership for Britain would be the inevitable rise in price of a vast range of foodstuffs. Instead of importing dairy produce from Commonwealth countries at a relatively low cost, Britain would be expected to absorb the EEC surpluses, thus dealing a severe blow to the economy of countries such as New Zealand.

Although refused admission to the EEC on several occasions by France, Britain would almost certainly make an important contribution to the further expansion of the Common Market, and particularly to the advance of technology among the member states. Britain's presence might also help towards a more even distribution of power. France, even after the departure of General de Gaulle, and Germany, with her strong economic position, have emerged as rival contenders for leadership; Britain could supply a much-needed balance.

European Free Trade Association (EFTA)

In May 1960, responding to the challenge posed by the EEC, Britain, Austria, Denmark, Norway, Portugal, Sweden, and Switzerland signed the Stockholm Convention setting up a European Free Trade Area. Finland became associated the following year, and Iceland applied for membership in 1968. Free trade between members in industrial products was inaugurated at the end of 1966, leaving each country to impose its own tariffs on products from outside EFTA. Agricultural products are excluded from the provisions of the association.

EFTA is a much smaller and more makeshift organization than the EEC and concerned solely with economic arrangements. In spite of an early success (trade doubled between EFTA members in the first year's operation of the free trade zone) Britain, Ireland, Denmark, and Norway now seek membership of the EEC for both political and economic reasons.

Council for Mutual Economic Assistance (COMECON)

COMECON was formed in 1949, as the communist response to the success of the Marshall Plan in rehabilitating Western Europe. Members are Bulgaria, Czechoslovakia, East Germany, Hungary, Poland, Rumania, the Soviet Union, and (outside Europe) Outer Mongolia. Special economic relations are also maintained with Yugoslavia, Cuba, North Korea, and North Vietnam. COMECON operates a system of specialized production by individual members, and inter-COMECON trade makes up about two thirds of the total foreign trade of the countries belonging to it. A successful move to establish external trading relationships independently of COMECON was made by Rumania in 1968.

Moves toward détente

Moves towards an East-West détente in Europe, the precursor of any association embracing both East and West, have been cautious. In 1957 the Polish Rapacki plan for withdrawing East-West

Divided Europe

○ Soviet bloc

● Other Communist countries

The political division of Europe into communist and non-communist countries was followed by the creation of two economic groups in the West (EFTA and EEC), and one (Comecon) in the East—see opposite.

Economic co-operation

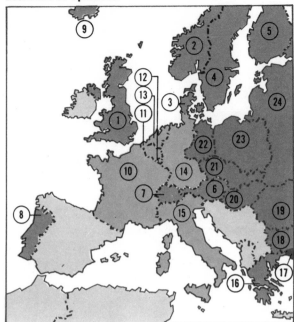

EFTA
1 UK
2 Norway
3 Denmark
4 Sweden
5 Finland (associate)
6 Austria
7 Switzerland
8 Portugal
9 Iceland

EEC
10 France
11 Belgium
12 Luxembourg
13 Netherlands
14 Germany (Federal Republic)
15 Italy
16 Greece (associate)
17 Turkey (associate)

Comecon
18 Bulgaria
19 Rumania
20 Hungary
21 Czechoslovakia
22 Germany (Democratic Republic)
23 Poland
24 USSR

military forces from central Europe seemed to offer hopes of progress. But the West never displayed much interest. The plan was followed by a modified proposal from the Polish leader Wladyslaw Gomulka, to "freeze" the existing level of forces in the area. On the Western side there have been unofficial proposals for a treaty to provide against surprise attack, and other measures have been suggested. But all have come to nothing with the apparent realization that a settlement in Europe must begin with a new relationship between the Soviet Union and the United States and also an easing of the situation in Germany. Western hopes of establishing closer economic and other relations with countries in the Soviet sphere received a sharp setback with the Soviet action against Czechoslovakia in 1968.

Economic Commission for Europe (ECE)
A regional commission of the United Nations, set up in 1947; the only European organization to embrace East and West Europe, plus the US.

Western European Union (WEU)
In March 1948 Belgium, Britain, France, Holland, and Luxembourg signed a mutual defence pact (which also called for collaboration in economic, social, and cultural matters) known as the Brussels Treaty. In May 1955 they were joined by Italy and West Germany and the group changed its name from Western Union to Western *European* Union. Used as a forum where Britain and members of the Common Market could discuss mutual problems.

Council of Europe
Founded in May 1949 by the Brussels Treaty countries, plus Denmark, Italy, Norway and Sweden. Later joined by Austria, Cyprus, Greece (resigned 1969), Iceland, Malta, Turkey, and Switzerland. Its membership clauses insist upon a state's adherence to the principles of freedom and human rights, thus effectively barring East European participation. Concerned with "safeguarding and realizing ideals and principles" of its members.

Organization for Economic Cooperation and Development (OECD)
Set up in 1948 as the Organization for European Economic Cooperation (OEEC) to distribute Marshall Aid. Main architect of European post-war economic recovery. Reformed into Organization for Economic Cooperation and Development (OECD) in 1961; 22 members—all non-communist countries of Europe, US, Canada, and Japan.

European Atomic Energy Community (Euratom)
Set up in 1958 by the six Common Market countries to coordinate their development of nuclear power for peaceful purposes. A tendency to handle advanced technology on a national rather than a supranational basis has led to its near-collapse.

European organizations: members and associates

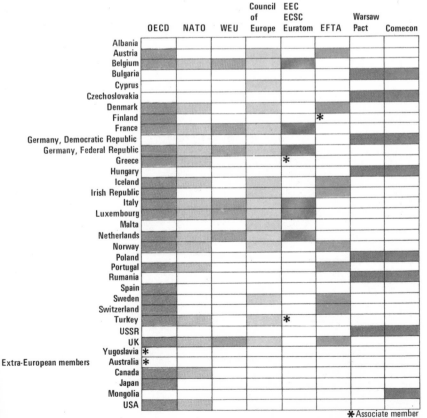

	OECD	NATO	WEU	Council of Europe	EEC ECSC Euratom	EFTA	Warsaw Pact	Comecon
Albania								
Austria	X			X		X		
Belgium	X	X	X	X	X			
Bulgaria							X	X
Cyprus				X				
Czechoslovakia							X	X
Denmark	X	X		X		X		
Finland	X					*		
France	X	X	X	X	X			
Germany, Democratic Republic							X	X
Germany, Federal Republic	X	X	X	X	X			
Greece	X	X		X	*			
Hungary							X	X
Iceland	X	X		X		X		
Irish Republic	X			X				
Italy	X	X	X	X	X			
Luxembourg	X	X	X	X	X			
Malta				X				
Netherlands	X	X	X	X	X			
Norway	X	X		X		X		
Poland							X	X
Portugal	X	X				X		
Rumania							X	X
Spain	X							
Sweden	X			X		X		
Switzerland	X			X		X		
Turkey	X	X		X	*			
USSR							X	X
UK	X	X	X	X		X		
Yugoslavia	*							
Australia	*							
Canada	X	X						
Japan	X							
Mongolia								X
USA	X	X						

Extra-European members

*Associate member

53

NORTH

SEA

BALTIC

Friesian Islands

Schiermonnikoog Ameland Terschelling Vlieland Texel

Den Helder Alkmaar Haarlem Leeuwarden Sneek Groningen Assen Meppel Hoorn Zaandam Kampen Zwolle Almelo

NETHERLANDS

The Hague Leiden Amsterdam Hilversum Utrecht Apeldoorn Deventer Enschede Hengelo

Hook of Holland Schiedam Gouda Arnhem Nijmegen

Rotterdam Dordrecht Breda 's Hertogenbosch Boxtel Bocholt

Flushing Zeebrugge Ostend Bruges Ghent Antwerp Turnhout Eindhoven Krefeld Duisburg

BELGIUM Mechelen Leuven Maastricht Heerlen M. Gladbach Essen Bochum Dortmund Hamm

Kortrijk Aalst Brussels Roubaix Liège Aachen Bonn Cologne (Köln) Wuppertal Remscheid

Lille Tourcoing Roubaix Namur Charleroi Verviers Malmedy

FLANDERS Mons Douai Valenciennes Cambrai

St. Quentin Hirson Charleville Mézières Sedan

LUX. Luxembourg Trier Longwy Thionville

Laon Soissons Aisne Metz

Reims Verdun SAAR Saarbrücken Neunkirchen

Château Thierry Épernay Châlons sur Marne Bar-le-Duc Toul Nancy LORRAINE

Troyes Aube St. Dizier Lunéville St. Dié Épinal Colmar

FRANCE Chaumont Langres Plateau de Langres

Avallon Montbéliard Belfort Mulhouse Schaffhausen

Dijon Côte d'Or Besançon Basle Winterthur

Autun Beaune Dôle Doubs Biel Solothurn Aarau Zürich

Le Creusot Chalon sur Saône FRANCHE COMTÉ Neuchâtel Luzern Schwyz

Mâcon Tournus Bourg Ain Yverdon Fribourg Bern Thun Interlaken

Villefranche **SWITZERLAND**

Lyons Rhône Villeurbanne Geneva Lausanne Montreux Sion Brig St. Gotthard P. Splügen P. St. Moritz Bernina Engadin

St. Étienne Vienne Annecy Aix-les-Bains Martigny Matterhorn Mte. Rosa Bellinzona

Chambéry Mt. Blanc Gt. St. Bernard P. Aosta Locarno Lugano L. Maggiore

Voiron Moûtiers D'AOSTA Gran Paradiso Ivrea Biella Varese Como Lecco

Grenoble Mt. Pelvoux Briançon Susa Turin Chivasso Casale Novara Vercelli LOMBARDY Bergamo Brescia

DAUPHINÉ Mt. Viso PIEDMONT Pinerolo Asti Alessandria Pavia Milan (Milano) Treviglio

Montélimar Embrun Cuneo Mondovì Saluzzo **ITALY** Piacenza Cremona Mantua (Mantova)

Viviers Nyons Gap Maritime Alps Col di Tenda San Remo Savona Genoa (Genova) Parma Reggio Modena

Orange Valence Martigues Col di Tenda Imperia Gulf of Genoa Spezia Carrara AEMILIA ROMAGNA Bologna

Nîmes Avignon Aix Cannes Nice Monaco & Monte Carlo Pistoia Prato Florence (Firenze) Lucca Pisa

Arles Martigues PROVENCE Verdon Riviera Fréjus Gulf of Genoa

Marseilles

LOWER SAXONY Oldenburg Bremen Lüneburg Celle Hanover (Hannover) Brunswick Salzgitter Hildesheim

Bremerhaven Harburg Hamburg Altona Elbe Lauenburg

Wilhelmshaven Emden Cuxhaven Weser Bremerhaven

Heligoland Heligoland Bay Norderney

SCHLESWIG-HOLSTEIN Flensburg Schleswig Rendsburg Kiel Kiel Bay Fehmarn Neumünster Glückstadt Brunsbüttel

Lübeck Lübeck Bay Warnemünde Rostock Wismar Schwerin Neu Brandenburg

Lolland Falster Gedser Fehmarn Belt

Rügen Stralsund Greifswald Sassnitz

Darlowo Koszalin Kolobrzeg Szczecin (Stettin) Goleniów Dabie Wolin Uznam/Uznojście

WEST GERMANY Osnabrück Herford Bielefeld Detmold Minden Hameln Paderborn Göttingen

NORTH RHINE WESTPHALIA Münster Gelsenkirchen Oberhausen Mülheim Hagen Kassel

RHINE LAND Düsseldorf Siegen Westerwald Eifel Ardennes

Koblenz Taunus Wiesbaden Mainz **Frankfurt** Offenbach Hanau Aschaffenburg

Hunsrück Kaiserslautern PALATINATE Worms Darmstadt Würzburg

Karlsruhe Heidelberg Mannheim Ludwigshafen Speyer Heilbronn Ansbach

Pforzheim Baden Baden **Stuttgart** Ludwigsburg Esslingen Donauwörth

Strasbourg BLACK FOREST Tübingen Reutlingen Ulm Augsburg Freising

Freiburg Rottweil Swabian Jura Biberach Iller Lech **Munich (München)**

BADEN WÜRTTEMBERG Tuttlingen Memmingen Ravensburg Rosenheim

Mulhouse Schaffhausen Konstanz Friedrichshafen Kempten Salzburg Bad Ischl

VORARLBERG Feldkirch Bregenz St. Gallen LIECHTENSTEIN Landeck Innsbruck TYROL

Bad Ischl Gmunden

HARZ MTS. 3750 Brocken Halberstadt Bernburg Dessau Wittenberg

Magdeburg Luckenwalde Zerbst Köthen

BERLIN Charlottenburg Potsdam Spandau Brandenburg Oranienburg Neustrelitz Neuruppin Rathenow

Stendal Havel Müritz Parchim Güstrow Prenzlau Eberswalde

EAST GERMANY Cottbus Frankfurt Forst Spremberg Zagan Glogów Zielona Góra

Leipzig Halle Merseburg Naumburg Zeitz Gera Jena Weimar Erfurt Gotha Eisenach Mühlhausen Nordhausen

THURINGIAN FOREST Meissen Dresden Görlitz Liberec Jablonec Hradec Králové

Reichenbach Zwickau Karl Marx Stadt (Chemnitz) Plauen Hof Erz Gebirge Teplice Usti nad Labem (Aussig)

Bayreuth Bamberg Erlangen Fürth **Nuremberg (Nürnberg)** Amberg Naab

Regensburg Ingolstadt Landshut Passau BAVARIA 4780 BOHEMIAN FOREST

Karlovy Vary (Karlsbad) Cheb Kladno **Prague (Praha)** Beroun Kolín Pardubice Labe (Elbe)

CZECHOSLOVAKIA BOHEMIA Plzeň (Pilsen) Příbram Tábor Písek Klatovy Havlíčkuv Brod Jihlava MORAVIAN Hts. Třebíč **Brno (Brünn)**

České Budějovice Třeboň Deggendorf Gmünd Zwettl Freistadt Linz UPPER AUSTRIA Ried Wels Steyr Enns

Znojmo 452 LOWER Horn Stockerau St. Pölten **Vienna (Wien)** Baden

AUSTRIA Salzburg Kufstein Landeck Ötztal Brenner P. 12461 Gr. Glockner Bad Gastein SALZBURG Mürzzuschlag Eisenerz Bruck Semmering P. 3215 Kapfenberg Leoben

TYROL Merano Bressanone Dolomites Carnic Alps Lienz CARINTHIA STYRIA BURGENLAND Graz Mur

Stelvio P. Ortles 12792 Marmolada 10965 Drave Villach Klagenfurt Bleiburg Maribor Nagykanizsa

Bolzano TRENTINO ALTO-ADIGE 11663 Trento Bassano Vittorio Veneto FRIULI-VENEZIA-GIULIA Udine Gorizia Triglav 9396 KARAWANKEN Celje Varazdin

Valtellina Adamello Rovereto VENETO Schio Vicenza Verona Belluno Treviso Trieste Ljubljana Zagreb

L. Como L. Garda Padua (Padova) Venice (Venezia) Rivaz Kranj Kočevje Karlovac Sisak

Brescia Mantua Rovigo Gulf of Venice Istria Rijeka Kupa

Crema Pavia Po Ferrara Chioggia Pula (Pola) C. Kamenjak Rovinj Krk Cres Lošinj Senj

Piacenza Modena Reggio Bologna Imola Faenza Forlì Ravenna Rubicone Cesena Rimini Pesaro Pag Zadar Dugi Otok

ADRIATIC SEA Troglav 6276

ft Land m Approximate

12,000 4000 9000 3000 6000 2000 4500 1500 3000 1000 1200 400 600 200 0 0 200 600 m ft Sea

Deployment of British forces, 1970

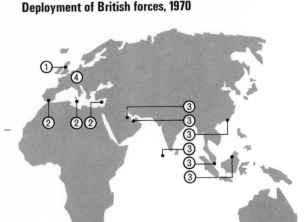

Location	Services		Total number of personnel
1 United Kingdom	Army	98,330	
	R A F	86,790	
	R N	52,330	
	R N at sea	22,250	259,700 total
2 Mediterranean and Near East	Army	7,780	
	R A F	8,500	
	R N	1,330	
	R N at sea	760	18,370 total
3 Middle and Far East (including Hongkong)	Army	30,320	
	R A F	10,170	
	R N	4,260	
	R N at sea	6,510	51,260 total
4 Continental Europe	Army	53,120	
	R A F	6,920	
	R N	160	60,200 total
Elsewhere	Army	4,250	
	R A F	1,350	
	R N	670	
	R N at sea	720	6,990 total

East-of-Suez

In October 1970 the new Conservative government modified plans to withdraw British forces East-of-Suez. Britain, although it has terminated its former unilateral commitment to defend Malaysia and Singapore, will now contribute to a five-power defence system for the area. The British contribution will be quite small—five small warships, a battalion group of troops, and a detachment of long range reconnaissance aircraft. But additional forces will visit the area regularly for training and, in consultation with the other powers, reinforcements may be sent in times of threat. Britain also continues to maintain a small garrison (about 5000 men) in the colony of Hongkong.

The other powers contributing to the system are Malaysia, Singapore, Australia, and New Zealand. In December 1970 plans for the Persian Gulf area were still to be worked out after discussions with leaders of the various Gulf states. Middle East headquarters and two battalions of infantry remained in Bahrain, and a long lease was held on the island of Masirah, off the Oman coast, for use as a staging post for military air routes to the Far East.

The other main British overseas bases are Dekhelia and Akrotiri in Cyprus (see p. 61).

Britain in Europe

The retention of a small force East-of-Suez has not altered the general direction of the British defence effort, which since 1967 has been concentrated on Europe.

The chief British contribution to the land defence of Europe is the Army of the Rhine, 48,500-strong. It consists of two armoured brigades and four infantry brigades. In addition, most British combat units (including infantry brigades and a parachute brigade) are formally committed to NATO, as is the greater part of the Royal Navy and the Royal Air Force. In addition to its 198,000 regular troops, Britain has 60,000 regular reserves and 45,000 Territorial and Army Volunteer reserves.

Nuclear forces

Britain's nuclear deterrent consists of four Polaris submarines, to which a fifth may be added shortly. At least one submarine, armed with 16 Polaris A-3 missiles, is on patrol at all times, while others are refitting, replenishing, or moving to their stations. The force is assigned to NATO and, according to policy laid down in 1965, cannot be used "independently".

Troubles in Northern Ireland

In 1969 Britain faced a serious internal security threat as a result of violence in the province of Ulster in Northern Ireland.

Ulster, with a population of 1·5 million people (two thirds of them Protestants) had remained part of the United Kingdom when the rest of Ireland, predominantly Roman Catholic, became a sovereign republic—Eire—in 1922.

In August 1969 civil rights grievances by the Ulster Catholic minority exploded in riots in the city of Londonderry, which quickly spread to the capital, Belfast. Great destruction was caused in both cities, and a large force of troops was dispatched from Great Britain to restore order.

During the troubles, which continued into 1971, more than a dozen people were killed and many thousands injured. At one time the security forces could be maintained only by temporary troop transfers from the Army of the Rhine.

Catholic and Republican extremists received aid from the Irish Republican Army, an organization banned by the Dublin government. But at no time was there a serious danger of intervention by the 13,000-strong defence force of the Irish Republic.

Below: Although the figure for British aid to developing countries shows an overall increase, the amount of aid expressed as a percentage of the GNP dropped from 1·3 per cent in 1965 to 0·97 per cent in 1969. The Pearson Report, produced for the World Bank, urges developed countries to earmark 1 per cent of their GNP for aid by 1975 or 1980 at the latest.

British overseas aid

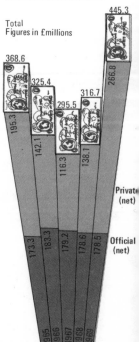

Total Figures in £millions

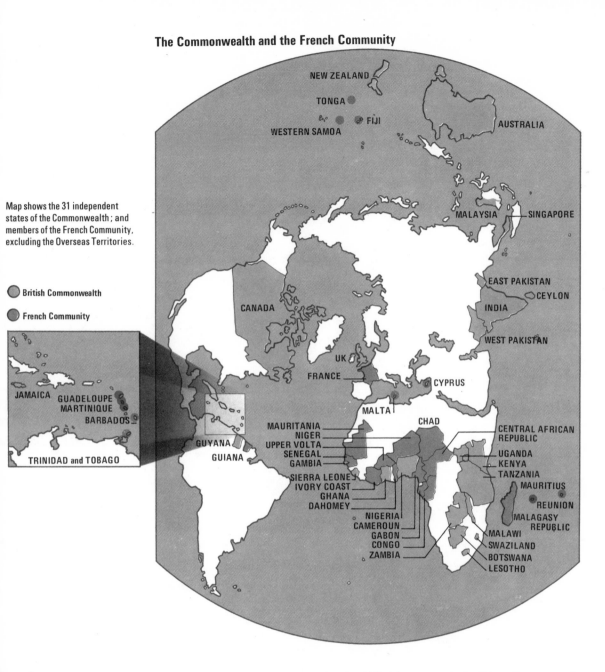

The Commonwealth and the French Community

Map shows the 31 independent states of the Commonwealth; and members of the French Community, excluding the Overseas Territories.

- British Commonwealth
- French Community

NEW ZEALAND

TONGA

WESTERN SAMOA · FIJI

AUSTRALIA

MALAYSIA — SINGAPORE

EAST PAKISTAN
CEYLON
INDIA
WEST PAKISTAN

CANADA

UK
FRANCE
CYPRUS
MALTA
CHAD
CENTRAL AFRICAN REPUBLIC
MAURITANIA
NIGER
UPPER VOLTA
SENEGAL
GAMBIA
UGANDA
KENYA
TANZANIA
MAURITIUS
REUNION
SIERRA LEONE
IVORY COAST
GHANA
DAHOMEY
MALAGASY REPUBLIC
NIGERIA
CAMEROUN
GABON
CONGO
ZAMBIA
MALAWI
SWAZILAND
BOTSWANA
LESOTHO

JAMAICA
GUADELOUPE
MARTINIQUE
BARBADOS
TRINIDAD and TOBAGO
GUYANA
GUIANA

Deployment of French forces

With the return to power in 1958 of the wartime leader, Charles de Gaulle, France speedily divested itself of its more intractable colonial problems, and began to act as an unofficial spokesman for small countries that felt threatened by the super-powers.

In 1968, a student revolt was ineptly handled by de Gaulle's ministers during his absence abroad. On his return, and in subsequent months, de Gaulle went some way towards meeting the grievances of students and workers, but in so doing he antag-onized the solid middle-class basis of his support. In 1969, he lost a referendum and resigned.

Although France withdrew from the permanent military organization of NATO in 1967, French forces—including a 328,000-strong army—are still available to the alliance in time of war. Under the Franco-German military treaty, two French

mechanized divisions remain in West Germany. A strategic reserve in France includes an air-portable division and an independent parachute regiment.

About 12,000 French combat troops are stationed overseas, including two regiments in the French Territory of the Afars and Issas (formerly French Somaliland); five regiments in other parts of Africa and in Madagascar; a detachment in Algeria; three battalions in French territories in the Indian Ocean and the Pacific; and one regiment in the Caribbean.

In 1970 a force of intermediate-range nuclear missiles became operational, supplementing the deterrent strategic air force of some 40 supersonic Mirage IV-A bombers, armed with small (9 kiloton) atomic bombs. The initial force of 16 missiles is deployed in underground launching sites in Haute-Provence, southeastern France. Four nuclear missile submarines are due for completion by 1975.

Europe Mediterranean lands

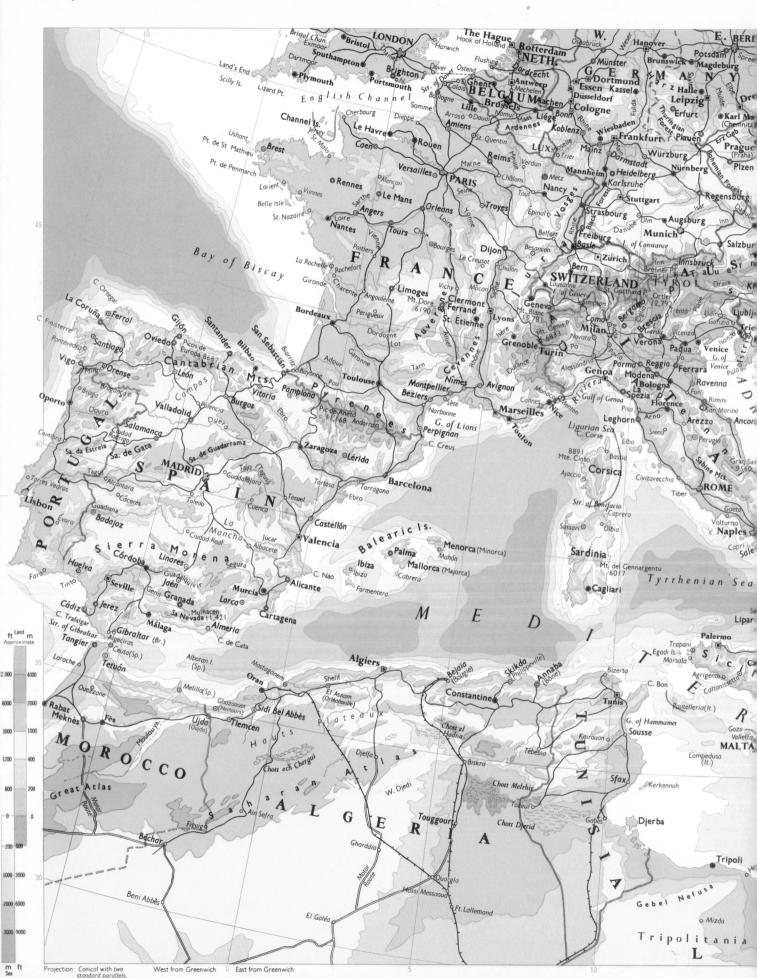

Projection: Conical with two standard parallels.   West from Greenwich   0   East from Greenwich

Scale 1:10,000,000

50   0   50   100   150   200 Statute Miles
50 0   100   200   300 Km

POLAND
Poznan   Plock   Warsaw (Warszawa)
Łódź   Wisła (Vistula)   Brest   Pinsk   Pripyat Marshes   Chernigov   Desna   Konotop   Sumy   Belgorod   Volgograd
Wrocław   Radom   Lublin   Bug   Goryn   Ipyat   Nezhin   Kazanskaya
Chorzow   Kielce   Lutsk   Rovno   Zhitomir   Kiev   Pereyaslav-Khmelnitski   Poltava   Kharkov
Kraków   Tarnów   Lvov   Dnepr   Belaya Tserkov   Slavyansk   Artemovsk   Donetz   Kamensk   Tsimlyansk Reservoir
Przemysl   U.   Vinnitsa   Cherkassy   Kremenchug (Dnieper)   Pavlograd   Lugansk (Voroshilovgrad)   Manych
OSTRAVA   Jablunka P.   Galicia   S.   Kamenets Podolski   Uman   Kirovograd   Dnepropetrovsk   Gorlovka   Makeyevka   Shakhty
HOS   Tatra 8737   Ruthenia   Kolomyia   Mogilev-Podolski   Pervomaysk   Krivoy Rog   Zaporozhye   Don   Novocherkassk
LOVAKIA   Košice   Carpathians   Prut   Balta   Voznesensk   Nikolayev   Melitopol   Zhdanov (Mariupol)   Taganrog   Azov   Rostov
Bratislava   Miskolc   Chernovtsy   Moldavia   Bug   Kherson   Perekop   Berdyansk   Tikhoretsk   Stavropol
HUNGARY   Debrecen   Iasi   Kishinev   Benderi   Tiraspol   Odessa   Sea of Azov   Kerch & Str   Krasnodar   Maykop   Armavir
Budapest   Oradea   Botosani   Pietrosul 7562   G. of Karkinitsk   Yeisk
Kecskemét   Cluj   Pietrosul 6896   Crimea   Yalta   Novorossiysk   Kuban   Tuapse
Szeged   Hódmezővásárhely   Arad   RUMANIA   C. Tarkhankut   Yevpatoriya   Simferopol   Feodosiya   Sukhumi
Pécs   Subotica   Sibiu   Negoiu 8317   Brasov (Orasul Stalin)   Galati   Izmail   Sevastopol   Balaklava   Poti
Timişoara   Transylvanian Alps   Braila   Sulina   BLACK SEA   Batumi
Novi Sad   Petrovaradin   Iron Gate   Turnu-Severin   Ploesti   Constanţa   Rize
BELGRADE   Craiova   Bucharest (Bucuresti)   Silistra   Trabzon
BOSNIA   Smederevo   Danube   Ruse   Tolbukhin   C. Ince   Sinop   Caník (Pontine) Mts.
Sarajevo   Vidin   Pleven   Türnovo   Varna   Inebolu   Samsun   Sebin Karahisar
Niš   Shipka P.   Sliven   Burgas   Giresun   Tirebolu
MONTENEGRO   Durmitor 8271   Sofia   BULGARIA   Zanguldak   Kastamonu   Amasya   Tokat   Sivas   Erzincan
Dubrovnik (Ragusa)   Musala 9596   Plovdiv   Eregli   Cankiri   Corum   Gürün
ALBANIA   Skopje   Rhodope   Maritsa   Edirne   Istanbul   Bolu   Ankara   Yozgat   TURKEY   Keban
Tirane   Bitolj   Strumica   Üsküdar   Izmit   Beypazari   Kirsehir   Kayseri   Firat
Shkoder   Elbasan   Serrai   Kavalla   Tekirdağ   Sea of Marmara   Iznik Gölü   Sakarya   Kütahya   Tuz Gölü   Erciyas Daği 12,848   Maras
Durrës   GREECE   Alexandroúpolis   Gelibolu (Gallipoli)   Bursa   Bilecik   Sivrihisar   Aksaray   Niğde   Gaziantep
Vlöre   Olympus 9570   Athos 6670   Imbroz   Dardanelles   Çanakkale   Balikesir   Eskişehir   Afyon Karahisar   Konya   Adana   Osmaniye
Pindus   Limnos   Bolvadin   Karaman   Tarsus   Mersin   Iskenderun   Aleppo
Lárisa   Vólos   N. Sporades   Lésvos   Ayvalik   Menderes   Egridir Gölü   Beysehir Gölü   Cilician Taurus   G. of Iskenderun   SYRIA
Návpaktos   Évvoia   Khíos   Manisa   Uşak   Isparta   Taurus Mountains   Silifke   Antakya
Levkás   Aegean Sea   Izmir   Alasehir   Egridir   Lycian Taurus   Antalya   Al Ladhiqiyah (Latakia)   Hama
Kefallinía   Athens   Sámos   Aydin   Burdur   Denizli   Elmali   G. of Antalya   Nicosia   Famagusta   Baniyas   Homs
Pátrai   G. of Corinth   Ikaría   Muğla   CYPRUS   Morphou   Larnaca   Tarabulus (Tripoli)   LEBANON
Kalamata   Sparti   Kikládhes   Síros   Andros   Ródhos (Rhodes)   Kastellorizon   Troodos 6405   Limassol   Beirut   Damascus
Morea   Náxos   Dodecanese   Ródhos (Rhodes)   Sidon   Mt. Hermon 9232   Jebel ed Druz
Pílos   C. Tainaron   Kíthira   Andikithira   Ios   Milos   Thíra   Karpáthos   Acre   Haifa   Busra
IONIAN SEA   Khaniá   Mt. Ídhi 8058   Iráklion   Crete   Tel Aviv-Jaffá   Jerusalem   Amman
ISRAEL   JORDAN   Dead Sea -1286   Korak (El Kerak)
Gaza   Petra   Ma'an
Darnah   El Marj (Barce)   Tobruk   G. of Bomba   Rosetta   El Burullus   Damietta   Port Said   El 'Arish   El Qantara
Benghazi   G. of Salūm   Matrūh   El 'Alamein   Mahalla el Kubra   Ismailia   Bitter Lakes   Desert el Tih   Eilat   'Aqaba
Gulf of Sidra   Cyrenaica   Salūm   Alexandria   Tanta   Suez   Sinai Pen.
MEDITERRANEAN SEA   CAIRO   Suez   G. of 'Aqaba
LIBYA   EGYPT (U.A.R.)   El Faiyûm   Beni Suef

Europe the Mediterranean flank

Strategic significance

The Mediterranean forms the southern flank of the NATO defence area—it also contains, on its eastern edge, the theatre of the Israeli-Arab conflict. However, one classical strategic aspect of the Mediterranean has been modified by time: it has ceased to be an indispensable highway for commerce between Europe and the East.

NATO forces

The main NATO force in the Mediterranean is the American Sixth Fleet. This comprises some 40 ships, and always includes at least one carrier, whose supersonic strike aircraft can reach targets within a radius of more than 1000 miles. The Sixth Fleet is independent of local bases, and draws its supplies from the eastern seaboard of the United States. In addition up to three American Polaris submarines may be in the Mediterranean at any one time, under direct control from Washington.

Backing the Sixth Fleet is an on-call force provided by the British, Italian, and Greek navies, and a maritime aerial reconnaissance command for tracking Soviet fleet movements in the Mediterranean. An American arms embargo, imposed on Greece after the Colonels' coup of 1967, was lifted in 1970, when concern about increasing Russian penetration of the Middle East, and the need to maintain effective bases in the eastern Mediterranean overcame any distaste the American government might have felt for the Greek junta.

About 15,000 British servicemen—half of them ground troops—are stationed at bases in Gibraltar, Malta, and Cyprus (see below). Military training and air-staging facilities in Libya were given up in 1970 after the deposition of King Idris. The new revolutionary government also required the United States to give up Wheelus Field air base near Tripoli.

Russian forces

The arrival in the late 1960s of significant numbers of Soviet warships in the Mediterranean poses many problems for NATO. Though much inferior to the US Sixth Fleet in striking power, the size of the Soviet fleet varies between 15 and 25 vessels. It sometimes includes tank-landing ships, and a helicopter-carrier of the Moscow class. Helicopter-carriers and landing-ships are a recent addition to the Soviet navy, and together with the formation of a small marine corps are widely seen as evidence of Russia's intention to match America's worldwide amphibious capability.

Soviet naval units use Egyptian facilities at Alexandria and Port Said, and also a deep-water anchorage in Salum Bay, near the UAR-Libyan border. Another anchorage used by the Russians is near the Greek island of Kithira, off the southern tip of the Peloponnese. On the Syrian coast the Russians use the naval base at Latakya, and work has been reported on additional facilities at Jeble, seven miles to the south. Other anchorages are available off the coasts of Algeria and Tunisia, and Russian long-range aircraft make maritime reconnaissance flights from Cairo, Aleppo, and other Arab airfields.

The Soviet naval expansion in the Mediterranean is part of a general extension of Soviet naval activity throughout the world. The aim is to establish a Soviet presence in what was formerly an American preserve. What the Soviet presence has done is to make it unlikely that the US can ever again undertake an operation such as the landing, in July 1958, of a force of marines to bolster Western interests in the Lebanon.

French forces

Although the French navy has ceased to use its former large naval base at Mers-el-Kebir, near

Military forces and bases

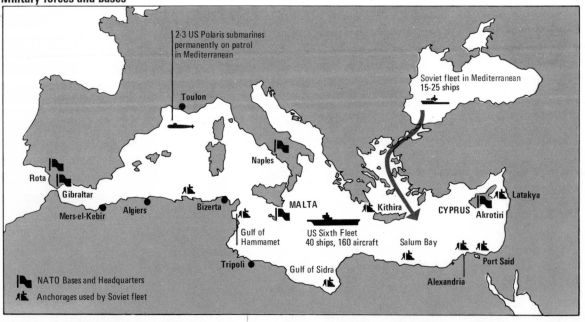

Now firmly established as a naval power in the Mediterranean, the Soviet Union supports its fleet there from bases in the Black Sea. Under the Montreux Convention of 1936, Russian warships may pass freely through the Turkish straits provided that advance notice is given to the Turkish government. The US Sixth Fleet, including a carrier task force, enjoys a great superiority in firepower. But small Russian surface-to-surface missile boats may present more of a threat than some Western naval authorities admit.

Oran (Algeria), and smaller installations at Bizerta in Tunisia, French naval forces based at Toulon (France) continue to make regular patrols of the North African coast. Under the Evian Agreement (1962) between France and Algeria, the French air force can continue to use the air base at Bou Sfar, near Mers-el-Kebir, until the mid-1970s.

France has two main aims in the Mediterranean: to restore the influence it had before Algeria, Morocco, and Tunisia won their independence; and to limit the Soviet naval challenge at the western end of the region. Like Yugoslavia, Algeria, and other Mediterranean countries, it would welcome the neutralization of the area, a situation that would require the complete withdrawal of both Russian and American naval forces.

Cyprus

Although Cyprus was a Turkish possession until acquired by Britain in 1878, four fifths of its 600,000 people are Greek. Independence was granted in 1960 after a bitter campaign against British rule by the Greek-Cypriot guerrilla organization EOKA. The new constitution guaranteed Turkish minority rights and provided for the stationing in Cyprus of balanced contingents of Greek and Turkish troops. It also allowed Britain to retain sovereign rights over two military bases in the south of the island—Dekhelia, an army base, and Akrotiri, used mainly by the Royal Air Force. Both bases serve British commitments to NATO and CENTO. Akrotiri is also an RAF staging post on the route to the Far East.

In 1963 a move by President Makarios to revise the constitution was seen by the Turkish minority as the preliminary to union (*enosis*) with Greece. In clashes arising from communal tension, terrible brutalities were committed by both sides. Peace was established by a United Nations emergency force, which included British troops.

Following further clashes in 1967, when Turkey threatened invasion, both Greece and Turkey agreed to withdraw their troops. But the United Nations force remains. Since 1968, relations between Cyprus and Greece have been complicated by the existence of the right-wing military government in Athens. Right-wing Greek Cypriots still desire *enosis,* but moderate elements, typified by President Makarios, now—temporarily—reject it. A right-wing attempt to assassinate the president was foiled in 1970.

Gibraltar

The Gibraltar promontory was ceded to Britain by the Treaty of Utrecht, which ended the War of the Spanish Succession in 1713. But Spain has repeatedly contested the treaty provision and its claim to the "Rock" was actively revived in the 1960s. Although Gibraltar has in fact lost much of its strategic importance with the advent of long-range air-power, Britain feels obliged to resist the Spanish claim in deference to the wishes of Gibraltar's inhabitants. In 1967 a United Nations committee voted for Gibraltar's "decolonization". But a referendum purported to show that only 44 Gibraltarians out of 12,138 supported union with Spain, at least under the regime of General Franco.

After the referendum, the Spanish authorities applied political and economic pressures on Gibraltar. They stopped the daily entry of 12,000 Spanish workers, halted tourist traffic, cut telephone communications, and forbade British aircraft to use nearby Spanish airspace.

In 1969, restrictions were eased. But in March 1970, the Spanish government announced that it did not intend to let the matter rest.

Gibraltar

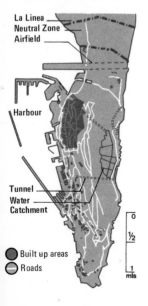

Built up areas
Roads

Rock shelters, a self-contained water supply, and elaborate harbour defences protect Gibraltar **(left)** against conventional attack. But the proximity of the airfield to Spanish airspace has led to international incidents.

Cyprus **(right)**, a member of the Commonwealth since 1960, lies only 40 miles south of Turkey. Since 1964 a United Nations force has been established in the island to keep the peace between Greek and Turkish Cypriots.

Cyprus

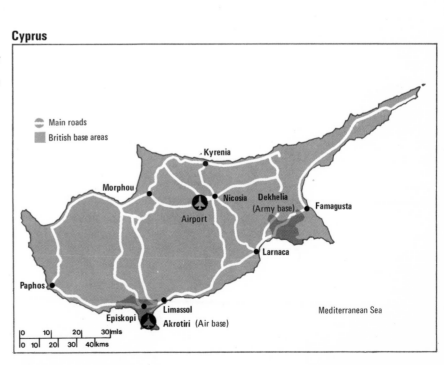

Main roads
British base areas

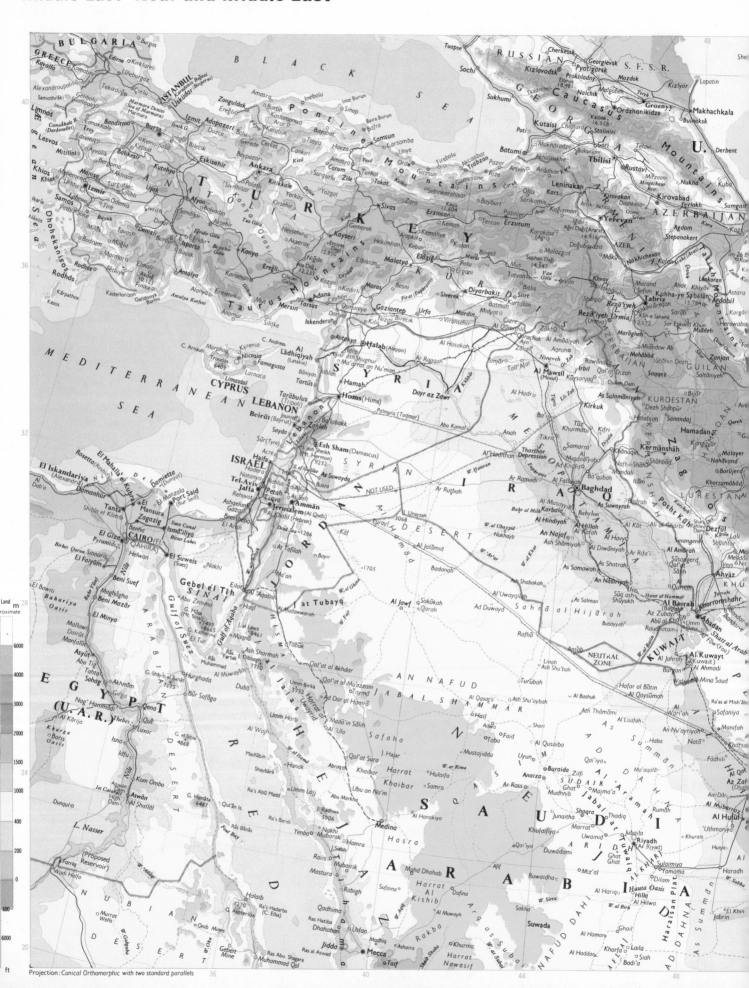

Projection: Conical Orthomorphic with two standard parallels

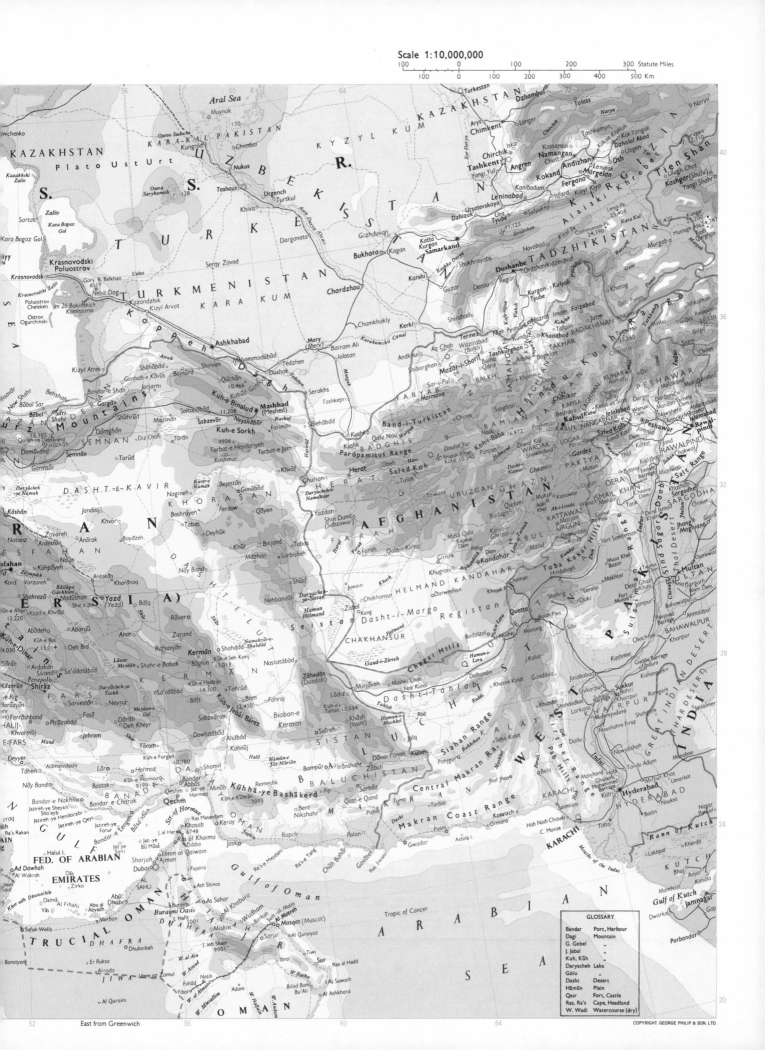

Middle East arms and strategy

Defensive alliances

The Middle East, which contains nearly two thirds of the world's reserves of petroleum, supplies Western Europe with most of its oil. The stability of the area is thus of particular concern to countries such as Britain and France, whose economic well-being depends to such a large extent on the maintenance of a steady flow of oil.

During the cold war, in the 1950s, it was widely assumed that the chief threat to the area came from the Soviet Union, and that the best way to prevent Russian penetration was to link the so-called "northern tier" of Middle Eastern countries in a military pact. So Britain took the lead in helping to bridge the long gap that lay between Turkey (in NATO) and Pakistan (in SEATO). The Baghdad Pact was thus formed in 1955, linking Turkey, Iraq, Iran, Pakistan, and Britain. It lost much of its effectiveness when a coup in 1958 led Iraq to withdraw, and the alliance had to be hastily renamed the Central Treaty Organization (CENTO).

The US is an associated member of CENTO and is represented on the Council of Military Deputies and on the Economic and Counter-subversion committees. The treaty aims to provide mutual cooperation for defence and security, but there is no international command structure as in NATO. Nuclear support is provided by Britain from Cyprus, and by the US Sixth Fleet.

Bilateral defence agreements also exist between the US and the three local CENTO members.

Although it has brought benefits such as joint road, railway, and telecommunications development among members, CENTO has failed to prevent Russian penetration of Middle East countries to the south of the CENTO area, and the creation of a Soviet presence in the Mediterranean.

Problems of the Arab world

Though the Arab world is readily identifiable by race, religion, language, and culture, Arab unity is something of a myth. Not till the end of World War II did complete independence come to the bulk of the Arab countries—and then only slowly.

In 1945 the Pact of the League of Arab States (better known as the Arab League) was signed by Egypt, Transjordan, Iraq, Syria, the Lebanon, Saudi Arabia, and the Yemen. The League was later joined by Libya, the Sudan, Morocco, Tunisia, Kuwait, and Algeria. Initially it made little impact and it was not until 1950—after their first defeat by Israelis in 1948–49—that the Arab countries signed a treaty for joint defence and economic cooperation. This treaty was never ratified, however, and it was not until after the Second Arab-Israeli War (1956), that the quest for unity recommenced. In 1958 Egypt and Syria joined together in the United Arab Republic, with President Gamal Abdul Nasser as supreme head of both countries. (For a short while the Yemen also joined the UAR.)

Since the Egyptian revolution of 1952, Nasser had been the most important figure in the Arab world. With his curious mixture of nationalism,

socialism, and idealism—and a skilful use of anti-Israel propaganda—he put himself at the forefront of the band of men in all Arab countries who sought far-reaching economic and social change. No nationalist revolutionary in the Arab world could afford to be hostile to Nasser; those who set themselves up against him were often swept away by popular revolution. In July 1958, Egypt's chief rival in the Arab world, Iraq, underwent a revolution that overthrew the monarchy, but did not remove Egyptian–Iraqi tensions.

In 1961, three years after the Egypt-Syria union, the United Arab Republic split up. Egypt alone retaining the name. The following year, with the emergence of independent Algeria, a new pole of attraction was created in the Arab world to rival Cairo. The Third Arab-Israeli War (1967) brought a measure of verbal unity in the councils of the Arab world, but in the aftermath (see p. 67) a serious split developed when Egypt and Jordan, under Soviet and American pressure, agreed to a cease-fire that would stop continuing border

Military forces of Middle Eastern countries

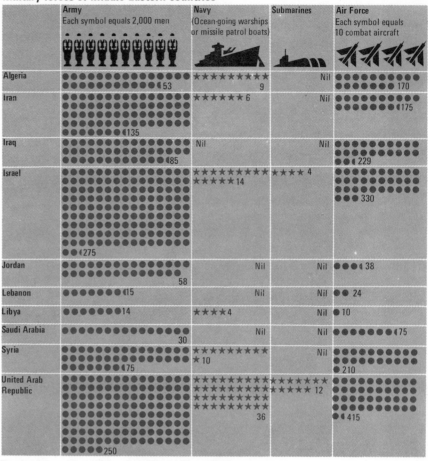

	Army Each symbol equals 2,000 men	Navy (Ocean-going warships or missile patrol boats)	Submarines	Air Force Each symbol equals 10 combat aircraft
Algeria	●●●●●●●●●●●●●●●●●●●●●●●●●● ◄53	★★★★★★★★★ 9	Nil	●●●●●●●●●●●●●●●●● ◄170
Iran	●● ◄135	★★★★★★ 6	Nil	●●●●●●●●●●●●●●●●● ◄175
Iraq	●● ◄85	Nil	Nil	●●●●●●●●●●●●●●●●●●●●●●● ◄229
Israel	●●● ◄275	★★★★★★★★★★★★ ★★★★★ 14	★★★ 4	●●●●●●●●●●●●●●●●●●●●●●●●●●●●●●●●● ●● ◄330
Jordan	●●●●●●●●●●●●●●●●●●●●●●●●●●●●●●●● 58		Nil	Nil	●●● ◄38
Lebanon	●●●●●●● ◄15		Nil	Nil	●● 24
Libya	●●●●●●● 14	★★★★4	Nil	● 10
Saudi Arabia	●●●●●●●●●●●●●●● 30	Nil	Nil	●●●●●●●● ◄75
Syria	●●●●●●●●●●●●●●●●●●●●●●●●●●●●●●●●●●●●●●● ◄75	★★★★★★★★★ ★ 10	Nil	●●●●●●●●●●●●●●●●●●●●● 210
United Arab Republic	●● 250	★★★★★★★★★★★★★★★★★★★ ★★★★★★★★★★★★★ 12 ★★★★★★★★★★ ★★★★★★★★★ 36		●●● ●◄ 415

Territorial and boundary disputes in North Africa

MOROCCO	ALGERIA	TUNISIA
	SPANISH SAHARA	

| 0 | 500 | 1000 mls |
| 0 | 800 | 1600 kms |

1. Algeria x Morocco
2. Morocco x Spain (Ifni)
3. Morocco x Spain (Spanish Sahara)
4. Tunisia x Algeria
(southern part of the Tunisia – Algeria border)

Map shows disputes that have affected relations between North African countries in recent years. The disputes between Algeria and Morocco (1) and Tunisia and Algeria (4) arise from the drawing of frontiers during the period of French rule. The dispute between Morocco and Spain over Ifni (2) was settled when Spain ceded the enclave to Morocco in 1969. Morocco's claim to the Spanish Sahara (3) became active after the discovery there in 1964 of what are possibly the world's largest phosphate deposits—reserves are estimated at 1000 million tons. In addition, Morocco claims the whole of the territory of adjoining Mauritania. (Disputes involving other areas of Africa are listed on p. 73.)

Suez Canal

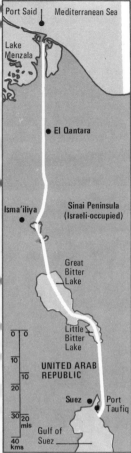

Port Said — Mediterranean Sea

Lake
Menzala

● El Qantara

Isma'iliya ●

Sinai Peninsula
(Israeli-occupied)

Great
Bitter
Lake

Little
Bitter
Lake

UNITED ARAB
REPUBLIC

Suez ●   ● Port
              Taufiq

Gulf of
Suez

0   0
10
    10
20
30 20
    mls
40
kms

Until June 1967, when the Suez
Canal (above) was closed, half the
oil exports from the Middle East
passed through the 101-mile-long
waterway. Today, giant tankers
from the Persian Gulf use the
longer route via the Cape of Good
Hope (see p. 69). Diagram (right)
shows arms expenditure by Middle
Eastern countries. Notice that
Israel, with only 3 million people,
can afford to spend about 10 times
as much per head as Egypt, whose
population is some 10 times
greater.

Military expenditure (1969) in relation to population

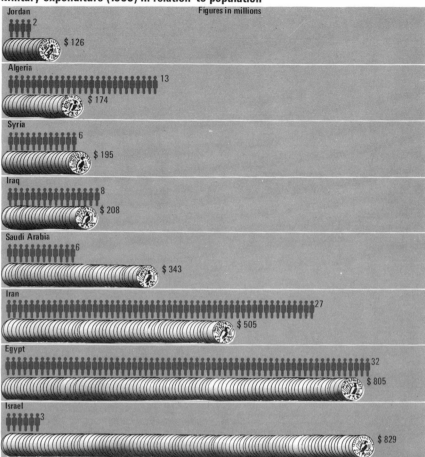

Figures in millions

Jordan   2
                $ 126

Algeria   13
                $ 174

Syria   6
                $ 195

Iraq   8
                $ 208

Saudi Arabia   6
                $ 343

Iran   27
                $ 505

Egypt   32
                $ 805

Israel   3
                $ 829

incidents with Israel and permit talks, under UN auspices, about a permanent settlement.

While the Jordanian monarchy was threatened by Palestinian "liberation" groups, the more militant Arab states—Algeria, Libya, Syria, and Iraq—denounced the cease-fire arrangement. They temporarily dropped their attacks following Nasser's death from a heart attack on September 28, 1970.

The Maghreb

The three Arab countries on the northwestern extremity of Africa—Tunisia, Algeria, and Morocco—have historical differences from the rest of the Arab world. Known collectively as the Maghreb, they continue to show strong traces of their former rule by France.

Algeria, which achieved its independence in 1962 after a long revolutionary war, now steers a middle course between East and West, although it maintains a high degree of revolutionary rhetoric. Most of its arms come from the Soviet Union, but it has good commercial relations with the United States. Relations with France—poor in the period

immediately after independence—have also been patched up. In 1969, for the first time, the Algerians arranged to buy French military aircraft. In 1965 the flamboyant President Ben Bella was deposed and succeeded by Houari Boumedienne, a much tougher man.

Morocco, independent since 1965, plays a somewhat passive role in Arab councils. Its chief international quarrels have been with Spain, though it has also laid a claim to neighbouring Mauritania. In 1969 Spain agreed to hand over its African territory of Ifni to Morocco, but no agreement was reached over Ceuta, Melilla, and Spanish Sahara.

Tunisia, ruled since 1956 by President Habib Bourguiba, who negotiated with France for Tunisian independence, has played little part in Arab politics, largely because of Bourguiba's dislike of the late President Nasser. Bourguiba long nourished hopes of a rapprochement between the Arabs and Israel, but was forced to abandon these after the Third Arab-Israeli War. In 1969, for the first time, he gave more than $50,000 to the Palestine Liberation Organization.

Middle East conflict over Palestine

Arabs versus Israelis

For several years the Middle East has been one of the world's most volatile regions, a potential flash point of World War III. The origin of the trouble goes back to 1917 when Britain, in the Balfour Declaration, undertook to establish a Jewish national home in Palestine.

Palestine was part of the Ottoman Empire until Britain wrested it from the Turks in World War I. The Balfour Declaration was a means of gaining the support of American Jewry for the war. But it conflicted with promises made to the Arabs by Colonel T. E. Lawrence, who led the Arab revolt that paved the way for the British victory.

After the war Britain received Palestine under a League of Nations mandate. The mandate provided for the setting up of a Jewish national home without injury to the Arab population. But this proved impossible when Jewish immigration, which had declined in the 1920s, revived as a result of Nazi persecution in Europe. Before, during, and after World War II, Britain virtually stopped all Jewish immigration into Palestine, but soon had to deal with increasing violence by Jewish and Arab guerrillas. In 1947 it announced its intention to withdraw from Palestine, leaving the United Nations to deal with the problem.

A United Nations plan to partition the country into Jewish and Arab states, with Jerusalem as an international city, was rejected by the Arabs. In May 1948, immediately after Britain's withdrawal, the Jews proclaimed the state of Israel—and the Arab countries invaded. The First Arab-Israeli War had begun.

In spite of their inferiority in numbers, the Israelis fought back, and by the time the United Nations could secure an armistice agreement in 1949, Israel had gained more ground than it had started with—including part of Jerusalem.

The Hashemite Kingdom of Transjordan (another former British mandate) also gained territory in central Palestine, became independent, and renamed itself Jordan. Egypt kept the Gaza Strip, an area of about 100 square miles near the Egyptian border. Hundreds of thousands of Arabs living in Israel became refugees and were mostly accommodated in United Nations refugee camps in the Gaza Strip and nearby Arab states. (The total today stands at about 1,500,000 refugees.) From 1949–56 Israel lived in a state of semi-war, while United Nations truce teams on its borders tried to keep the peace.

The Second Arab-Israeli War (1956) was precipitated by the Anglo-American withdrawal of offers to help finance Egypt's great dam at Aswan, followed by the Egyptian nationalization of the Anglo-French Suez Canal company. Russia at once promised finance for the dam, and began supplying Egypt with aircraft and tanks.

On October 29, 1956, concerned at Egypt's growing military strength and by the formation of an Egyptian-Syrian-Jordanian joint command, the Israelis invaded the Sinai Desert, routed the Egyptian army, and advanced towards the Suez Canal. Next day Britain and France presented the Egyptians with a demand to occupy points along the canal, ostensibly to protect it and to separate the combatants. When Egypt ignored this ultimatum, Anglo-French forces bombed Egyptian installations and, after a clumsy concentration of forces, made a landing, on November 5, at Port Said.

Despite official denials, it later became clear that the British and French governments had connived in Israeli plans for the attack, and had tried to hide their intentions from the United States. When the Americans learned that the operation had been launched, they threatened to withdraw support from sterling and the franc, unless the British and French (and Israelis) complied with a United Nations ceasefire call. The action was ended in under 24 hours.

The Suez expedition was politically and militarily disastrous: the Egyptians blocked the canal by sinking 40 ships; the Russians used the occasion to divert world opinion from their brutal repression of a revolt in Hungary; and the way was paved for Russia's deep penetration of the Arab world.

In December the Anglo-French forces were replaced by a 6000-strong United Nations force. Israel evacuated Sinai and the Gaza Strip. The canal remained closed until April 1957.

The Third Arab-Israeli War was partly precipitated by Egypt's refusal to allow Israeli ships or cargoes through the Suez Canal and Egyptian territorial waters. Until 1967, Israeli vessels continued to pass through the Gulf of Aqaba to the Israeli port of Eilat, the terminal of a commercially important pipeline for oil imports. But on May 22, 1967 the Egyptians announced a blockade of the Strait of Tiran, thus blocking access to Eilat. The Israelis declared that they would open the strait.

Israel's conquests in Six-Day War

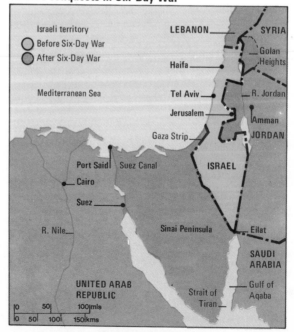

Map shows that territory won during Six-Day War gives Israel a valuable bargaining counter in any settlement with the Arabs. If Russia and US were to guarantee it against attack, Israel might negotiate about certain areas. If the territory concerned were demilitarized, Israel might return Golan Heights to Syria, much of Sinai to UAR. A Palestine state might even be set up on West Bank of Jordan and in Gaza Strip, so providing a home for over two million refugees.

The war began early on June 5 with a pre-emptive Israeli air strike. The Egyptian air force was destroyed within a few hours. Almost simultaneously Israeli tanks entered Sinai and within four days (see map) had eliminated seven Egyptian divisions. In a subsidiary attack against Jordan the Israeli army captured Jerusalem and cleared the whole west bank of the river Jordan by June 8. An advance into Syria, against great natural obstacles, secured the Golan Heights—a natural battlement of volcanic rock that had for years dominated the Israeli-Syrian frontier and provided an artillery base for shelling Israeli settlements. Fighting ended on June 11.

Though the Six-Day War confirmed Israel's superiority in military skill and courage, the material losses of the Arab states were soon made good by Russia in less than 12 months. Subsequent attempts by the US, Britain, and France to persuade the Israelis to give up their conquests in return for international guarantees of their security have failed due to Israel's insistence on direct talks with the Arabs, which would involve Arab recognition of Israel. The Arabs have long refused such recognition, but appeared to be relenting when Egypt and Jordan agreed to the 1970 cease-fire talks (see below).

The war did not bring peace to the Middle East. After 1967, fighting continued sporadically on all Israel's borders, and especially across the Suez Canal. There was also a marked increase in activity by Palestinian guerrilla organizations.

In August 1970 Palestinian guerrilla activity reached a new intensity when a small "commando" group hi-jacked and destroyed four Western air-liners, three of them in Jordan. The Jordanian army moved against the guerrillas in an attempt to reassert the government's authority; and in two weeks' fighting some 3000 people were killed. During the fighting, Syrian tank units intervened briefly to aid the guerrillas but were withdrawn after the Israelis threatened to commit their air force. The fighting left King Hussein in power but with diminished authority.

The guerrillas' aim had almost certainly been to sabotage the agreement by Jordan and Egypt to a US-sponsored cease-fire with Israel, in which the Soviet Union also showed interest. On the Suez Canal front the cease-fire provided for a "standstill" zone extending 32 miles either side of the canal.

Within hours of going into operation the cease-fire threatened to break down when the Egyptians advanced surface-to-air missile batteries (SAM sites) to points from which they commanded air space over Israel's Bar-Lev defence line (see map). To save the agreement the US had to rectify the military balance by deliveries of new equipment to Israel. In January 1971 Israel, under US pressure, agreed to return to talks with the UN Jarring mission on a more permanent settlement. The good faith of Russia, which had supplied, and in some cases manned, the Egyptian missiles had been seriously impugned.

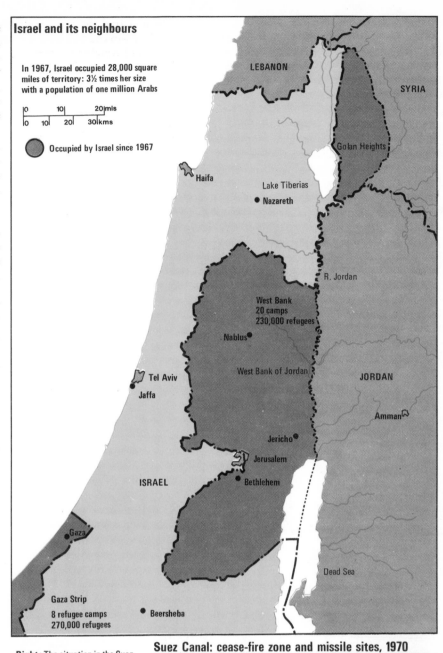

Israel and its neighbours

In 1967, Israel occupied 28,000 square miles of territory: 3½ times her size with a population of one million Arabs

Occupied by Israel since 1967

Right: The situation in the Suez Canal zone in December 1970, five months after the first Soviet-built missiles were set up there (see this page.)

Suez Canal: cease-fire zone and missile sites, 1970

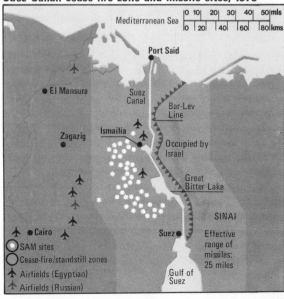

SAM sites
Cease-fire/standstill zones
Airfields (Egyptian)
Airfields (Russian)

Middle East oil and stability

Supplies and sales
No highly industrialized state can survive without adequate supplies of oil. The Soviet Union is self-supporting in oil, as is the United States, but Western Europe has practically none of its own. Most of the world's reserves are in its poorer areas, thousands of miles from where the bulk of the oil is actually consumed. Consequently the shipment of oil accounts for a high percentage of the world's shipping. There are more oil tankers afloat than any other kind of large ship.

The world's oil industry is dominated by seven companies. Five of these are American; the other two are Anglo-Dutch Shell; and British Petroleum, a firm in which the British government has a 49 per cent holding.

Middle Eastern oil was first found in Persia (Iran) in 1908. Important finds were registered in Iraq in 1927 and in Bahrain in 1932. Although Anglo-French interests initially controlled the concessions, it was not long before the large American companies moved in. Today the Middle East dominates the world oil market, holding 75 per cent of the known reserves and 46 per cent of production. It is the cheapest oil in the world to produce, as the figures (per barrel) show:

Kuwait	6·26 US cents
Middle East (average)	15 cents
Venezuela	51 cents
Soviet Union	80 cents
United States	131 cents

The 1971 oil crisis
In 1971 a confrontation developed between oil producers and oil consumers when the Organization of Petroleum Exporting Countries (OPEC) demanded an all-round increase in oil prices and a rise in the tax rate on oil companies' net income from 50 to 55 per cent. The oil companies insisted that any deal must guarantee the stability of prices for at least five years. Refusing to be bound by any agreement, the OPEC countries threatened to cut off oil supplies if price increases were not paid to Iran and the Gulf states. Thus Western Europe was again reminded of its industrial dependence on Middle East supplies.

The "posted" price of oil
OPEC also demanded the removal of differences between the "posted" prices of oil—the nominal price on the basis of which oil royalties are normally paid by oil companies. The idea of the posted price originated in 1948 when Venezuela—then the largest exporting country—introduced a tax reform whereby the profits of the oil industry were to be divided equally between the oil companies and the government. The idea caught on in the Middle East where, in order to improve relations with the producer countries, the companies agreed to "post" an official export price for oil, which was actually based at the time on the selling price of oil in the United States. After subtracting the cost of production, the company and the producer government

then shared the profit equally between them. The policy worked well until a surplus of oil later in the decade brought consumer prices down and made the "posted prices" look ridiculously high.

In 1959 President Eisenhower, under pressure from defence planners who felt that the United States was beginning to rely too much on oil imports, imposed compulsory controls on the import of oil into the US. American companies who produced overseas were forced to find new markets, and initially they concentrated on Western Europe. The price fell.

In consequence the companies, for the first and last time, reduced the "posted prices", to the fury of the producer governments, whose budgets were geared strictly to the continuing high price of oil. In September 1960, President Abdul Kerim Kassem of Iraq called for a conference of oil-producing countries. The result was the setting up of OPEC —an almost unique producers' cartel that gives the producing countries a considerable amount of leverage with regard to the oil companies.

Rivalries in the Persian Gulf
About one third of the world's oil comes from the Persian Gulf. The loss of supplies could be extremely serious to Western Europe which, apart from its large investments in the Middle East oil industry, meets three quarters of its needs from the area.

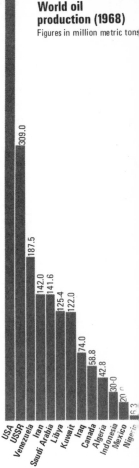

World oil production (1968)
Figures in million metric tons

USA	526·0
USSR	309.0
Venezuela	187.5
Iran	142.0
Saudi Arabia	141.6
Libya	125.4
Kuwait	122.0
Iraq	74.0
Canada	58.8
Algeria	42.8
Indonesia	30·0
Mexico	20·0
Nigeria	6·3

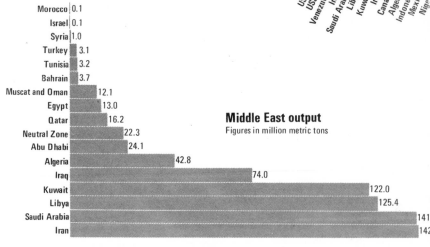

Middle East output
Figures in million metric tons

Morocco	0.1
Israel	0.1
Syria	1.0
Turkey	3.1
Tunisia	3.2
Bahrain	3.7
Muscat and Oman	12.1
Egypt	13.0
Qatar	16.2
Neutral Zone	22.3
Abu Dhabi	24.1
Algeria	42.8
Iraq	74.0
Kuwait	122.0
Libya	125.4
Saudi Arabia	141.
Iran	142.

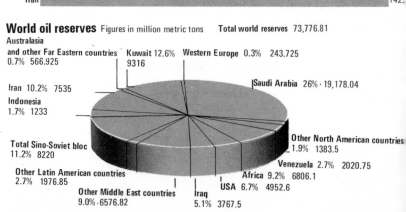

World oil reserves Figures in million metric tons   Total world reserves 73,776.81

Australasia and other Far Eastern countries 0.7% 566.925
Kuwait 12.6% 9316
Western Europe 0.3% 243.725
Iran 10.2% 7535
Saudi Arabia 26%· 19,178.04
Indonesia 1.7% 1233
Total Sino-Soviet bloc 11.2% 8220
Other North American countries 1.9% 1383.5
Venezuela 2.7% 2020.75
Africa 9.2% 6806.1
Other Latin American countries 2.7% 1976.85
USA 6.7% 4952.6
Other Middle East countries 9.0%·6576.82
Iraq 5.1% 3767.5

The flow of oil could be endangered if gross instability were to follow the withdrawal of British military forces which, through a complicated treaty system, have helped to police the Gulf for more than a century.

The Gulf states protected by British treaties are Bahrain (pop. 185,000); Qatar (pop. 80,000); and the Trucial States (pop. 180,000).

The Trucial States (taking their name from a 19th century agreement to end piracy and the slave trade) are: Abu Dhabi, Dubai, Sharjah, Ajman, Umm al Qaiwain, Ras al Khaimah, and Fujairah.

Under the treaties Britain became responsible for the foreign relations of the Gulf states, through a Political Resident in Bahrain.

Kuwait (pop. 470,000) dropped British protection in 1961 and became totally independent. It is now the world's seventh largest oil-producer.

Three territorial claims have given cause for anxiety about Persian Gulf stability in recent years: that of Iran to sovereignty over Bahrain; that of Iraq to Kuwait; that of Saudi Arabia to the Buraimi oasis on the border of Abu Dhabi.

The Iranian claim to Bahrain was relinquished in 1970. But Iran, Iraq, and Saudi Arabia could be drawn into active rivalry if a "power vacuum" were to follow Britain's withdrawal. To avoid this danger, Britain in 1968, encouraged the "protected" Gulf states—Bahrain, Qatar, and the Trucial States—to set about forming a federation. Preliminary agreement was reached in February, but local rivalries prevented further progress.

In August 1970 a new element entered the picture with a coup in the Sultanate of Muscat and Oman, deposing the aged and autocratic ruler in favour of his son. Oman, as it is now simply called, has newly found oil wealth and a population of 750,000.

It is clearly a state to which others may wish to attach themselves in some alternative to federation. First, however, it must solve the problem of insurgency in the Dhofar region, where a revolt provoked by the old Sultan's misrule has been supported with arms from the South Yemen.

A further threat to stability in the Gulf arises from the spread of revolutionary politics from Baathist Iraq, the chief source of skilled labour for the smaller states' oilfields, and from Egypt, whose schools and universities have trained the many Palestinians now serving the Gulf States as teachers and civil servants.

Threat to Saudi Arabia

A threat to Saudi Arabia arose in the early 1960s when Egyptian forces supported the revolt against royalist rule in the neighbouring Yemen. In spite of Egyptian strength in armour and modern weapons, the royalists, aided from Saudi Arabia, succeeded in the hinterland. In 1968 dissensions between Egypt and the republican Yemenite leaders led to Egyptian forces being withdrawn.

The inherent contest between Arab monarchism, represented by Saudi Arabia, and Arab socialism, represented by Egypt, has yet to be resolved. In the meantime Saudi Arabia is an important donor of funds for the Arab struggle with Israel and to compensate Egypt for the loss of Suez Canal revenues.

Autocratically governed, but undergoing reforms since the accession of King Faisal in 1964, Saudi Arabia possesses not only vast oil wealth but also, in Mecca, the holiest shrine of the Muslim world.

A move to remedy its military backwardness was made with the acquisition of British jet fighters and anti-aircraft missiles in the late 1960s.

Territorial and boundary disputes

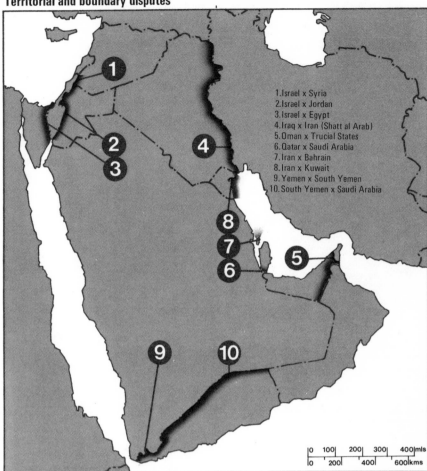

1. Israel x Syria
2. Israel x Jordan
3. Israel x Egypt
4. Iraq x Iran (Shatt al Arab)
5. Oman x Trucial States
6. Qatar x Saudi Arabia
7. Iran x Bahrain
8. Iran x Kuwait
9. Yemen x South Yemen
10. South Yemen x Saudi Arabia

Suez Canal closure

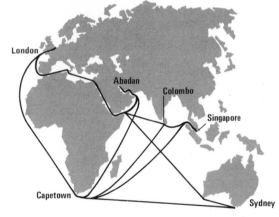

London	via Suez	via Cape
to Abadan		
miles	7,527	13,744
days	17 ¼	31 ½
to Colombo		
miles	7,691	11,984
days	17 ½	27 ½
to Singapore		
miles	9,495	13,440
days	21 ¾	30 ¾
to Sydney		
miles	13,222	15,369
days	30 ¼	33
distances are in miles, not nautical miles – Speed 16 knots		

Effect on international shipping times of closure of the Suez Canal in June 1967. Closure has stimulated the construction of tankers and other bulk-carriers too large for the canal. Russia and other Comecon countries—which import increasing amounts of Middle East oil—are keen to get the canal reopened, a job that could take as little as two months. Map **(top)** shows location of various territories and boundaries in the Middle East that have been the subject of dispute in recent years.

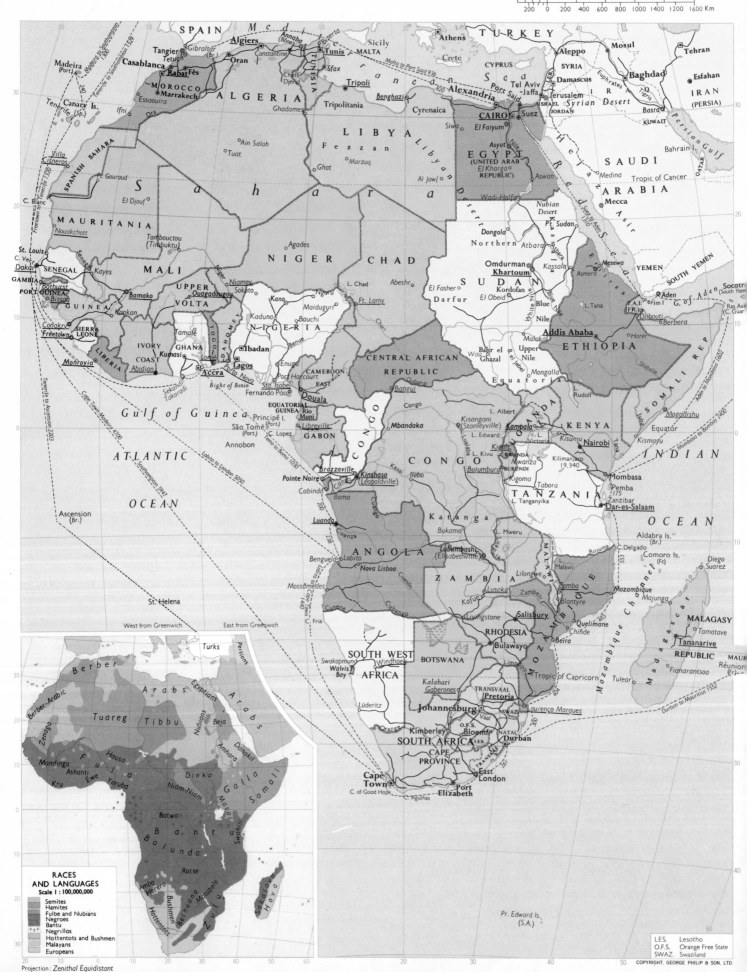

Africa political

Scale 1:40,000,000

200   0   200   400   600   800   1000 Statute Miles
200   0   200   400   600   800 1000 1200 1400 1600 Km

SPAIN
Madeira (Port.)
Tangier
Tetuan
Casablanca
Rabat Fès
MOROCCO
Marrakech
Essaouira
Ifni
Canary Is. Tenerife (Sp.)
C. Blanc
SPANISH SAHARA
Villa Cisneros
MAURITANIA
Nouakchott
St. Louis
C. Ver.
Dakar
SENEGAL
Kayes
GAMBIA
Bathurst
PORT. GUINEA
Bissau
Conakry
Freetown
SIERRA LEONE
LIBERIA
Monrovia
IVORY COAST
Kumasi
Abidjan
Sekondi-Takoradi

Algiers
Oran
Constantine
Annaba (Bône)
Bizerta
TUNISIA
Tunis
Sfax
Tripoli
Tripolitania
Ghadames
Ghat

ALGERIA
Sahara
Ain Salah
Tuat
El Djouf
Ft. Gouraud
Tombouctou (Timbuktu)
Agades
MALI
Bamako
Ouagadougou
UPPER VOLTA
Niamey
Sokoto
GUINEA
Kankan
Niger
Kano
Kaduna
Bauchi
Maiduguri
NIGERIA
Tamale
GHANA
TOGO DAHOMEY
Lomé
Porto Novo
Accra
Lagos
Ibadan
Benue
Enugu
Port Harcourt
CAMEROON
EAST
Sta. Isabel
Fernando Póo
Douala

Malta to Port Said 936
Athens
Sicily
MALTA
Crete
Benghazi
Cyrenaica
LIBYA
Fezzan
Marzuq
Al Jawf

TURKEY
CYPRUS
Aleppo
Mosul
SYRIA
Damascus
Baghdad
Tel Aviv-Jaffa
ISRAEL
Jerusalem
JORDAN
Alexandria
Port Said
Cairo
Suez
El Faiyum
EGYPT (UNITED ARAB REPUBLIC)
El Kharga
Asyut
Aswan
Wadi-Halfa
Nubian Desert
Pt. Sudan
Dongola
Northern
Atbara
Omdurman
Khartoum
Kassala
SUDAN
Kordofan
El Obeid
El Fasher
Darfur
Abeshr
L. Chad
Ft. Lamy
Nguru
Chari
CHAD
NIGER

Tehran
IRAN (PERSIA)
Esfahan
Basra
KUWAIT
SAUDI ARABIA
Medina
Mecca
Bahrain I.
QATAR
Tropic of Cancer
Red Sea
YEMEN
SOUTH YEMEN
Aden
Perim
T.A.I. (FR.)
Djibouti
Berbera
Socotra (South Yem.)
Ras Asir (C. Guar.)
G. of Aden

CENTRAL AFRICAN REPUBLIC
Bangui
Ubangi
Congo
CONGO
Brazzaville
Pointe Noire
Cabinda
Boma
Mbandaka
Kasai
Ilebo
Bukama
Katanga
Lubumbashi (Elisabethville)
Bahr el Ghazal
Wau
Bahr el Jebel
Equatoria
Mongalla
Upper Nile
Malakal
White Nile
Blue Nile
L. Tana
Addis Ababa
Harer
ETHIOPIA
Mesewa
Asmera
Eritrea
SOMALI REP.
Mogadishu
Kismayu

EQUATORIAL GUINEA
Rio Muni
Libreville
GABON
São Tomé (Port.)
Príncipe I. (Port.)
Annobon
C. Lopez
Gulf of Guinea

UGANDA
Kampala
L. Albert
Kisangani (Stanleyville)
L. Edward
L. Kivu
RWANDA
Kigali
Bujumbura
BURUNDI
Kigoma
L. Tanganyika
Tabora
TANZANIA
Kilimanjaro 19,340
L. Victoria
Mwanza
Kisumu
KENYA
Nairobi
Mombasa
Pemba
Zanzibar
Dar-es-Salaam
L. Rudolf
Equator
Tana

ATLANTIC OCEAN
Ascension (Br.)
St. Helena

Luanda
Cuanza
Benguela
Lobito
Nova Lisboa
Mossâmedes
ANGOLA
Cunene
Cubango

Bie
ZAMBIA
Lusaka
Kafue
Livingstone
MALAWI
L. Mweru
Ruvuma
C. Delgado
Comoro Is. (Fr.)
L. Malawi
Lilongwe
Zomba
Blantyre
Chinde
Quelimane
MOZAMBIQUE
Mozambique
Majunga
Mozambique Channel
Aldabra Is. (Br.)
Diego Suarez
MALAGASY REPUBLIC
Tamatave
Tananarive
Fianarantsoa
MAUR.
Réunion (Fr.)
Madagascar
INDIAN OCEAN

West from Greenwich   East from Greenwich

SOUTH WEST AFRICA
Swakopmund
Windhoek
Walvis Bay
Lüderitz
Kalahari
BOTSWANA
Gaberones
Salisbury
Bulawayo
RHODESIA
Beira
Limpopo
Tropic of Capricorn
Tulear

TRANSVAAL
Pretoria
Johannesburg
Kimberley
Vaal
Bloemfontein
O.F.S.
SWAZ.
NATAL
Durban
Lourenço Marques
Orange
SOUTH AFRICA
CAPE PROVINCE
Cape Town
C. of Good Hope
C. Agulhas
Port Elizabeth
East London

Durban to Mauritius 1532

Pr. Edward Is. (S.A.)

RACES AND LANGUAGES
Scale 1:100,000,000

Semites
Hamites
Fulbe and Nubians
Negroes
Bantu
+++ Negrillos
Hottentots and Bushmen
Malayans
Europeans

Berber
Berber-Arabic
Zenaga
Tuareg
Tibbu
Arabs
Egyptians
Nubians
Beja
Amhara
Danakil
Galla
Somali
Mandingo
Fula
Hausa
Ashanti
Kru
Ewe
Yoruba
Niam-Niam
Dinka
Masai
Swahili
Batwa
Bantu
Balunda
Ambo
Herero
Bechuana
Matabele
Rotse
Zulu
Hottentots
Bushmen
Hova
Sakalava

Turks
Persians
Arabs

Projection: Zenithal Equidistant

LES.   Lesotho
O.F.S.   Orange Free State
SWAZ.   Swaziland

Pakistan

Pakistan, an Islamic republic of over 130 million people, consists of two major provinces—East and West Pakistan—separated by 1000 miles of Indian territory.

Since 1958, when General Ayub Khan took over as president, the country has been governed by a military dictatorship. Economic progress has been hampered by lack of mineral and industrial resources, a high rate of illiteracy (75 per cent of all people over the age of 15), and poor communications. Nevertheless, Pakistan had made considerable advances until checked in 1965 by the costly war with India over Kashmir.

In 1970 a new president, General Yahya Khan, launched an ambitious development programme and promised general elections. The programme, scheduled to cover a period of five years, aims to achieve an annual growth rate of 7.5 per cent in East Pakistan and 5.5 per cent in West Pakistan.

If successful, it will mean an increase of rather more than 150 per cent over the outlay achieved during the previous five-year plan. A significant aspect of the programme is its emphasis on heavy industry and the intention to allocate more money to social services.

Pakistan's relations with India have been embittered since both countries' independence in 1947. Since 1957 the United Nations has urged that a plebiscite should be held in Kashmir to decide its future. India has refused to agree unless Pakistan first withdraws its troops. In August 1965 tension over Kashmir led to war between Pakistan and India. With Russian help, a cease-fire was agreed at Tashkent, in the south of the Soviet Union, in 1966, but no final settlement is yet in prospect.

Following the 1965 war, Pakistan has received military aid, including T–54 tanks and Mig–19 aircraft, from China, and has ceased to play an active role in Western alliances.

Kashmir

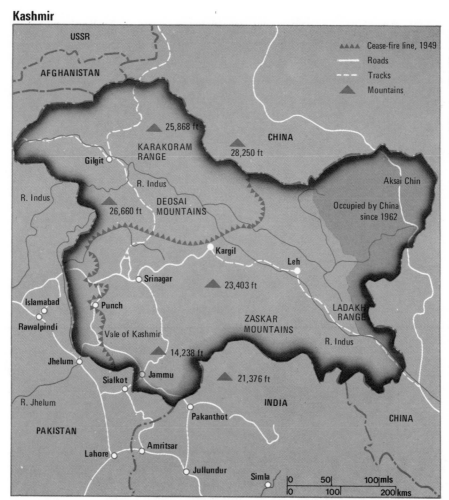

Kashmir (**left**) is not only the focal point of a long-standing quarrel (see text). The allocation, between India and Pakistan, of water from rivers that rise in or flow through the state was successfully resolved in 1960 by the Indus Waters Treaty. Under this treaty, the three eastern rivers of the Indus system were allocated to India, the three western to Pakistan. Such an example of effective cooperation between the two countries suggests that the Kashmir dispute is not beyond solution.

Asia China

Post-revolutionary problems

Since 1949, when the Communists won final control of the Chinese mainland, China (population 750 million, the world's largest) has threatened to dominate Asia. Despite the fiasco of the Great Leap Forward (1958–60) and the disruption caused by the "cultural revolution" (1966–9) it possesses, after Japan and the Soviet Union, the largest industrial capability in Asia.

Fears of Chinese expansionism, first aroused by Chinese participation in the Korean War (p. 93), were sharply reinforced by the invasion of Tibet, in 1950, and of India in 1963. But China lacks the means to deploy its vast military manpower (see map, below), and has hitherto preferred to seek objectives in Asia by aid or exhortation to others.

The United States has consistently refused to recognize the Peking government and has resisted communist China's admission to the United Nations. (China's seat on the Security Council is held by the Nationalist government in Taiwan.) Since 1955, however, United States and Chinese ambassadors have met intermittently in Warsaw.

Chinese-Soviet relations deteriorated sharply in the late 1950s following Russia's refusal to supply China with nuclear weapons and technology. The revival of ancient frontier claims (p. 88) also served to sharpen the growing ideological conflict between the two countries, each struggling for leadership of the communist world.

In mid-1970 China began to send a number of its ambassadors back to their posts from which they had been hurriedly recalled during the cultural revolution. Other signs of a return to normality included the reappearance in Europe of Chinese trade missions; the readmission of journalists and officially approved tourists to China; and the release of a number of foreign political prisoners.

Below: The deployment of China's conventional armed forces. The People's Liberation Army (PLA) embraces all three services, and includes a force of 118 front-line divisions. It has a total strength of 2,450,000 men. The navy (150,000 men) is divided into three fleets, and includes 29 fleet submarines. The air force (180,000 men) has 2800 combat aircraft.

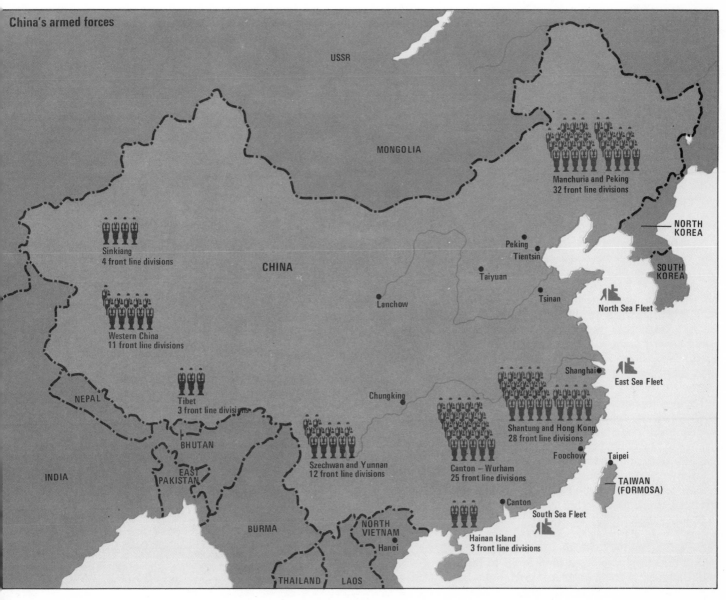

China's armed forces

USSR

MONGOLIA

Manchuria and Peking
32 front line divisions

NORTH KOREA

SOUTH KOREA

Sinkiang
4 front line divisions

CHINA

Peking
Tientsin

Taiyuan

Lanchow

Tsinan

North Sea Fleet

Western China
11 front line divisions

Shanghai

East Sea Fleet

Chungking

Tibet
3 front line divisions

NEPAL

BHUTAN

Shantung and Hong Kong
28 front line divisions

Foochow

Taipei

EAST PAKISTAN

INDIA

Szechwan and Yunnan
12 front line divisions

Canton – Wurham
25 front line divisions

TAIWAN (FORMOSA)

Canton

South Sea Fleet

BURMA

NORTH VIETNAM

Hanoi

Hainan Island
3 front line divisions

THAILAND   LAOS

Dispute with Russia

China and Russia have a common frontier that stretches for 4150 miles and was drawn in the 19th century in an area of Asia that had never been properly surveyed. For nearly 100 years Chinese governments have regarded the relevant frontier treaties as invalid and "un-equal".

As long as Sino-Soviet relations remained friendly there was no need to face the issue of demarcation. But with the growth of the ideological quarrel, the problem became acute.

Late in 1963 attempts were made to resolve the dispute at talks in Peking; but these broke down six months later when Mao Tse-tung attacked Soviet "territorial ambitions".

The fall of Khrushchev, in October 1964, was followed by a pause. But the dispute flared up again in March 1966, when China refused to attend the Soviet Communist Party's 23rd Congress. In 1966, after a number of incidents, both sides began to build up forces along the border. By December, the Soviet Union had at least 12 divisions along the frontier, and China 50. Border incidents increased in frequency and violence, culminating in 1969 in armed clashes on the Ussuri river in March and in the Ili river area of Sinkiang in August.

Despite an unprecedented outburst of mutual accusations, when Russia went so far as to make diplomatic representations about China in Western capitals, and China launched a "prepare for war" campaign at home, the Soviet Union suggested in March 1969 that the 1963-64 border talks should be resumed. After seven months of wrangling, the talks opened in Peking. A commission was set up and was continuing to meet in 1971.

The military confrontation

Any estimate of the Soviet threat to China and *vice versa* must take account of China's great size and population. With an area of 9.6 million square miles it is a million square miles larger than the Soviet Union, including the whole of Siberia; and its population of more than 700 million is three times greater than Russia's. The Soviet forces could never "occupy" China. On the other hand, the Chinese forces are materially ill-equipped to fight the heavily armed divisions that Russia can muster on its Asia frontier.

Though threatened at the height of the Sino-Soviet quarrel, a limited attack against Chinese nuclear installations could hardly be made without risking a much larger war and serious political consequences in the communist world.

Soviet nuclear launchers are reported to have been deployed in Mongolia and at other points on the frontier. China exploded its first nuclear device in October 1964, an H-bomb in 1967, and launched a satellite in April 1970. By 1973 it would be technically possible for China to develop a 6000-mile ICBM that would put large areas of the US and Canada, as well as the USSR, India, and Australia, within range of its nuclear warheads.

Foreign aid programmes

The end of the cultural revolution has been followed by renewed Chinese efforts to penetrate areas of the underdeveloped world, especially in Africa and the Middle East. In 1970 China began its largest foreign aid programme yet undertaken—the financing and building of the £169 million Tanzania-Zambia railway (see p. 77). Somalia, the Sudan, and Congo (Brazzaville) have also secured substantial economic aid agreements from Peking. The building of the Tan-Zam railway will require the presence of 3000 Chinese technicians, and Tanzania and Zambia are likely to receive large quantities of Chinese goods as part of a complicated loan repayment agreement. In Zanzibar the Chinese have virtually a free field following the departure of Russian and East German aid missions. On the political front the Chinese have supported the rebel secessionist movement in Eritrea, and dissidents led by the Luo tribal leader, Odinga-Odinga, in Kenya. In the Middle East, China now has diplomatic missions in eight of the 13 countries of the Arab League. Chinese advisers have helped the rebel movement in the Dhofar region of Oman, and are active in Southern Yemen. Contact has also been established with Palestinian guerrilla leaders following Soviet involvement in the US Middle East peace plan of 1970.

China's growing industrial strength **(see below)** can draw on huge reserves of coal (263,000 million metric tons) and iron ore (20,000 million tons). Since 1960 production of crude petroleum has more than trebled to some 14 million tons a year, reducing China's dependence on Soviet imports.

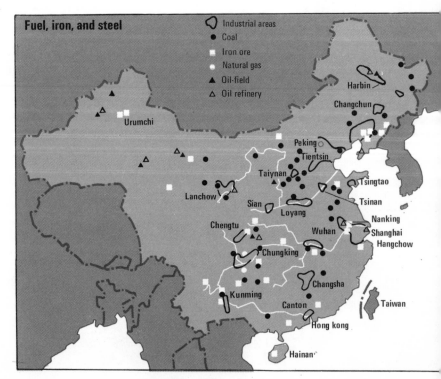

Fuel, iron, and steel

- Industrial areas
- Coal
- Iron ore
- Natural gas
- Oil-field
- Oil refinery

Hongkong

The last relic of the British colonial empire in Asia, Hongkong survives because of communist China's interest in its prosperity. Through remittances sent by Chinese workers to their families in China proper, and by the importation of Chinese goods, foodstuffs, and raw materials, it provides China with valuable foreign exchange. The British forces stationed in Hongkong are primarily to maintain internal security. They could not be expected to repel an invasion by the Chinese army. Hongkong Island was annexed from China by Britain in 1841, and the mainland peninsula of Kowloon in 1860. The so-called New Territories—another mainland peninsula and some other islands—were obtained from China on a lease that expires in 1997. Refugees from the mainland have swollen the population to almost four million (nearly 10,000 people to each square mile). In recent years there have been frequent political disturbances, largely organized by the Chinese Communist Party, which operates legally in the colony. The Bank of China and other communist enterprises are also permitted to trade.

Macao

Less than 50 miles west of Hongkong lies the tiny (six square miles) Portuguese territory of Macao, with a Chinese population of 200,000. Macao consists of a peninsula and two islands. Its chief sources of income are tourism and gambling. Macao has been a Portuguese settlement since 1557. Like Hongkong, it provides communist China with foreign exchange; and although the Portuguese are powerless to defend it, China shows little sign of wishing to take it over.

Taiwan

Taiwan (called Formosa by the Japanese) has been the only major territory held by the Chinese Nationalists since General Chiang Kai-shek was forced to abandon the mainland after the communist revolution in 1949. Its 13 million people—largely Chinese, but with a minority of indigenous Formosans—include about 500,000 Nationalist troops.

Taiwan was ceded to Japan in 1895, but was recovered for China by Chiang Kai-shek in 1945. Communist threats to invade and take over the island were countered when, after the outbreak of the Korean War in 1950, President Truman ordered the United States Seventh Fleet to protect it.

Since then, the United States has guaranteed Taiwan's security on condition that the Nationalists do not launch an unauthorized attack on the mainland. A mutual security pact was signed with America in 1954, paving the way for an era of prosperity. The Nationalist government continues to occupy China's seat on the United Nations Security Council; and the Peking government has repeatedly declared that it cannot contemplate UN membership unless the Nationalists are expelled.

In addition to Taiwan itself, which lies about 100 miles off the southeast coast of China, the Nationalists hold the Pescadores Islands, and the offshore islands of Quemoy and Matsu, which overlook the approaches to the mainland ports of Amoy and Foochow.

Taiwan and the off-shore islands

Hongkong and the New Territories

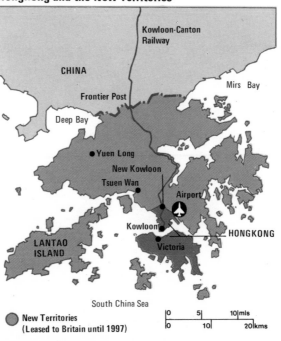

Taiwan (far left), with a population of nearly 14 million people, is controlled by the Nationalist government of Chiang Kai-shek. Communist China has repeatedly asserted its right to possession, but the island is protected by the US Seventh Fleet. Left: the industrial complex of Hongkong and the New Territories. Textiles account for half the colony's domestic exports.

Asia Pacific Ocean

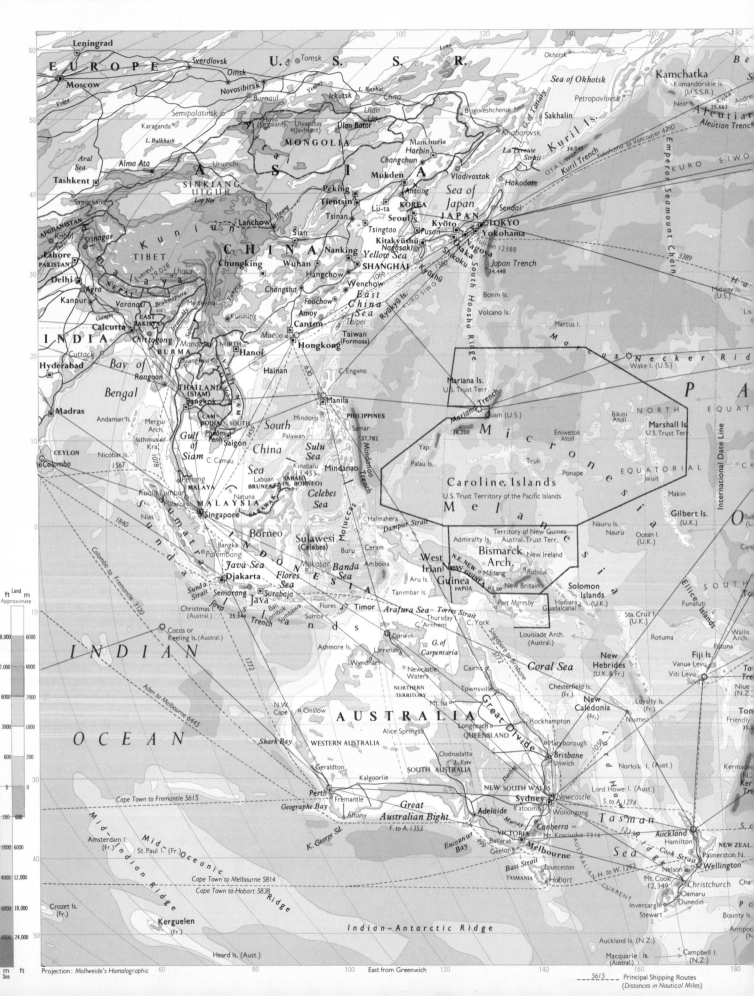

Projection: Mollweide's Homolographic

East from Greenwich

_____ 5615 _____ Principal Shipping Routes
(Distances in Nautical Miles)

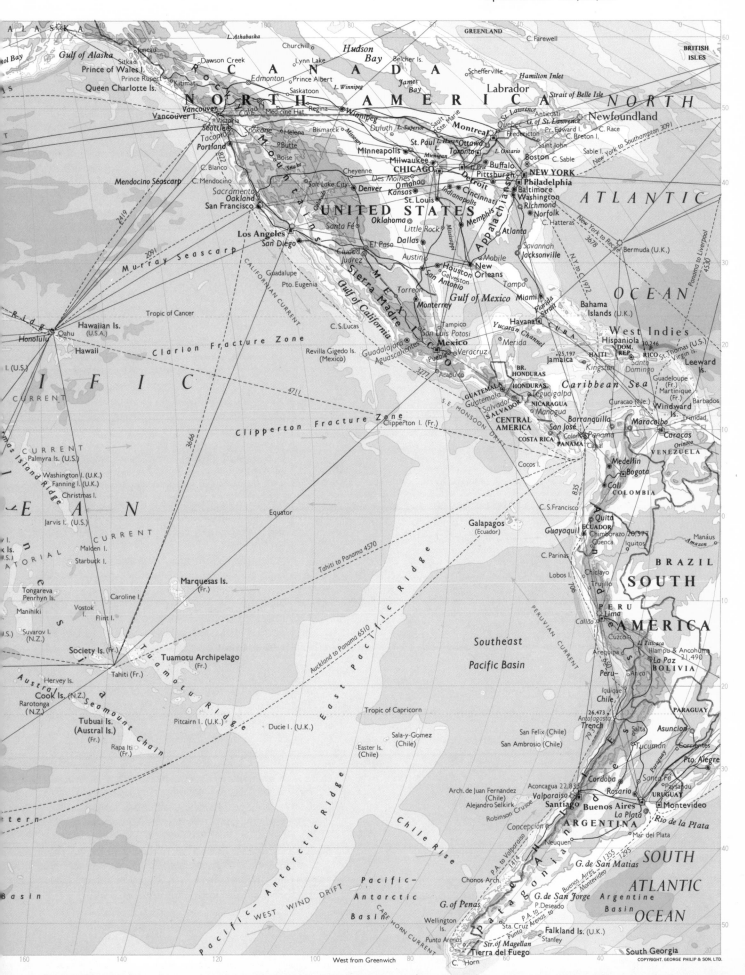

Equatorial Scale 1:60,000,000

COPYRIGHT. GEORGE PHILIP & SON. LTD.

West from Greenwich

Economic "miracle"
Since Japan's defeat in World War II, political and military issues have been subordinated to the task of restoring and expanding the economy; as a result, the gross national product increased by an average of more than 10 per cent annually during the 1960s. In 1969 the growth rate was 14 per cent, compared with 4 per cent for the United States. At some $200,000 million, the GNP is now the third highest in the world, behind the US ($932,000 million) and the Soviet Union ($600,000 million).

Japanese economic prosperity is not without qualification, however. In terms of per capita income the country lies 20th in the world league, with about $1395 per head per annum in 1970; and the mass of its 102 million people have some way to go before they can enjoy a general standard of living equal to the rest of the industrialized world.

Like Britain, Japan has to import enormous quantities of raw materials for its industries. Since the end of World War II, it has concentrated on promoting exports, which have increased sixfold since 1955, or about twice as fast as world trade as a whole. Yet Japan still exports only just over 10 per cent of its GNP.

The government has consistently encouraged investment in industries with the highest export growth potential—motor vehicles, electronics, chemicals, and so on—and total exports now exceed $15,000 million. But that emphasis is beginning to shift as the government makes plans to boost the imports of raw materials on which Japan's livelihood so absolutely depends. Supplies come from only four areas—the United States, Canada, the Near and Middle East, and Southeast Asia. Japan is 100 per cent dependent on overseas sources for its raw cotton, wool, bauxite, nickel ore, and natural gas; it has to import 99 per cent of its crude oil, and 88 per cent of its iron ore (almost half of it from Australia).

Fears of military revival
The upsurge of economic strength tends to revive fears that Japan may once again become the dominant power in Asia. Till recently this seemed unlikely. The 1947 constitution imposed by the US restricts Japan to defensive forces, which at present number about 250,000. But a new five-year defence plan, due to take effect from 1972, envisages a doubling of military expenditure with emphasis on ship, aircraft, and tank procurement. The military budget will still be only about two thirds the size of the 1971 British defence budget: but the concept of a mere "self-defence" force is vanishing. Japan has already joined the space club by launching its first scientific satellite, and is capable of producing both long-range missiles and nuclear warheads if it chooses.

Support for an increased defence programme has been publicly given by leading Japanese industrialists. But more alarming in some Western eyes is the development of private armies and right-wing military groups such as the *Tatenokai,* or Shield Society, founded by the novelist Yukio Mishima, who committed ritual suicide in 1970.

In November 1969, the Japanese prime minister, Eisaku Sato, flew to Washington to request the return of the Ryukyus Islands (which include Okinawa, where the US maintains a powerful nuclear base) to Japan. He secured a promise that control of Okinawa, the largest island in the group, would revert to Japan (with no nuclear bases) in 1972. Claims for the return of the Soviet-occupied Kuril Islands (see map) have met with less success.

In external affairs, too, many problems await solution. Japan's trade and investment in Asia, and in parts of Latin America and Africa, is considerable. Its foreign aid programme ($1400 million in 1970) is second only to that of the United States. But Japan's ability to act on a major scale in the Far East is still restricted by uncertainty about American intentions in Asia.

Map (right) shows the islands (dark grey) that make up the Japanese empire. The inset map depicts the "Northern Territories"—the islands of Shikotan and the Habomai group, the Kunashiri and Etorofu, the most southerly of the Kuril Islands. Russia has suggested it might return Shikotan and Habomai as part of a final peace settlement (Japan and the USSR have not yet signed a treaty of peace). But it refuses to discuss the future of Etorofu (a Soviet military base) and Kunashiri.

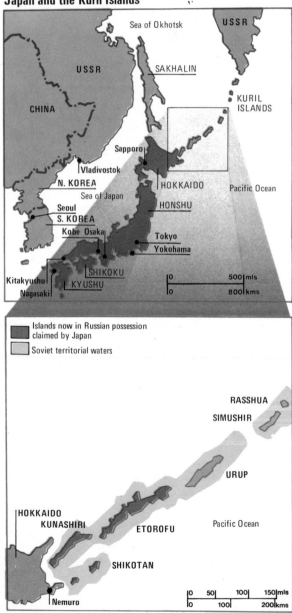

Japan and the Kuril Islands

Islands now in Russian possession claimed by Japan

Soviet territorial waters

War and division in Korea

Korea, a Japanese dependency from 1910 to 1945, occupies a strategic position between Japan and China. In the northeast it extends to within 30 miles of the Soviet port of Vladivostok, and with Japan it controls the Korea Strait, through which pass Russian ships moving south to the China Sea.

The country's division at the 38th parallel dates from the Japanese surrender in 1945. After Japan's capitulation, American forces occupied the southern half of the country and Russian forces the northern half, with an understanding that elections would be held to choose a government for the whole country. But Russian support for the North Korean communist régime in the north raised numerous difficulties. In 1948, elections held only in the South led to the setting up of a South Korean government in the national capital, Seoul. (The North Korean government made Pyongyang its capital.) Early in 1950 the Americans and Russians withdrew.

In June 1950, encouraged by hints that Korea was excluded from US defence commitments, communist forces invaded from the north. The Security Council—meeting without the participation of Russia, which was boycotting the Council—demanded their withdrawal. When the demand was ignored, the Council declared North Korea an aggressor, and UN member states were asked to send forces to resist the invasion.

American forces had already been dispatched: but before these could establish a defence line, the Communists succeeded in overrunning the whole of South Korea except for a small area round the port of Pusan. It was not until September 1950 that the UN forces, under the American supremo, General Douglas MacArthur, broke out of the Pusan perimeter and moved northwards.

When the 16-nation UN force (predominantly American and South Korean, but with strong British Commonwealth and Turkish contingents) crossed the 38th parallel and approached the Chinese border, the Peking government dispatched "volunteer" divisions to repel it. The Chinese onslaught drove the UN forces deep into the south again, and it was five more months before the latter could fight their way back to the area of the parallel. The Chinese then agreed to peace talks.

The talks dragged on two years, and were accompanied by some of the bitterest fighting in the war. In July 1953 the Korean armistice established a cease-fire line from just north of Inchon in the west to Kosong in the east. The line has since been maintained despite frequent clashes between North Korean and South Korean forces, occasionally involving American units also. American forces remain in South Korea under a bilateral security pact: but other UN forces were withdrawn after the armistice. Chinese forces were also withdrawn from North Korea. In the Sino-Soviet quarrel, North Korea—like North Vietnam—has maintained close relations with Russia, from which it derives military and economic aid.

Korea's neighbours

Map **(left)** shows the location of Korea in relationship to Japan, China, and the Soviet Union. Map **(below)** includes the respective military strengths of North and South Korea today, more than 17 years after the armistice was signed. The four small maps show the main stages of the war (see text).

The Korean War and its aftermath

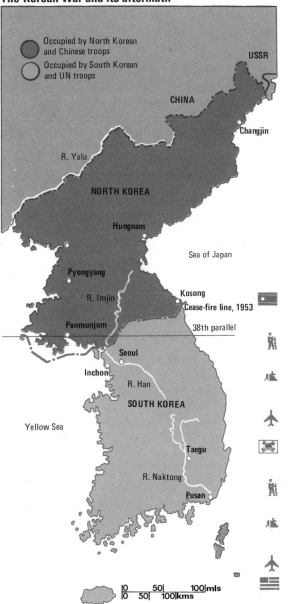

Occupied by North Korean and Chinese troops
Occupied by South Korean and UN troops

June 25 1950   September 15 1950

January 12 1951   July 27 1953

REGULAR FORCES

North Korea
Peoples Democratic Republic
population 13.0 millions

Army: 370,000
2 armoured divisions
20 infantry divisions

50 torpedo boats
4 missile patrol boats
4 submarines

580 combat aircraft
including 90 MiG 21s

South Korea
Republic of Korea
population 31 millions

Army: 570,000
2 armoured divisions
19 infantry divisions

3 destroyers
7 escorts and frigates
20 landing ships

200 combat aircraft

Also 2 US infantry divisions, missile command, and elements of 5th Air Force

War in Vietnam

Indochina, the area of Southeast Asia embracing Vietnam, Cambodia, and Laos, has been ravaged by war for more than a quarter of a century. The First Indochina War (1945–54) began as a popular uprising against the French colonial administration. Despite American "anti-colonial" sentiment the United States acceded to French requests for aid after the communist invasion of South Korea. US help was limited to material, however, and when a large French force was encircled by Vietminh (communist) forces at Dien Bien Phu in 1954, the US refused to intervene militarily.

Following the fall of Dien Bien Phu, a peace settlement was reached at the 1954 Geneva conference, attended by China, Russia, the United States, and the United Kingdom. Vietnam was given full independence and temporarily divided along the 17th parallel, pending elections for a government of the whole country. Laos and Cambodia also received their independence, and the conference members, with Britain and Russia as co-chairmen, pledged themselves to support the two countries' neutrality. French forces were withdrawn from Indochina. But the Geneva settlement broke down when the South Vietnamese government of Ngo Dinh Diem refused to take part in the promised elections on the ground that those in the communist-held north would not be free. In 1955 a worsening border situation led the United States to start arms deliveries to South Vietnam.

In 1959 the military arm of the South Vietnamese Communists (the Vietcong) began a campaign of assassination against government officials and local leaders in the South Vietnam countryside. The Diem régime had meanwhile relapsed into increasing corruption and repression; and in 1961 President Kennedy felt obliged to dispatch "advisers" to train and lead the South Vietnamese security forces and avert a complete breakdown.

By 1963 there were 25,000 American advisers in Vietnam; but the internal situation continued to worsen as the North Vietnamese sent in regular troops to counter the US intervention.

In November 1963 Diem was assassinated, and was followed by a succession of military rulers. In August 1964 North Vietnamese torpedo boats attacked an American destroyer in the Gulf of Tonkin—an action that changed the whole war when used by President Lyndon B. Johnson to secure from Congress the authority to take all necessary steps to assist South Vietnam.

In February 1965, US aircraft, operating from the Seventh Fleet, began the regular bombing of targets in North Vietnam. In March the first US combat formations were dispatched to Saigon. Between 1965 and 1969, American forces in Vietnam rose to over 500,000. The war was characterized by the unprecedented use of American firepower. But the determining factors were the stubbornness of the Vietnamese guerrillas and their possession of a protected supply line—the

Vietnam: forces and principal military bases

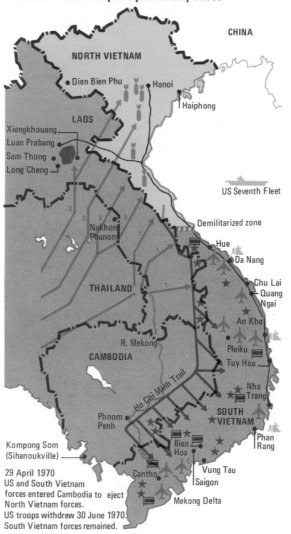

★ Vietcong strongholds
▭ South Vietnamese military bases
⚓ US naval bases
✈ US air bases

💣 US bomber strikes

↗1 American B 52s bomb Ho Chi Minh trail North Vietnam's main supply route

↗2 US fighter bombers based in Thailand support Laotian forces

⬤ 1969 Communist forces recapture Plain of Jars which controls major roadways

Units of US Seventh Fleet mount air strike against North Vietnamese targets

29 April 1970
US and South Vietnam forces entered Cambodia to eject North Vietnam forces. US troops withdrew 30 June 1970. South Vietnam forces remained.

Ho Chi Minh Trail—in adjacent Laotian and Cambodian territory.

The US bombing of North Vietnam was finally halted in 1969, when peace talks began in Paris. But ground and air operations in South Vietnam continued.

In September 1970 the communist delegation to the peace talks put forward a plan including a demand for total US withdrawal by June 1971. They offered to negotiate with a provisional coalition government in Saigon if existing leaders were excluded. Three weeks later President Nixon offered to negotiate a formal date for US withdrawal subject to an internationally supervised cease-fire. Though neither offer produced an immediate response, these moves were seen as necessary preliminaries in a lengthy process of bargaining.

By January 1971 American war losses were 44,000 dead. The South Vietnamese had lost more than 110,000 dead, and the North Vietnamese and Vietcong an estimated 700,000. No reliable figure was available for the hundreds of thousands of civilians killed on both sides.

Countries with troops in South Vietnam include the United States, Australia, New Zealand, Thailand, South Korea, and the Philippines. Both Russia and China supply massive military aid to the North, which also gets valuable economic assistance from members of Comecon. As the US withdraws most of its troops, the South Vietnamese forces will be left to continue the fight on their own.

Asia **War and division in Southeast Asia**

Laos

The 1954 Geneva Agreement, which ended the Indochina war, established Laos as an independent state under a coalition between the communist nationalist Pathet Lao (a movement akin to that of the Vietcong) and the right-wing "neutralists". But the coalition quickly broke down, and despite attempts in 1962 to impose a truce and guarantee Laotian neutrality under the Geneva Agreement, intermittent fighting has occurred ever since. The Pathet Lao has controlled the eastern half of the country, which includes the Ho Chi Minh Trail carrying communist reinforcements from North to South Vietnam. The Royal Laotian Army, advised and equipped by the United States, has controlled the western half.

Pathet Lao forces, supported by troops from North Vietnam, have tended to advance each year in the dry season, and to retire towards the Vietnam frontier when the rains set in. In September 1969, however, government forces scored an unexpected victory when they drove the Pathet Lao and North Vietnamese from the Plain of Jars (which controls the country's major roadways).

In the following February a communist offensive recaptured the Plain, threatening Laotian-United States bases to the south. About the same time, the United States government admitted that the Central Intelligence Agency had been training several thousand guerrillas led by the Laotian General Vang Pao. In addition to bombing the Ho Chi Minh Trail, the US Air Force had also been bombing the communist-held province of Sam Neua. The bombing led to large numbers of refugees being forced out of the Pathet Lao-held areas. Early in 1970 there were half a million refugees in Laos—out of an estimated population of three million.

Laos could provide the Communists with a base from which to infiltrate across the Mekong river into Thailand.

Cambodia

In March 1970, the left-wing Cambodian leader, Prince Norodom Sihanouk, was deposed by his prime minister, General Lon Nol. The new Cambodian government proclaimed its neutrality and its intention of stopping North Vietnamese use of Cambodian territory as a base for operations against South Vietnam. Two weeks later, the United States—apparently seeking to relieve pressure on its forces in South Vietnam and so to facilitate their repatriation—moved into Cambodia to "clean up" the North Vietnamese/Vietcong base area. The operation was completed and US troops withdrew from Cambodia in six weeks. But South Vietnamese troops remained. Cambodia, meanwhile, faced a desperate-looking situation as communist forces gathered for a counter-attack against its small, ill-equipped army.

Thailand

Unlike most other Asian countries, Thailand (formerly Siam) has never been colonized. Its old social structure remains virtually intact, and the conservatism of its people is reinforced by a widespread system of agricultural freeholding. Crops are abundant and there is no population pressure. In World War II Thailand was allied with Japan; since 1954 it has been linked with the United States through the South-East Asian Treaty Organization, whose headquarters are in Bangkok.

In 1965, US airfields established in Thailand under SEATO were used to bomb targets in North Vietnam. In return the Thai government demanded, and received, fresh guarantees of Thailand's security. In 1970 nearly 50,000 American servicemen were reportedly stationed in the country.

In the late 1960s Thailand faced a growing insurgency problem, mainly in the north and east where communist guerrillas had been able to exploit the grievances of an ethnic minority—the Meo tribesmen. There is also guerrilla activity on the southern border by communist bands surviving from the Malayan emergency of the 1950s.

Singapore and Malaysia

Singapore, a thriving, independent island state at the foot of the Malay peninsula, possesses, in its harbour, the fifth largest seaport in the world.

Three quarters of its two million people are Chinese. The Malays (some 290,000) form the largest minority group, followed by Indians and Pakistanis (180,000). Under its popular prime minister, Lee Kuan Yew, Singapore has survived

Below: The percentage of Nanyang (overseas) Chinese—among the different countries of Southeast Asia. The number of Chinese outside China itself probably exceeds 30 million.

The overseas Chinese

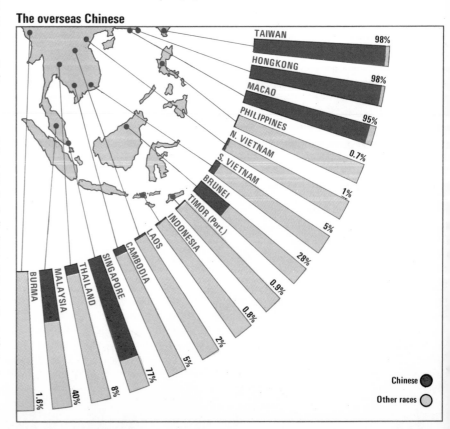

TAIWAN	98%
HONGKONG	98%
MACAO	95%
PHILIPPINES	
N. VIETNAM	0.7%
S. VIETNAM	1%
BRUNEI	5%
TIMOR (Port.)	
INDONESIA	28%
LAOS	0.9%
CAMBODIA	0.8%
SINGAPORE	
THAILAND	2%
MALAYSIA	17%
BURMA	8%
	40%
	1.6%

Chinese ●
Other races ○

the economic consequences of the closure of the large British naval base. But with a high birth rate and limited land resources, the island faces grave problems unless tariff barriers are removed in overseas markets and an outlet provided for its manufactures.

Malaysia, a federation of the former state of Malaya and the former British colonies of North Borneo and Sarawak, is also ethnically divided —between a Malay majority and a large Chinese minority. It was largely from the poorer Chinese that the Communists drew their strength during the Malayan emergency of 1948–60. Singaporean concern for Chinese minority rights in Malaysia, and Malaysian concern for Malays in Singapore, are a source of friction between the two states. Communal tensions partly accounted for Singapore's departure from the Malaysia federation in 1965.

In Eastern Malaysia (the Malaysian part of Borneo) the indigenous population of Dyaks and other non-Malay peoples has yet to be brought into political life, and the failure of the Malaysian government to win their support is a continuing source of weakness. (For Singapore/Malaysia defence problems see p. 100.)

The Nanyang (overseas) Chinese play a leading part in the economic life of Southeast Asia and number about 15 million out of the region's 230 million inhabitants. In Singapore they constitute a majority; in Malaysia they form about 40 per cent of the total population, and in Thailand and the Philippines they form sizeable, and commercially powerful, minorities.

The Philippines

The Philippines has had a remarkable history— conquered by Spain in 1565, ceded to America in 1898, and occupied by Japan in World War II, it gained independence in 1946. Its territory comprises 7100 islands, 880 of them inhabited, of which the two largest—Luzon in the north and Mindanao in the far south—account for 69 per cent of the area. Luzon is the political and economic heartland.

In international politics the Philippines has been closely allied with the United States, while maintaining a somewhat volatile relationship with its regional neighbours. It is a member of SEATO, the Association of South-East Asian Nations (ASEAN), and the Asian and Pacific Council (ASPAC). Internally, the republic is a parliamentary democracy, regularly holding elections, and there is a two-chamber Congress on American lines. An attempt by the communist-led Hukbalahaps to seize power in the late 1940s and early 1950s was crushed, but dissidence continues in central Luzon. Ethnic and religious differences have caused disturbances in the southern Philippines. The vast majority of the population of 35 million is Roman Catholic; but there are Aglipayan (national Catholic) and Moslem minorities. More than half the population is under the age of 20.

SEATO

The South-East Asia Collective Defence Treaty was signed in 1954 by Australia, France, New Zealand, Pakistan, the Philippines, Thailand, the United Kingdom, and the United States. The treaty set up the South-East Asia Treaty Organization (SEATO)—with headquarters at Bangkok —and provides for collective action should external aggression (or internal subversion) occur against any of the eight signatories. It covers the general region of Southeast Asia, including the entire home area of the Asian signatories and the general locality of the southwest Pacific south of 21° 31′ N. (Hongkong and Taiwan, which lie just north of this latitude, are thus excluded.) The treaty is of indefinite duration, but any member may withdraw after one year's notice. In an accompanying note the US limited its definition of aggression to communist aggression. A protocol to the treaty states that Laos, Cambodia, and South Vietnam are covered by its defence provisions and eligible for membership of economic programmes, though subsequently Laos and Cambodia disavowed SEATO protection.

SEATO, however, is a much less effective instrument than its paper organization suggests. France and Pakistan have long ceased to be active members. Since 1962 military action in the treaty area has in fact been planned for in bilateral as well as in general terms. Mao Tse-tung has called SEATO a "paper tiger". But in Vietnam SEATO has given the US some legal justification for action.

Main roads

Railway

Built up areas

Singapore

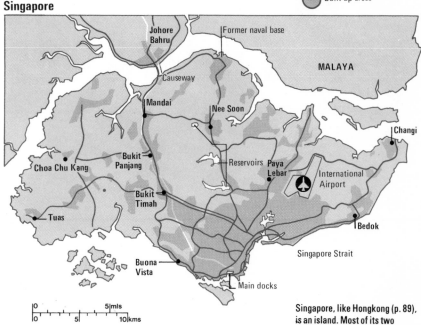

Singapore, like Hongkong (p. 89), is an island. Most of its two million people live in the city itself, which is situated at the southern end of the island. A causeway 1100 yards long connects the island to the Malayan mainland, and carries a road, a railway, and water supply lines.

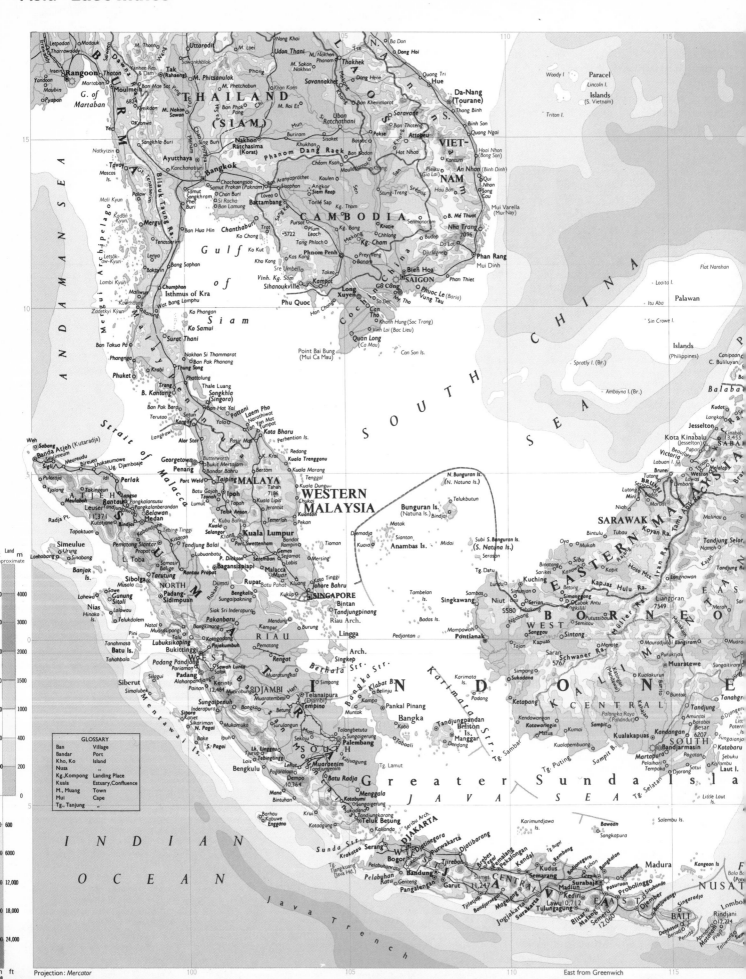

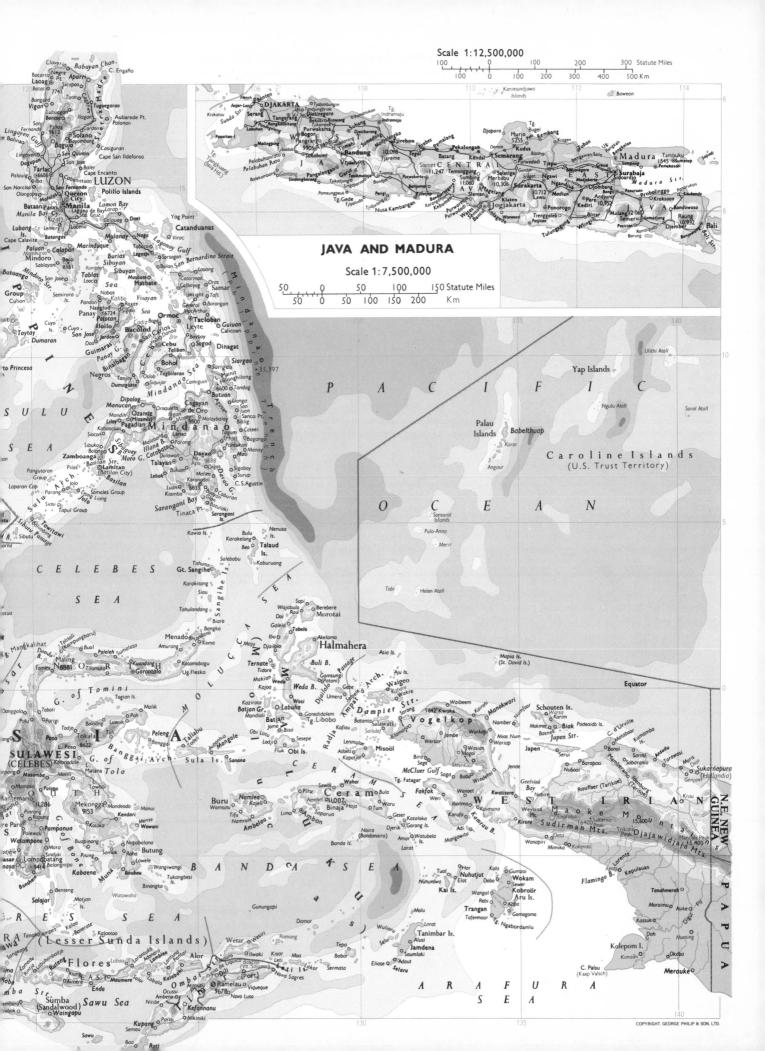

National awareness

Few nations live with a keener sense of geography than the Australians. Dwellers in a largely empty continent, separated from the lands of their origin by thousands of sea-miles, they must live in neighbourliness with the crowded countries of Asia and look for security to diplomacy rather than force.

Only two Australian cities have populations above 750,000 (Sydney, 2,450,000, Melbourne 2,100,000). The nationwide average population density is only four persons per square mile. The total population of 12 million includes 80,000 Aborigines, who enjoy full political rights. But there are restrictions on immigration by non-Europeans.

Immigration and a high birth rate could double the population to 25 million by the year 2000. Recent discoveries of large mineral deposits—particularly iron and oil—could lead to a corresponding expansion of the economy.

But it will require a technological miracle to transform Australia's desert interior; and it is an illusion to suppose that "empty" Australia could support Asia's millions.

In the post-war period, with Britain's slow withdrawal East-of-Suez and the rise of new forces in Asia, it was inevitable that the United States, which is both closer and more powerful, should replace Britain as Australia's chief ally.

The ANZUS pact, committing the US to the defence of Australia and New Zealand, is now the cornerstone of Australian defence policy; and the commitment of Australian and New Zealand troops to America's side in Vietnam might be seen as a down-payment on the ANZUS guarantee.

The "forward" policy of involvement in Southeast Asia has also been justified by reference to Australia's interest, as a trading nation, in safeguarding stability over a wide area.

The policy was severely tested during the Indonesian confrontation of Malaysia in 1963–7. By providing only token support for the Malaysians under Commonwealth defence arrangements, Australia contrived to maintain good relations with Indonesia, which at the time appeared capable of threatening New Guinea.

Indonesia and Malaysia

A major threat to peace in the 1960s was the military confrontation between Indonesia and Malaysia. Before it ended in 1966 some 50,000 British troops and 14,000 Malaysian troops and police were involved in defending Malaysia against incursions by Indonesian-trained guerrillas. In the North Borneo territory of Sarawak an additional threat came from the Clandestine Communist Organization (CCO)—recruited largely from underprivileged local Chinese. The trouble began with the foundation of Malaysia itself.

In 1961 Tunku Abdul Rahman, prime minister of Malaya (which had gained independence in 1957) proposed a federation of Malaya, Singapore, and

the three British dependencies in Borneo (North Borneo, now called Sabah; Sarawak, and Brunei). A referendum in Singapore, and elections in Sabah and Sarawak, favoured federation, but the Sultan of Brunei rejected the plan. At an early stage opposition was voiced by the Philippines, which claims sovereignty over a large part of Sabah. A more serious problem, however, was the opposition of Indonesia, which saw the federation as a rival power centre likely to attract secessions from its own loosely knit territories.

In December 1962 an Indonesian-backed revolt broke out in Brunei, but was suppressed with the aid of British troops. Malaysia came into being in September 1963; the Indonesian government, under President Sukarno, thereupon announced the policy of "confrontation", a complex economic, military, and political campaign involving the recruitment and training of local dissidents.

Four years of counter-insurgency operations, mainly in Borneo but later against guerrilla groups landed in the Malay peninsula, resulted in the killing of 2000 guerrillas for the loss of about 150 men of the security forces.

Confrontation ended after Indonesian army chiefs deposed President Sukarno, alleging his connivance in an attempted coup by the Peking-backed Indonesian Communist Party (PKI) in September 1965. The dramatic eclipse of the PKI, which had seemed to be steadily growing in strength, was seen as a major setback to Chinese efforts to penetrate Southeast Asia.

In 1965 Singapore withdrew from Malaysia after continuous frictions within the federation. A contributing factor was the widespread belief by Singapore's Chinese population that the federal government was acting against Chinese interests.

Below, right: The countries of Southeast Asia diagrammatically shown in proportion to their population. For example, Australia (2,267,883 square miles) appears much the same size as Ceylon (25,332 square miles) because both countries have approximately the same number of people (i.e. about 12 million). As might be expected, the more densely populated countries tend to have a lower nutritional standard. The differences in calorie intake are shown by the shading.

Malaysia, Singapore, Indonesia and New Guinea

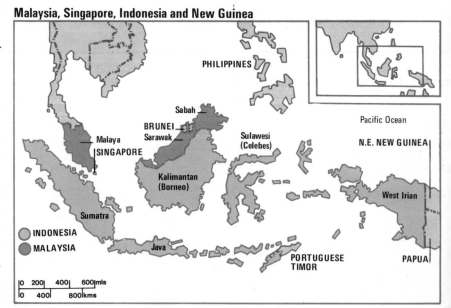

RE7/0361 M. BEAZLEY OBSERVER ATLAS' SHEET 5.

Southeast Asia: population densities

0 400 800 1200 mls
0 500 1000 1500 kms

People per sq. mile	People per sq. km
under 2	under 1
2–64	1–25
64–512	25–200
over 512	over 200

Hungry people

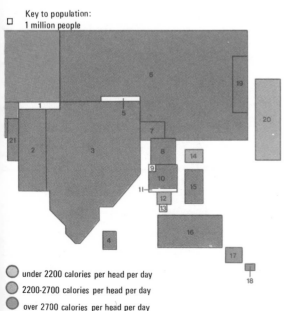

Key to population:
□ 1 million people

Population
Figures in millions

1	Afghanistan	16.1M
2	Pakistan	130 M
3	India	540 M
4	Ceylon	11.9M
5	Nepal	10.3 M
6	China	750 M
7	Burma	26.4 M
8	Thailand	33.7 M
9	Laos	2.8 M
10	Vietnam	35.2 M
11	Cambodia	6.5 M
12	Malaysia	10.3 M
13	Singapore	2 M
14	Taiwan	13.3 M
15	Philippines	35.9 M
16	Indonesia	112.8 M
17	Australia	12 M
18	New Zealand	2.7 M
19	Korea	43.4 M
20	Japan	102 M
21	Iran	26.9 M

○ under 2200 calories per head per day
○ 2200-2700 calories per head per day
○ over 2700 calories per head per day

The "green revolution"

More than half the people in the world today—around 2000 million—live in Asia, a continent that has for centuries existed in the everpresent shadow of famine. According to the UN Food and Agriculture Organization, something like half of them are underfed. In particular they are desperately short of protein (meat, milk, eggs, etc.)—and the total population is doubling every 25 years. Obviously there can be little future or stability for Asia until the twin problems of food and population are brought into a satisfactory balance.

In the mid-1960s, agricultural experts working at the International Rice Institute in the Philippines managed to develop new varieties of rice seed that point the way to what can be done to produce more food if sufficient world resources are devoted to the job. One of these new varieties, known as IR–8, can increase rice yields—granted certain ideal conditions—by as much as 10 to 15 times. This possibility prompted in the late 1960s optimistic talk of a "green revolution" in producing food supplies. In 1964 and 1965 only 200 acres had been sown with IR–8, but three years later that area had increased to the astonishing figure of 20 million acres—about 10 per cent of all the land in Asia devoted to cereal crops.

In Asia, as elsewhere, the problem of improving food output on a sufficiently intensive scale and for a sustained period of time is essentially social and technological. To succeed, the so-called "miracle" rice seeds require enormous new irrigation schemes and the application of huge amounts of fertilizer, most of which must be supplied by the rich countries, at least to begin with. The difficulties are immense. For example, studies have shown that if India alone (population, 540 million) were to use fertilizer at the same rate per head as the Netherlands (admittedly the world's most intensively farmed country) it would consume half the present world production of fertilizer.

Irrigation, the other essential ingredient for success, is no less of a problem. In a world that is increasingly short of fresh water, nuclear-powered desalination plants (drawing their supplies from the sea) probably offer the most efficient and effective method of attack. E. A. Mason, of the Oak Ridge National Laboratories, Tennessee, has estimated that merely to keep pace with today's world population growth would involve spending, in the next five years, at least $315,000 million on desalination plants.

Statistical profiles

The following pages give basic facts and figures about the countries of the world. The information comes either from the governments of the countries concerned or from United Nations sources. Figures for defence expenditure are based either on 1969 appropriations (most Western countries) or on estimates made by the Institute of Strategic Studies in London. Where any set of figures is unobtainable for a particular country that item is numbered in the table but left blank. Where information is not applicable, the item itself is omitted. Like much statistical information, the data vary considerably in reliability; the most dependable come from the developed countries. Figures for GNP per head of population are particularly difficult to estimate, and should be used with caution. Figures shown thus: (67), (68), (69), etc, indicate year of origin. (Abbreviations: GNP, Gross National Product (the total annual output of goods and services); kg, kilogrammes; km, kilometres; M, millions; sq, square.)
The information is set out as follows:

COUNTRY
1 Status
2 Languages
3 Area: sq miles, sq km
4 Population
5 Capital and population
6 Date of independence or creation
Economy
1 GNP
2 GNP per head of population
3 Principal exports
4 Energy consumption per head in coal equivalent
Defence
1 Annual expenditure or budget
2 Size of armed forces
3 Principal multilateral treaty affiliations
4 Military service

STATISTICAL EQUIVALENTS

Currency
£1 million = $2.4 million
$1 million = £416,667

Square measure
1 square mile = 2.59 square kilometres
1 square kilometre = 0.386 square mile

Length
1 mile = 1.609 kilometre
1 kilometre = 0.621 mile

Miscellaneous
1 megaton = 1 million tons. A 1-megaton bomb has an explosive power equivalent to 1 million tons of TNT
1 kiloton = 1000 tons. A 1-kiloton bomb has an explosive power equivalent to 1000 tons of TNT

AFGHANISTAN
1 Kingdom
2 Pashto, Persian
3 249,000 sq miles 647,497 sq km
4 16,113,000 (68)
5 Kabul 456,300
Economy
1 $874M (63)
2 $60 (63)
3 Tea, sugar, textiles, wheat, petroleum products
4 27 kg (67)
Defence
1 $21M (67)
2 86,000
4 1–2 years (selective)

ALBANIA
1 Republic
2 Literary Albanian, dialects
3 11,100 sq miles 28,748 sq km
4 2,019,000 (68)
5 Tirane 161,300
6 1912
Economy
1
2
3 Petroleum, chrome ore, tobacco
4 359 kg (67)
Defence
1 $105M (69)
2 38,000
4 2 years (army)

ALGERIA
1 Republic
2 French, Arabic
3 919,586 sq miles 2,381,741 sq km
4 12,943,000 (68)
5 Algiers 943,200
6 1962
Economy
1 $2743M (63)
2 $245 (63)
3 Wine, petroleum, citrus fruit
4 421 kg (67)
Defence
1 $174M (69)
2 57,000
4 Limited conscription

ANDORRA
1 Republic under joint rule of France and Spain
2 Catalan, French, Spanish
3 175 sq miles 453 sq km
4 18,000 (68)
5 Andorra 1300
Economy
1
2
4

ANGOLA
1 Portuguese overseas territory
2 Portuguese
3 481,350 sq miles 1,246,700 sq km
4 5,258,000 (67)
5 S. Paulo de Luanda 225,000
Economy
1 $358M (63)
2 $71 (63)
3 Coffee, diamonds, maize
4 102 kg (67)
Defence
Defence controlled by Portugal

ARGENTINA
1 Republic
2 Spanish
3 1,072,073 sq miles 2,776,656 sq km
4 23,617,000 (68)
5 Buenos Aires 7,984,000
6 1816
Economy
1 $18,733M (66)

2 $818 (66)
3 Meat, wheat, other cereals, wool
4 1380 kg (67)
Defence
1 $428.6M (68)
2 120,000
4 1 year (army)

AUSTRALIA
1 Commonwealth
2 English
3 2,267,883 sq miles 7,686,810 sq km
4 12,031,000 (68)
5 Canberra 100,100
6 1901
Economy
1 $26,692M (67)
2 $2260 (67)
3 Wool, wheat, meat, metal ores, fruit, vegetables
4 4791 kg (67)
Defence
1 $1225M (69–70)
2 87,150
3 SEATO, ANZUS
4 2 years (selective)

AUSTRIA
1 Republic
2 German
3 32,374 sq miles 83,849 sq km
4 7,349,000 (68)
5 Vienna 1,636,600
6 1955
Economy
1 $10,635M (67)
2 $1452 (67)
3 Machinery, manufactured goods, iron, steel, textiles, timber
4 2660 kg (67)
Defence
1 $144M (69)
2 50,000
4 9 months

BAHAMAS
1 British colony
2 English
3 5386 sq miles 13,950 sq km
4 145,900 (67)
5 Nassau 81,000
Economy
1
2
3 Pulpwood, crawfish, rum, salt
4 4729 kg (67)
Defence
Defence controlled by Britain

BARBADOS
1 Independent state
2 English
3 166 sq miles 430 sq km
4 250,700 (67)
5 Bridgetown 12,300
6 1966
Economy
1 $107M (66)
2 $433 (66)
3 Sugar
4 498 kg (67)
Defence
2 250
4 Voluntary

BELGIUM
1 Kingdom
2 Flemish, French
3 11,781 sq miles 30,513 sq km
4 9,619,000 (68)
5 Brussels 1,079,200
6 1830
Economy
1 $22,900M (69)
2 $2039 (67)

3 Iron, steel, non-ferrous metal goods, textiles
4 4670 kg (67)
Defence
1 $519M (69)
2 102,400
3 NATO
4 12–15 months

BERMUDA
1 British colony
2 English
3 20 sq miles 53 sq km
4 50,100 (67)
5 Hamilton 3000
Economy
1
2
3 Concentrated essences
4 3667 kg (67)
Defence
Defence controlled by Britain

BOLIVIA
1 Republic
2 Spanish, Quechua, Aymara
3 424,162 sq miles 1,098,581 sq km
4 4,680,000 (68)
5 La Paz 360,300 (68)
6 1825
Economy
1 $719M (67)
2 $189 (67)
3 Tin, lead, zinc, silver, sulphur
4 234 kg (67)
Defence
1 $15.8M (65)
2 15,000
4 1 year

BOTSWANA
1 Republic
2 English, Tswana
3 231,804 sq miles 600,372 sq km
4 611,000 (68)
5 Gaberones 14,500
6 1966
Economy
1 $55M (66)
2 $96 (66)
3 Meat, hides, skins
4

BRAZIL
1 Republic
2 Portuguese
3 3,286,473 sq miles 8,511,965 sq km
4 92,000,000 (68)
5 Brazilia 200,000
6 1822
Economy
1 $27,711M (66)
2 $333 (66)
3 Coffee, cotton, iron ore
4 392 kg (67)
Defence
1 $1008.5M (68)
2 180,000
4 1 year

BRITISH HONDURAS
1 British colony
2 English, Spanish
3 8866 sq miles 22,963 sq km
4 114,300 (66)
5 Belize 38,500
Economy
1 $34M (63)
2 $335 (63)
3 Sugar, citrus fruits, timber
4 407 kg (67)
Defence
Defence controlled by Britain

BRUNEI
British protected state (sultanate)
Malay, English
2226 sq miles 5800 sq km
130,000 (68)
Brunei 30,000
Economy
1 $82M (58)
2 $1075 (58)
3 Petroleum, petroleum products, rubber
4 2306 kg (67)

BULGARIA
Republic
Bulgarian, Turkish
42,822 sq miles 110,912 sq km
8,370,000 (68)
Sofia 923,400
Economy
1 $8000M (68)
2 $996 (68)
3 Oil, machinery, tractors, cosmetics
4 3054 kg (67)
Defence
1 $234M (69)
2 154,000
3 Warsaw Pact
4 2 years (army)

BURMA
Union
Burmese
261,793 sq miles 678,033 sq km
26,389,000 (68)
Rangoon 821,800
1948
Economy
1 $1803M (67)
2 $70 (67)
3 Rice, hardwoods, ores, cotton, rubber
4 52 kg (67)
Defence
1 $111M (68)
2 142,500
4 Voluntary

BURUNDI
Republic
French, Kirundi, Kiswahili
10,747 sq miles 27,834 sq km
3,406,000 (68)
Bujumbura 71,000
1962
Economy
1 $123M (63)
2 $40 (63)
3 Coffee, ores, cotton, beverages
4 7 kg (67)
Defence
1 $3.1M (68)
2 3000
4 Voluntary

CAMBODIA
Kingdom
Cambodian, French
69,894 sq miles 181,035 sq km
6,557,000 (68)
Phnom-Penh 394,000
1955
Economy
1 $917M (66)
2 $146 (66)
3 Rice, rubber, maize
4 51 kg (67)
Defence
1 $64M (69)
2 38,500
4 Voluntary

CAMEROON
Federal republic
French, English
183,591 sq miles 475,500 sq km
5,350,000 (67)
Yaoundé 90,000

---

6 1960
Economy
1 $603M (63)
2 $120 (63)
3 Coffee, cocoa
4 83 kg (68)
Defence
1 $21.9M (69)
2 4350
4 Voluntary

CANADA
1 Dominion
2 English, French
3 3,851,794 sq miles 9,976,139 sq km
4 20,772,000 (68)
5 Ottawa 508,000
6 1867
Economy
1 $57,329M (67)
2 $2805 (67)
3 Manufactures, non-ferrous metals, wheat
4 8060 kg (67)
Defence
1 $1678M (69–70)
2 98,300
3 NATO
4 Voluntary

CENTRAL AFRICAN REPUBLIC
1 Republic
2 French, Bantu, Sudanic dialects
3 240,540 sq miles 622,984 sq km
4 1,488,000 (68)
5 Bangui 150,000
6 1960
Economy
1 $148M (63)
2 $113 (63)
3 Diamonds, cotton, coffee
4 36 kg (67)
Defence
1 $4.5M (38)
2 1100
4 2 years

CEYLON
1 Republic
2 English, Sinhalese, Tamil
3 25,332 sq miles 65,610 sq km
4 11,964,000 (68)
5 Colombo 546,200
6 1948
Economy
1 $1796M (67)
2 $153 (67)
3 Tea, rubber
4 112 kg (67)
Defence
1 $12M (67)
2 2980
4 Voluntary

CHAD
1 Republic
2 Sudanic dialects, French
3 495,750 sq miles 1,284,000 sq km
4 3,460,000 (68)
5 Fort-Lamy 99,000
6 1960
Economy
1 $213M (63)
2 $66 (63)
3 Cotton, cattle
4 16 kg (67)
Defence
1 $6.9M (68)
2 2650
4 2 years

CHINA
1 People's republic
2 Chinese, plus dialects
3 3,691,500 sq miles 9,561,000 sq km
4 750,000,000 (68)

---

5 Peking 4,010,000
Economy
1
2
3 Silk, meat, rice, soya
4
Defence
1 Unknown (estimated to be about $4800M)
2 2,821,000–3,300,000 (rough estimate)
4 4–6 years (selective)

CHILE
1 Republic
2 Spanish
3 299,255 sq miles 756,945 sq km
4 9,050,000 (67)
5 Santiago 2,447,700
6 1818
Economy
1 $5343M (67)
2 $585 (67)
3 Copper, copper bars, iron ore
4 1163 kg (67)
Defence
1 $109M (68)
2 60,000
4 1 year

COLOMBIA
1 Republic
2 Spanish, Indian dialects
3 456,535 sq miles 1,138,914 sq km
4 19,825,000 (68)
5 Bogota 2,206,100
6 1830
Economy
1 $6209M (66)
2 $334 (66)
3 Coffee, crude petroleum
4 521 kg (67)
Defence
1 $135.5M (68)
2 64,000
4 1 year

CONGO (Brazzaville)
1 Republic
2 French, Bantu dialects
3 132,050 sq miles 342,000 sq km
4 870,000 (68)
5 Brazzaville 136,200
6 1960
Economy
1 $153M (63)
2 $188 (63)
3 Wood, diamonds, wood veneer
4 188 kg (67)
Defence
1 $7M (66)
2 1600
4 Voluntary

CONGO (Kinshasa)
1 Republic
2 Kiswahili, dialects
3 905,568 sq miles 2,345,409 sq km
4 16,730,000 (68) (African population only)
5 Kinshasa 901,500
6 1960
Economy
1 $1730M (66)
2 $108 (66)
3 Copper, coffee, palm oil, diamonds, cobalt
4 76 kg (67)
Defence
1 $54M (69)
2 38,250
4 Voluntary

COSTA RICA
1 Republic
2 Spanish
3 19,575 sq miles 50,700 sq km

---

4 1,640,000 (68)
5 San José 349,500
6 1821
Economy
1 $674M (67)
2 $423 (67)
3 Coffee, bananas, sugar
4 327 kg (67)
Defence
1 $2.3M (65)

CUBA
1 Republic
2 Spanish, English
3 44,222 sq miles 114,524 sq km
4 8,500,000 (70)
5 Havana 1,565,700
6 1898
Economy
1
2
3 Sugar, tobacco, minerals
4 1033 kg (67)
Defence
1 $250M (67)
2 121,000
4 3 years

CYPRUS
1 Republic
2 Greek, Turkish, English
3 3572 sq miles 9251 sq km
4 622,000 (68)
5 Nicosia 109,000
6 1960
Economy
1 $460M (67)
2 $750 (67)
3 Copper, crude fertilizer, fruit, potatoes, wine
4 1054 kg (67)
Defence
1 $7.3M (67)
2 2000
4 6 months

CZECHOSLOVAKIA
1 Federal socialist republic
2 Czech, Slovak, German, Hungarian, Ukrainian, Polish
3 49,366 sq miles 127,869 sq km
4 14,362,000 (68)
5 Prague 1,027,100
6 1918
Economy
1 $26,800M (68)
2 $1914 (68)
3 Machinery, consumer goods
4 5487 kg (67)
Defence
1 $1576M (69)
2 230,000
3 Warsaw Pact
4 2 years (army)

DAHOMEY
1 Republic
2 French, Sudanese, dialects
3 43,480 sq miles 112,622 sq km
4 2,571,000 (68)
5 Porto-Novo 74,500
6 1960
Economy
1 $167M (63)
2 $75 (63)
3 Palm kernels, groundnuts, palm oil
4 29 kg (67)
Defence
1 $4M (66)
2 1800
4 Voluntary

DENMARK
1 Kingdom
2 Danish
3 16,629 sq miles 43,069 sq km

---

4 4,870,000 (68)
5 Copenhagen 1,377,900
Economy
1 $15,300M (69)
2 $2497 (67)
3 Meat, dairy produce, machinery
4 4264 kg (67)
Defence
1 $336M (69)
2 45,500
3 NATO
4 12–14 months

DOMINICAN REPUBLIC
1 Republic
2 Spanish
3 18,816 sq miles 48,734 sq km
4 4,029,000 (68)
5 Santo Domingo 615,000
6 1821
Economy
1 $1068M (67)
2 $275 (67)
3 Sugar, coffee, cocoa, fruit, bauxite, tobacco
4 178 kg (67)
Defence
1 $31.1M (67)
2 17,000
4 Voluntary

ECUADOR
1 Republic
2 Spanish, Quechua, Jibaro
3 109,487 sq miles 283,561 sq km
4 5,695,000 (68)
5 Quito 401,800
6 1830
Economy
1 $1270M (67)
2 $231 (67)
3 Bananas, coffee, cocoa
4 219 kg (67)
Defence
1 $22.7M (65)
2 19,000
4 11 months (selective)

EL SALVADOR
1 Republic
2 Spanish
3 8,260 sq miles 21,393 sq km
4 3,266,000 (68)
5 San Salvador 317,600
6 1841
Economy
1 $882M (67)
2 $280 (67)
3 Coffee, cotton, sugar
4 170 kg (67)
Defence
1 $10.5M (66)
2 5630
4 12 months (selective)

EQUATORIAL GUINEA
1 Republic
2 Spanish, Portuguese, English
3 9828 sq miles 28,051 sq km
4 268,000 (70)
5 Santa Isabel 19,900
6 1968
Economy
1 $70M (68)
3 Cocoa, coffee
4 155 kg (67)

ETHIOPIA
1 Empire
2 Amharic, English
3 471,777 sq miles 1,221,900 sq km
4 23,900,000 (68)
5 Addis Ababa 644,100
Economy
1 $1483M (66)
2 $64 (66)

3 Coffee, hides, skins, pulses
4 19 kg (67)
Defence
1 $40.5M (66)
2 43,210
4 Voluntary

FINLAND
1 Republic
2 Finnish, Swedish, Lapp
3 130,123 sq miles 337,009 sq km
4 4,688,000 (68)
5 Helsinki 652,000
6 1917
Economy
1 $8711M (67)
2 $1868 (67)
3 Paper, timber, wood pulp
4 3013 kg (67)
Defence
1 $131M (69)
2 36,400
4 7–11 months

FRANCE
1 Republic
2 French
3 211,210 sq miles 547,026 sq km
4 49,920,000 (68)
5 Paris 8,196,800
Economy
1 $141,000M (69)
2 $2324 (67)
3 Base metals, manufactures, transport equipment, food, tobacco, textiles, beverages
4 3093 kg (67)
Defence
1 $5586M (69)
2 503,000
3 NATO, SEATO
4 12–16 months (selective)

FRENCH GUIANA
1 French overseas department
2 French
3 23,000 sq miles 90,000 sq km
4 44,330 (67)
5 Cayenne 24,600
Economy
1
2
3 Timber, rum, gold, shrimps, balata rubber
4 868 kg (67)
Defence
Defence controlled by France

GABON
1 Independent republic
2 French, Bantu
3 101,400 sq miles 267,000 sq km
4 466,000 (66)
5 Libreville 53,000
6 1960
Economy
1 $184M (66)
2 $392 (66)
3 Timber, petroleum, cocoa, gold
4 397 kg (67)
Defence
1 $5.5M (69)
2 1050
4 1 year

GAMBIA
1 Independent state
2 English
3 4003 sq miles 10,368 sq km
4 343,000 (67)
5 Bathurst 40,000
6 1965
Economy
1 $26M (63)
2 $81 (63)
3 Oil seeds, vegetable oils, groundnuts
4 44 kg (67)

GERMANY (Democratic Republic)
1 Republic
2 German
3 41,658 sq miles 107,901 sq km
4 17,089,900 (67)
5 East Berlin 1,080,800
6 1949
Economy
1 $30,000M (68)
2 $1500 (68)
3 Machinery, equipment, fuel, raw materials, consumer goods, food products
4 5336 kg (67)
Defence
1 $1873M (69)
2 137,000
3 Warsaw Pact
4 18 months (army)

GERMANY (Federal Republic)
1 Federal republic
2 German
3 95,746 sq miles +186 sq miles 247,973 sq km +481 sq km West Berlin
4 58,015,000 +2,150,000 (West Berlin) (69)
5 Bonn 138,200
6 1955
Economy
1 $164,200M (69)
2 $2021 (67)
3 Machinery, vehicles, chemicals, iron, steel, consumer goods, food products
4 4199 kg (67)
Defence
1 $5301M (69)
2 465,000
3 NATO
4 18 months

GREECE
1 Monarchy (monarch in exile since 1967)
2 Greek
3 50,944 sq miles 131,944 sq km
4 8,716,400 (67)
5 Athens 1,852,700
6 1830
Economy
1 $7092M (67)
2 $814 (67)
3 Foodstuffs, fruits, beverages, tobacco, minerals, chemicals, manufactures
4 867 kg (67)
Defence
1 $382M (69)
2 159,000
3 NATO
4 30 months (army)

GUATEMALA
1 Republic
2 Spanish, Indian dialects
3 42,042 sq miles 108,889 sq km
4 4,864,000 (68)
5 Guatemala City 577,100
6 1821
Economy
1 $1417M (67)
2 $300 (67)
3 Coffee, bananas, cotton
4 218 kg (67)
Defence
1 $14.4M (66)
2 9000
3 Treaty alliance with El Salvador, Honduras, Nicaragua
4 2 years

GHANA
1 Republic
2 English, Aban, Ewe
3 92,097 sq miles 238,537 sq km

4 8,376,000 (68)
5 Accra 758,300
6 1957
Economy
1 $2052M (67)
2 $252 (67)
3 Cocoa, wood, diamonds, manganese
4 109 kg (67)
Defence
1 $38.7M (68)
2 17,000
4 Voluntary

GUADELOUPE
1 French overseas department
2 French
3 583 sq miles 1510 sq km
4 312,700 (67)
5 Basse-Terre 15,000
Economy
1
2
3 Sugar, rum, bananas
4 412 kg (67)
Defence
Defence controlled by France

GUINEA
1 Republic
2 French
3 95,000 sq miles 245,857 sq km
4 3,702,000 (67)
5 Conakry 120,000
6 1958
Economy
1 $333M (63)
2 $99 (63)
3 Bauxite, iron ore, coffee
4 97 kg (67)
Defence
1 $9.5M (66–67)
2 5400
4 2 years

GUYANA
1 Republic
2 English
3 83,000 sq miles 214,969 sq km
4 710,000 (68)
5 Georgetown 186,800
6 1966
Economy
1 $213M (66)
2 $322 (66)
3 Sugar, bauxite, alumina, rice
4 964 kg (67)
Defence
1 $6.3M (66)
2 1000
4 Voluntary

HAITI
1 Republic
2 French, Creole
3 10,714 sq miles 27,750 sq km
4 4,768,000 (69)
5 Port-au-Prince 240,000
6 1804
Economy
1 $383M (67)
2 $84 (67)
3 Coffee, sisal, sugar
4 33 kg (67)
Defence
1 $7M (65)
2 5500
4 Voluntary

HONDURAS
1 Republic
2 Spanish, Indian dialects
3 43,277 sq miles 112,088 sq km
4 2,413,000 (68)
5 Tegucigalpa 170,500
6 1838

Economy
1 $576M (67)
2 $236 (67)
3 Bananas, coffee, timber, minerals, cattle
4 407 kg (67)
Defence
1 $6.7M (66)
2 4725
3 Treaty alliance with El Salvador, Guatemala, Nicaragua
4 8 months

HONGKONG
1 British colony
2 English, Cantonese
3 398 sq miles 1032 sq km
4 3,926,500 (68)
5 Victoria 675,000
Economy
1 $1174M (63)
2 $335 (63)
3 Textiles, clothing
4 787 kg (67)

HUNGARY
1 Republic
2 Hungarian
3 35,919 sq miles 93,030 sq km
4 10,255,000 (68)
5 Budapest 1,980,000 (67)
Economy
1 $12,700M (68)
2 $1270 (68)
3 Machinery, fuel, consumer goods, raw materials, foodstuffs
4 2563 kg (67)
Defence
1 $457M (69)
2 97,000
3 Warsaw Pact
4 3 years maximum

ICELAND
1 Republic
2 Icelandic
3 39,800 sq miles 103,000 sq km
4 200,000 (68)
5 Reykjavik 90,800
6 1944
Economy
1 $541M (67)
2 $2720 (67)
3 Fish, fish products
4 3824 kg (67)
Defence
3 Treaty with NATO allows American bases in Iceland

INDIA
1 Republic (Union of States)
2 Hindi, Urdu, English
3 1,261,815 sq miles 3,268,090 sq km
4 537,000,000 (68)
5 New Delhi 3,780,000
6 1947
Economy
1 $43,842M (66)
2 $88 (66)
3 Tea, vegetable oils, cotton goods, jute, leather footwear, textiles
4 176 kg (67)
Defence
1 $1491M (69–70)
2 925,000
4 Voluntary

INDONESIA
1 Republic
2 Bahasa Indonesia
3 575,896 sq miles 1,491,564 sq km
4 112,825,000 (68)
5 Djakarta 2,906,500
6 1945
Economy
1 $10,649M (66)

2 $99 (66)
3 Rubber, petroleum, tin, copra, tea, coffee, kernels, tobacco
4 99 kg (67)
Defence
1 $229M (69)
2 365,000
4 Emergency compulsory service

IRAN
1 Shahdom
2 Persian, French, English
3 636,300 sq miles 1,648,000 sq km
4 26,985,000 (68)
5 Tehran 2,719,700
Economy
1 $7439M (67)
2 $283 (67)
3 Petroleum, carpets, cotton, wool, hides, skins
4 451 kg (67)
Defence
1 $505M (69–70)
2 221,000
3 CENTO
4 2 years

IRAQ
1 Republic
2 Arabic, Kurdish, English
3 169,240 sq miles 434,924 sq km
4 8,634,000 (68)
5 Baghdad 1,745,300
6 1958
Economy
1 $2199M (66)
2 $262 (66)
3 Petroleum, dates
4 610 kg (67)
Defence
1 $280M (69)
2 78,000
4 2 years

IRISH REPUBLIC
1 Republic
2 Irish, English
3 27,136 sq miles 70,283 sq km
4 2,910,000 (68)
5 Dublin 650,200
6 1918
Economy
1 $3107M (67)
2 $1072 (67)
3 Live animals, foodstuffs, manufactured goods
4 2634 kg (67)
Defence
1 $33M (68–69)
2 13,000
4 Voluntary

ISRAEL
1 Republic
2 Hebrew, Arabic
3 7993 sq miles 20,700 sq km
4 2,745,000 (68)
5 Jerusalem 266,300
6 1948
Economy
1 $3979M (67)
2 $1491 (67)
3 Citrus fruits and by-products, textiles, wines
4 2262 kg (67)
Defence
1 $829M (69–70)
2 68,000
4 20–36 months

ITALY
1 Republic
2 Italian
3 116,345 sq miles 301,225 sq km
4 52,750,000 (68)
5 Rome 2,602,000

Economy
1 $80,700M (69)
2 $1279 (67)
3 Fruit, vegetables, textiles, footwear, clothing
4 2129 kg (67)
Defence
1 $1930M (69)
2 420,000
3 NATO
4 15 months (army)

IVORY COAST
1 Republic
2 French, local dialects
3 124,504 sq miles 322,463 sq km
4 4,100,000 (68)
5 Abidjan 282,000
6 1960
Economy
1 $1005M (66)
2 $256 (66)
3 Coffee, cocoa, timber, bananas
4 151 kg (67)
Defence
1 $16.7M (67)
2 3800
4 Voluntary

JAMAICA
1 Independent state
2 English
3 4232 sq miles 10,962 sq km
4 1,913,000 (68)
5 Kingston 376,500
6 1962
Economy
1 $975M (67)
2 $520 (67)
3 Bauxite, alumina sugar, bananas, tobacco, rum,
4 951 kg (67)
Defence
1 $4.5M (65–66)
2 1500
4 Voluntary

JAPAN
1 Empire
2 Japanese
3 142,766 sq miles 369,765 sq km
4 102,000,000 (69)
5 Tokyo 11,172,000
Economy
1 $200,000M (70)
2 $1395 (70)
3 Iron, steel, ships, textiles, motor vehicles, electronic goods
4 2323 kg (67)
Defence
1 $1344M (69–70)
2 250,000
4 Voluntary

JORDAN
1 Kingdom
2 Arabic
3 37,738 sq miles 97,740 sq km
4 2,102,000 (68)
5 Amman 330,200
Economy
1 $575M (67)
2 $268 (67)
3 Phosphates, fruit, vegetables, tobacco
4 265 kg (67)
Defence
1 $126M (69)
2 55,000
4 2 years (selective)

KENYA
1 Republic
2 Swahili, English
3 224,960 sq miles 582,644 sq km
4 10,209,000 (68)

---

5 Nairobi 479,000
6 1963
Economy
1 $1158M (67)
2 $117 (67)
3 Coffee, sisal, timber
4 144 kg (67)
Defence
1 $17.9M (68)
2 4200
4 Voluntary

KOREA, SOUTH
1 Republic
2 Korean
3 38,024 sq miles 98,477 sq km
4 30,470,000 (68)
5 Seoul 3,805,300
6 1948
Economy
1 $4829M (67)
2 $162 (67)
3 Metal ores, plywood
4 567 kg (67)
Defence
1 $290M (69)
2 620,000
4 2 years (army)

KOREA, NORTH
1 Democratic people's republic
2 Korean
3 46,540 sq miles 120,538 sq km
4 13,000,000 (68)
5 Pyongyang 653,100
6 1948
Economy
1 $2800M (68)
2 $200 (68)
3 Metal ores, metal products
4
Defence
1 $692M (69)
2 384,500
4 3–4 years

KUWAIT
1 Sheikhdom
2 Arabic, English
3 6200 sq miles 16,000 sq km
4 540,000 (68)
5 Kuwait 295,300
6 1914
Economy
1 $1700M (66)
2 $3463 (66)
3 Oil, skins, wool, entrepôt trade
4 6648 kg (67)
Defence
1 $60.2M (67)
2
4 Voluntary

LAOS
1 Kingdom
2 Lao, French
3 91,400 sq miles 236,800 sq km
4 2,825,000 (69)
5 Vientiane 162,300
6 1949
Economy
1 $168M (63)
2 $67 (63)
3 Tin, coffee
4 41 kg (67)
Defence
1 $19.8M (69)
2 65,000
4 Selective conscription

LEBANON
1 Republic
2 Arabic, English, French
3 4000 sq miles 10,400 sq km
4 2,580,000 (68)

---

5 Beirut 700,000
6 1941
Economy
1 $775M (63)
2 $339 (63)
3 Fruit, vegetables, wool, tobacco
4 648 kg (67)
Defence
1 $44.6M (68)
2 15,000
4 Voluntary

LESOTHO
1 Kingdom
2 English, Basuto
3 11,720 sq miles 30,355 sq km
4 910,000 (68)
5 Maseru 18,000
6 1966
Economy
1 $75M (66)
2 $88 (66)
3 Wool, mohair, diamonds
4
Defence
Defence controlled by South Africa

LIBERIA
1 Republic
2 English
3 43,002 sq miles 111,369 sq km
4 1,130,000 (68)
5 Monrovia 81,000
Economy
1 $229M (66)
2 $210 (66)
3 Rubber, iron ore and concentrates, industrial diamonds
4 331 kg (67)
Defence
1 $4.4M (69)
2 4150
4 Voluntary

LIBYA
1 Kingdom
2 Arabic
3 679,362 sq miles 1,759,540 sq km
4 1,803,000 (68)
5 Tripoli 247,400
  Benghazi 137,300
6 1951
Economy
1 $1535M (67)
2 $883 (67)
3 Groundnuts, hides, skins, oil
4 390 kg (67)
Defence
1 $45.9M (69–70)
2 15,000
4 3 years

LIECHTENSTEIN
1 Principality
2 German
3 62 sq miles 157 sq km
4 21,000 (69)
5 Vaduz 3500
Economy
1
2
3 Textiles, ceramics, precision instruments, pharmaceuticals

LUXEMBOURG
1 Grand Duchy
2 German, French, Luxembourgeois
3 998 sq miles 2586 sq km
4 336,000 (67)
5 Luxembourg 77,100
Economy
1 $722M (67)
2 $2155 (67)
3 (As for Belgium)
4 (As for Belgium)

Defence
1 $8M (69)
2 560
3 NATO
4 9 months (voluntary)

MALAGASY REPUBLIC
1 Republic
2 French, Malagasy
3 229,233 sq miles 594,180 sq km
4 6,777,000 (67)
5 Tananarive 321,700
6 1960
Economy
1 $737M (67)
2 $116 (67)
3 Foodstuffs, textiles, mineral products
4 66 kg (67)
Defence
1 $13.9M (69)
2 4500
4 2 years

MALAWI
1 Republic
2 English, Bantu, local dialects
3 45,483 sq miles 117,800 sq km
4 4,285,000 (68)
5 Zomba 19,700 (66)
6 1964
Economy
1 $213M (67)
2 $51 (67)
3 Tobacco, tea, groundnuts, cotton
4 48 kg (67)
Defence
1 $1.3M (68)
2 1150
4 Voluntary

MALAYSIA, Federation of
West Malaysia
1 Malay states
2 Malay, Chinese, English
3 50,840 sq miles 131,676 sq km
4 8,840,000 (69)
5 Kuala Lumpur 316,200
6 1957
Economy
1 $2623M (66)
2 $316 (66)
3 Rubber, tin, iron ore
4 424 kg (67)
Defence
1 $132M (69)*
2 30,000
4 Voluntary
*Defence figures for entire federation

East Malaysia
SABAH
1 State
2 Malay, Chinese, English
3 29,388 sq miles 76,115 sq km
4 591,000 (67)
5 Kota Kinabalu 21,700
6 1963
Economy
1 $188M (66)
2 $332 (66)
3 Rubber, timber, copra
4 275 kg (67)

SARAWAK
1 State
2 Malay, Chinese, English
3 48,250 sq miles 121,400 sq km
4 902,000 (67)
5 Kuching 70,000
6 1963
Economy
1 $247M (66)
2 $286 (66)
3 Rubber, timber, sago, pepper, crude oil
4 426 kg (67)

MALI
1 Republic
2 French, Sudanic dialects, Hamitic
3 478,760 sq miles 1,240,000 sq km
4 4,787,000 (68)
5 Bamako 175,000
6 1960
Economy
1 $329M (63)
2 $75 (63)
3 Cotton, live animals, vegetable oil
4 22 kg (67)
Defence
1 $10.3M (68–69)
2 3500
4 Voluntary

MALTA
1 State
2 Maltese, English
3 122 sq miles 316 sq km
4 319,000 (67)
5 Valletta 15,500
6 1964
Economy
1 $187M (67)
2 $587 (67)
3 Foodstuffs, textile threads and yarns, clothing, fabrics
4 781 kg (67)
Defence
Defence controlled by Britain

MARTINIQUE
1 French overseas department
2 French
3 420 sq miles 1090 sq km
4 320,000 (67)
5 Fort-de-France 99,100
Economy
1
2
3 Sugar, bananas, rum
4 436 kg (67)
Defence
Defence controlled by France

MAURITANIA
1 Republic
2 French, Semitic
3 419,232 sq miles 1,085,805 sq km
4 1,100,000 (68)
5 Nouakchott 20,000
6 1960
Economy
1 $200M (68)
2 $107 (63)
3 Iron ore, dried and salted fish, gum arabic
4 53 kg (67)
Defence
1 $4.9M (68)
2 1530
4 2 years (selective)

MAURITIUS
1 Independent state
2 Creole, English, French
3 720 sq miles 1865 sq km
4 782,000 (67)
5 Port Louis 136,200
6 1968
Economy
1 $199M (67)
2 $257 (67)
3 Sugar
4 141 kg (67)
Defence
1 $0.4M (67)

MEXICO
1 Federal republic
2 Spanish, Indian dialects
3 761,604 sq miles 1,972,546 sq km
4 47,267,000 (68)

5 Mexico City 3,418,500 (68)
6 1821
Economy
1 $24,112M (67)
2 $528 (67)
3 Foodstuffs, sugar, cotton, coffee, ores, petroleum
4 1073 kg (67)
Defence
1 $153M (65)
2 68,500
4 1 year

MONACO
1 Principality
2 French
3 0.6 sq mile 1.49 sq km
4 23,000 (69)
5 Monaco 2000
Economy
1
2
4

MONGOLIA
1 People's republic
2 Mongolian
3 604,200 sq miles 1,565,000 sq km
4 1,210,000 (68)
5 Ulan Bator 195,300
6 1921
Economy
1 $550M (68)
2 $450 (68)
3 Livestock, wool, hides, skins, furs
4
Defence
1 $20M
2 17,500
4 2 years

MOROCCO
1 Kingdom
2 Arabic, Spanish, French
3 171,835 sq miles 445,050 sq km
4 14,580,000 (68)
5 Rabat-Sale 410,000
6 1956
Economy
1 $2706M (67)
2 $191 (67)
3 Phosphates, fish products
4 178 kg (67)
Defence
1 $80M (69)
2 55,000
4 18 months

MOZAMBIQUE
1 Portuguese overseas territory
2 Portuguese, Bantu
3 297,846 sq miles 771,124 sq km
4 8,000,000 (70)
5 Lourenco Marques 178,000
Economy
1 $482M (63)
2 $71 (63)
3 Sugar, cotton, cashew nuts
4 113 kg (67)
Defence
Defence controlled by Portugal

NEPAL
1 Constitutional monarchy
2 Nepáli, Hindi
3 54,600 sq miles 141,400 sq km
4 10,294,000 (66)
5 Káthmándu 195,300
Economy
1 $1075M (67)
2 $102 (67)
3 Food, jute, timber, oilseeds
4 10 kg (67)
Defence
1 $5.4M (67)
2 20,000
4

NETHERLANDS
1 Kingdom
2 Dutch
3 12,976 sq miles 33,612 sq km
4 13,000,000 (70)
5 Amsterdam 857,600
Economy
1 $28,200M (69)
2 $1804 (67)
3 Foodstuffs, fruit, vegetables, consumer goods, chemicals
4 3751 kg (67)
Defence
1 $940M (69)
2 124,000
3 NATO
4 16–18 months (army)

NEW ZEALAND
1 Dominion
2 English, Maori
3 103,736 sq miles 268,675 sq km
4 2,751,000 (68)
5 Wellington 173,200
Economy
1 $5456M (67)
2 $2001 (67)
3 Wool, meat, dairy produce
4 2590 kg (67)
Defence
1 $98M (69)
2 13,135
3 SEATO, ANZUS
4 Voluntary (selective for army)

NICARAGUA
1 Republic
2 Spanish
3 50,190 sq miles 130,000 sq km
4 1,842,000 (68)
5 Managua 262,000
6 1838
Economy
1 $641M (67)
2 $359 (67)
3 Cotton, coffee, timber, meat
4 271 kg (67)
Defence
1 $8.9M (65)
2 7100
4 Selective

NIGER
1 Republic
2 French, Sudanic dialects, Hamitic
3 489,200 sq miles 1,267,000 sq km
4 3,806,000 (66)
5 Niamey 60,000
6 1960
Economy
1 $260M (63)
2 $81 (63)
3 Groundnuts, live animals
4 13 kg (67)
Defence
1 $3.7M (69)
2 2100
4 2 years

NIGERIA
1 Republic
2 English, Fulani, Ibo, Yoruba Hausa
3 356,669 sq miles 923,768 sq km
4 53,700,000 (69)
5 Lagos 665,200
6 1960
Economy
1 $4603M (66)
2 $77 (66)
3 Groundnuts, vegetable oil, cocoa
4 32 kg (67)
Defence
1 $308M (68)
2 163,500
4 Voluntary

NORWAY
1 Kingdom
2 Norwegian
3 125,182 sq miles 324,219 sq km
4 3,819,000 (68)
5 Oslo 579,500
6 1905
Economy
1 $10,800M (69)
2 $2199 (67)
3 Non-ferrous metals and manufactures, machinery, transport equipment, pulp, paper
4 3964 kg (67)
Defence
1 $344M (69)
2 38,000
3 NATO
4 12 months (army)

OMAN
1 Sultanate
2 Arabic
3 82,000 sq miles 212,400 sq km
4 750,000 (64)
5 Muscat 6000
Economy
1 $34M (58)
2 $62 (58)
3 Dates, oil, fish
4 32 kg (67)
Defence
1
2
4

PAKISTAN
1 Republic
2 Bengali, English
3 365,526 sq miles 946,716 sq km
4 130,000,000 (69)
5 Islamabad (new capital, in process of construction and habitation)
6 1947
Economy
1 $15,600M (69)
2 $120 (68)
3 Jute, cloth, raw cotton, jute manufactures
4 92 kg (67)
Defence
1 $542M (69)
2 324,000
3 CENTO, SEATO
4 Voluntary

PANAMA
1 Republic
2 Spanish
3 29,762 sq miles* 77,082 sq km
4 1,372,200* (68)
5 Panama 373,200
6 1903
*including canal zone
Economy
1 $773M (67)
2 $581 (67)
3 Bananas, fish, coffee, fuel
4 1249 kg (67)
Defence
Defence controlled by USA

PAPUA and NEW GUINEA
1 Australian trust territories
2 English
3 86,100 sq miles 222,998 sq km
  92,160 sq miles 238,694 sq km
5 Port Moresby 50,000
Economy
1
2
3 Copra, rubber, coffee, cocoa
4 132 (68) 111 (68)

PARAGUAY
1 Republic
2 Spanish, Guarani
3 157,048 sq miles 406,752 sq km
4 2,231,000 (68)
5 Asuncion 411,500
6 1811
Economy
1 $485M (67)
2 $224 (67)
3 Meat products, timber, oils, tobacco, cotton
4 127 kg (67)
Defence
1 $9.9M (66)
2 20,200
4 2 years

PERSIAN GULF STATES
Bahrain
1 U.K. protectorate
2 Arabic
3 231 sq miles 598 sq km
4 182,200 (65)
5 Manama 79,100
Economy
1
2
3 Oil
4 2115 kg (68)

Qatar
1 U.K. protectorate
2 Arabic
3 4000 sq miles 10,360 sq km
4 80,000 (69)
5 Doha 65,000
Economy
1
2
3 Oil
4 1425 kg (68)

Trucial Oman
1 U.K. protectorate
2 Arabic
3 32,300 sq miles 83,600 sq km
4 180,200 (65)
5 Dubai 60,000
Economy
1
2
3 Oil
4 924 kg (68)
Defence
1
2
4

PERU
1 Republic
2 Spanish, Quechua, Aymara
3 496,224 sq miles 1,285,216 sq km
4 12,772,000 (68)
5 Lima 2,072,800
6 1821
Economy
1 $3507M (67)
2 $283 (67)
3 Minerals, fishmeal, cotton, sugar, coffee
4 620 kg (67)
Defence
1 $119M (66)
2 54,650
4 2 years

PHILIPPINES
1 Republic
2 Tagalog, English, Spanish
3 115,600 sq miles 299,400 sq km
4 35,993,000 (68)
5 Quezon 501,800
6 1946

Economy
1 $9645M (67)
2 $278 (67)
3 Sugar, copra, logs, timber fibres, abaca, metal ores
4 236 kg (67)
Defence
1 $123M (69)
2 32,500
3 SEATO
4 Selective

POLAND
1 Republic
2 Polish
3 120,665 sq miles 312,520 sq km
4 32,426,000 (68)
5 Warsaw 1,275,600 (67)
6 1918
Economy
1 $38,000M (68)
2 $1171
3 Fuels, rolling stock, ships, foodstuffs
4 3642 kg (67)
Defence
1 $2080M (69)
2 275,000
3 Warsaw Pact
4 2 years (army)

PORTUGAL
1 Republic
2 Portuguese
3 35,515 sq miles 91,971 sq km
4 10,000,000 (70)
5 Lisbon 826,500
Economy
1 $4619M (67)
2 $489 (67)
3 Cork, wine, sardines, woodpulp
4 565 kg (67)
Defence
1 $321M (69)
2 182,000
3 NATO
4 18–48 months (army)

PORTUGUESE GUINEA
1 Portuguese overseas territory
2 Creole, Portuguese
3 13,948 sq miles 36,125 sq km
4 529,000 (68)
5 Bissau 55,000
Economy
1 $37M (63)
2 $71 (63)
3 Peanuts, coconuts, timber, beeswax
4 57 kg (67)
Defence
Defence controlled by Portugal

REUNION
1 Overseas department of France
2 French, Creole
3 969 sq miles 2510 sq km
4 430,000 (69)
5 St-Denis 85,400
Economy
1 $115M (63)
2 $310 (63)
3 Sugar, rum
4 251 kg (67)

RHODESIA
1 Republic
2 English, Afrikaans, Bantu dialects
3 150,333 sq miles 389,361 sq km
4 4,500,000 (68)
5 Salisbury 330,000
6 1965 Unilateral Declaration of Independence
Economy
1 $1053M (67)
2 $233 (67)
3 Copper, tobacco, asbestos, chrome ore, meat

4 491 kg (67)
Defence
1 $23.6M (69–70)
2 4600
4 12 months (white population)

RUMANIA
1 Republic
2 Rumanian
3 91,699 sq miles 237,500 sq km
4 19,721,000 (69)
5 Bucharest 1,518,700
Economy
1 $18,100 (68)
2 $905 (68)
3 Fuels, metals, machinery, consumer goods, foodstuffs
4 2279 kg (67)
Defence
1 $574M (69)
2 193,000
3 Warsaw Pact
4 1 year (army)

RWANDA
1 Republic
2 French, Kinyarwanda, Kiswahli
3 10,169 sq miles 26,338 sq km
4 3,405,000 (67)
5 Kigali 4300
6 1962
Economy
1 $117M (63)
2 $40 (63)
3 Coffee
4 8 kg (67)
Defence
1 $3.2M (68)
2 2750
4 2 years

ST HELENA
1 British colony
2 English
3 47 sq miles 121 sq km
4 4700 (67)
5 Jamestown 1600
Economy
1
2
3 Flax fibre, tow, rope, twine
4

TRISTAN DA CUNHA and ASCENSION
1 Dependencies of St Helena
2
3 40 sq miles 104 sq km
34 sq miles 88 sq km
4 260 (64) 480 (66)

SAN MARINO
1 Republic
2 Italian
3 24 sq miles 61 sq km
4 18,000 (68)
5 San Marino 3800
Economy
1
2
3 Wine, textiles, tiles, ceramics
4

SÃO TOMÉ and PRINCIPE
1 Portuguese overseas province
2 Portuguese
3 372 sq miles 964 sq km
4 64,100 (60)
5 São Tomé 5700
Economy
1
2
3 Cocoa, coffee, coconuts
4 123 (68)
Defence
Defence controlled by Portugal

SAUDI ARABIA
1 Kingdom
2 Arabic
3 830,000 sq miles 2,149,690 sq km
4 6,000,000 (68)
5 Riyadh 225,000
Economy
1 $2700M (68)
2 $4500
3 Crude oil
4 440 kg (67)
Defence
1 $343M (69)
2 34,000
4 Voluntary

SENEGAL
1 Republic
2 French
3 75,754 sq miles 196,192 sq km
4 3,685,000 (68)
5 Dakar 374,700
6 1960
Economy
1 $811M (66)
2 $227 (66)
3 Groundnuts, groundnut oil, phosphates, salt
4 138 kg (67)
Defence
1 $18M (68)
2 5850
4 Voluntary

SEYCHELLES
1 British colony
2 English, French, Creole
3 145 sq miles 376 sq km
4 46,500 (64)
5 Victoria 10,000
Economy
1
2
3 Copra, patchouli, vanilla, cinnamon bark
4 183 kg (68)

SIERRA LEONE
1 Independent state
2 English
3 27,925 sq miles 71,740 sq km
4 2,475,000 (68)
5 Freetown 163,000
6 1961
Economy
1 $295M (63)
2 $128 (63)
3 Diamonds, iron ore, palm kernels
4 49 kg (67)
Defence
1 $2.5M (67)
2 1600
4 Voluntary

SINGAPORE
1 Republic
2 English, Malay, Chinese, Tamil
3 224 sq miles 581 sq km
4 2,000,000 (69)
5 Singapore 1,955,600
6 1965
Economy
1 $1264M (67)
2 $646 (67)
3 Entrepôt trade
4 637 kg (67)
Defence
1 $109M (69–70)
2 14,250
4 2 years

SOMALI REPUBLIC
1 Republic
2 Somali, Arabic, Italian, English
3 246,201 sq miles 637,657 sq km
4 2,500,000 (69)
5 Mogadiscio 172,700

6 1960
1 $160M (63)
2 $69 (63)
3 Bananas, livestock, hides, skins
4 24 kg (67)
Defence
1 $8.9M (67)
2 12,000
4 Voluntary

SOUTH AFRICA
1 Republic
2 Afrikaans, English
3 471,444 sq miles 1,221,037 sq km
4 18,733,000 (67)
5 Cape Town (legislative) 807,211
Pretoria (administrative) 422,590
6 1909
Economy
1 $14,000M (68)
2 $700 (68)
3 Food, live animals, wool, metal, metal manufactures, diamonds
4 2687 kg (67)
Defence
1 $380.2M (69–70)
2 43,800
4 9–12 months in Citizen Force

SOUTHERN YEMEN
1 Republic
2 Arabic
3 111,074 sq miles 287,683 sq km
4 2,000,000 (67)
5 Madinet al-Shaab 300,000
6 1967
Economy
1 $179M (63)
2 $166 (63)
3 Cotton, hides, skins
4 2023 kg (67)
Defence
1
2 10,000
4 Voluntary

SOUTH WEST AFRICA
1 Mandated territory of Republic of South Africa
2 Afrikaans, Nama
3 318,261 sq miles 824,292 sq km
4 610,000 (66)
5 Windhoek 36,100
Economy
1
2
3 Diamonds, lead
4

SPAIN
1 State
2 Spanish
3 194,883 sq miles 504,750 sq km
4 33,000,000 (69)
5 Madrid 2,764,500
6 1936 (statehood)
Economy
1 $26,435M (67)
2 $822 (67)
3 Foodstuffs, fruit, vegetables, wine, textiles, manufactured goods
4 1264 kg (67)
Defence
1 $273M (68)
2 289,500
4 18 months

SPANISH WEST AFRICA: Ifni
1 Spanish overseas province
2 Spanish
3 580 sq miles 1500 sq km
4 47,600 (61)
5 Sidi Ifní 12,800

Spanish Sahara
1 Spanish overseas province
2 Spanish
3 102,680 sq miles 266,000 sq km
4 48,600 (66)
5 Aaiún 4500
Economy
(No figures available)

SUDAN
1 Republic
2 Arabic, English
3 967,500 sq miles 2,505,813 sq km
4 14,770,000 (69)
5 Khartoum 189,000
6 1956
Economy
1 $1333M (63)
2 $104 (63)
3 Cotton, gum arabic, sesame, groundnuts
4 87 kg (67)
Defence
1 $55.3M (68)
2 20,000
4 Voluntary

SURINAM
1 Associate state of Netherlands
2 Dutch, English, Hindi, Javanese, Chinese, Surinamese
3 55,143 sq miles 163,265 sq km
4 324,200 (64)
5 Paramaribo 123,000
Economy
1 $115M (63)
2 $363 (63)
3 Bauxite, alumina, rice
4 1942 kg (67)
Defence
Defence controlled by Netherlands

SWAZILAND
1 Monarchy
2 Siswati, English, Afrikaans
3 6704 sq miles 17,366 sq km
4 389,500 (66)
5 Mbabane 8000
6 1968
Economy
1 $67M (66)
2 $178 (66)
3 Sugar, asbestos, rice, iron ore, wood pulp

SWEDEN
1 Kingdom
2 Swedish
3 173,666 sq miles 449,793 sq km
4 8,000,000 (70)
5 Stockholm 1,274,700
Economy
1 $23,926M (67)
2 $3041 (67)
3 Machinery, transport equipment, crude materials, wood, pulp, paper, steel
4 4787 kg (67)
Defence
1 $1099M (69–70)
2 750,000
4 9–15 months (army, navy)

SWITZERLAND
1 Republic
2 German, French, Italian, Romansch
3 15,941 sq miles 41,288 sq km
4 6,147,000 (68)
5 Berne 254,900
Economy
1 $15,765M (67)
2 $2597 (67)
3 Machinery, chemicals, watches, textiles
4 2762 kg (67)
Defence
1 $412M (69)
2 644,500
4 4 months

SYRIA
1 Republic
2 Arabic
3 71,498 sq miles 185,180 sq km
4 5,738,000 (68)
5 Damascus 578,600
Economy
1 $1308M (68)
2 $235 (68)
3 Cereals, cotton, tobacco, manufactures, foodstuffs
4 393 kg (67)
Defence
1 $195M (69)
2 70,500
4 2 years

TAIWAN
1 Republic
2 Chinese
3 13,885 sq miles 35,961 sq km
4 13,297,000 (68)
5 Taipei 1,221,100
Economy
1 $3604M (67)
2 $274 (67)
3 Sugar, bananas, textiles
4 726 kg (67)
Defence
1 $302M (68)
2 555,000
4 2 years

TANZANIA
1 United Republic
2 Swahili, English
3 362,820 sq miles 939,702 sq km
4 12,590,000 (68)
5 Dar es Salaam 272,800
6 Tanganyika 1961 Zanzibar 1964
Economy
1 $843M (67)
2 $69 (67)
3 Coffee, cotton, sisal, diamonds
4 117 kg (67)
Defence
1 $10.9M (68)
2 7900
4 Voluntary

THAILAND
1 Kingdom
2 Thai
3 198,500 sq miles 514,000 sq km
4 33,693,000 (68)
5 Bangkok 1,608,300
Economy
1 $5079M (67)
2 $155 (67)
3 Rice, rubber, tin, maize, teak, jute, tapioca products
4 175 kg (67)
Defence
1 $154M (68)
2 126,400
3 ASPAC, SEATO
4 2 years

TOGO
1 Republic
2 Ewe, Mina, Hamitic
3 21,853 sq miles 56,600 sq km
4 1,724,000 (67)
5 Lomé 86,000
6 1960
Economy
1 $135M (63)
2 $86 (63)
3 Phosphates, cocoa, coffee
4 57 kg (67)
Defence
1 $2.7M (69)
2 1250
4 2 years

TRINIDAD AND TOBAGO
1 Independent state
2 English, Hindi, French, Spanish
3 1980 sq miles 5128 sq km
4 973,920 (65)
5 Port-of-Spain 94,000
6 1962
Economy
1 $757M (66)
2 $761 (66)
3 Sugar, cocoa beans, petroleum products, natural asphalt
4 4215 kg (67)
Defence
1 $2.8M
2 1000
4 Voluntary

TUNISIA
1 Republic
2 Arabic
3 63,379 sq miles 164,150 sq km
4 4,660,000 (69)
5 Tunis 469,000
6 1957
Economy
1 $948M (67)
2 $208 (67)
3 Iron ore, phosphates, olive oil
4 235 kg (67)
Defence
1 $20M (68)
2 16,000
4 1 year (selective)

TURKEY
1 Republic
2 Turkish, Kurdish
3 301,382 sq miles 780,576 sq km
4 36,000,000 (67)
5 Ankara 978,900
Economy
1 $11,540M (67)
2 $353 (67)
3 Tobacco, fruit, cotton, minerals, cereals
4 422 kg (67)
Defence
1 $510M (69–70)
2 483,000
3 NATO, CENTO
4 2 years

UGANDA
1 Republic
2 English, Kiswahili
3 91,134 sq miles 236,036 sq km
4 8,133,000
5 Kampala 170,000
6 1962
Economy
1 $754M (67)
2 $95 (67)
3 Coffee, cotton, copper, tea, tobacco, groundnuts
4 53 kg (67)
Defence
1 $14.5M (67)
2 5700
4 Voluntary

UNION OF SOVIET SOCIALIST REPUBLICS
1 Federal republic
2 Russian, plus 57 others
3 8,649,287 sq miles 22,402,200 sq km
4 240,000,000 (70)
5 Moscow 6,563,000
Economy
1 $430,000M (68)
2 $1800 (68)
3 Clocks, watches, machinery, manufactures, wheat, petroleum products, cotton
4 3957 kg (67)

Defence
1 $42,140M* (69)
2 3,300,000
3 Warsaw Pact
4 2 years (army, air force)
*Declared defence expenditure only. Figure excludes cost of nuclear warheads, research and development of advanced weapons, military elements of space programmes, etc.

UNITED ARAB REPUBLIC
1 Republic
2 Arabic
3 386,660 sq miles 1,001,449 sq km
4 31,680,000 (68)
5 Cairo 4,219,900
Economy
1 $5690M (66)
2 $189 (66)
3 Cotton, rice, petroleum
4 267 kg (67)
Defence
1 $805M (69)
2 207,000
4 3 years

UNITED KINGDOM
1 Kingdom
2 English
3 94,222 sq miles 244,030 sq km
4 55,283,000 (68)
5 London 7,880,800
Economy
1 $92,700M (69)
2 $1977 (67)
3 Machinery, vehicles, textiles, beverages, plastics, non-ferrous metals
4 5003 kg (67)
Defence
1 $5438M (69–70)
2 405,000
3 NATO, SEATO, CENTO
4 Voluntary

UNITED STATES OF AMERICA
1 Federal republic
2 English
3 3,615,196 sq miles 9,363,353 sq km
4 204,100,000 (70)
5 Washington D.C. 2,704,100
6 1776
Economy
1 $932,000M (69)
2 $4600 (69)
3 Machinery, vehicles, cereals, chemicals, aircraft
4 9828 kg (67)
Defence
1 $78,475M (69–70)
2 3,454,000
3 NATO, CENTO, SEATO
4 2 years (selective)

UPPER VOLTA
1 Republic
2 French, Sudanese
3 105,869 sq miles 274,200 sq km
4 5,175,000 (68)
5 Ouagadougou 77,500
6 1960
Economy
1 $245M (66)
2 $49 (66)
3 Livestock, preserved fish, groundnuts
4 12 kg (67)
Defence
1 $4.2M (69)
2 1800
4 2 years

URUGUAY
1 Republic
2 Spanish
3 72,172 sq miles 186,926 sq km
4 2,818,000 (68)

5 Montevideo 1,154,500
6 1828
Economy
1 $1686M (66)
2 $613 (66)
3 Wool, meat, meat products, hides, skins
4 847 kg (67)
Defence
1 $13.1M (66)
2 13,850
4 Voluntary

VENEZUELA
1 Republic
2 Spanish
3 352.144 sq miles 912,050 sq km
4 9,686,000 (68)
5 Caracas 1,959,000
6 1830
Economy
1 $8515M (67)
2 $911 (67)
3 Petroleum, iron ore, coffee
4 2220 kg (67)
Defence
1 $172M (66)
2 30,500
4 2 years

VIETNAM, NORTH
1 Democratic republic
2 Vietnamese, French
3 61,294 sq miles 158,750 sq km
4 17,800,000 (67)
5 Hanoi 643,600
6 1954
Economy
1 $2200M (68)
2 $110 (68)
3 Coal, phosphates, cotton and silk goods
Defence
1 $500M (69)
2 457,000
4 3 years minimum

VIETNAM, SOUTH
1 Republic
2 Vietnamese, French, English
3 67,112 sq miles 173,809 sq km
4 17,414,000 (68)
5 Saigon 1,639,800
6 1954
Economy
1 $1503M (63)
2 $98 (63)
3 Rubber, tea
4 296 kg (67)
Defence
1 $715.5M (69)
2 472,500
4 3 years

YEMEN
1 Republic
2 Arabic
3 75,300 sq miles 195,000 sq km
4 5,000,000 (68)
5 San'a 60,000
Economy
1 $240M (58)
2 $48 (58)
3 Coffee, hides, skins, cereals
4 10 kg (67)
Defence
1 $10M (68)
2
4

YUGOSLAVIA
1 Socialist republic
2 Serbo-croat, Macedonian, Slovene
3 98,766 sq miles 255,804 sq km
4 20,186,000 (68)
5 Belgrade 585,200
6 1918

Economy
1 $9600M (68)
2 $480 (68)
3 Timber, non-ferrous metals, animals, animal produce, machinery, metal products
4 1153 kg (67)
Defence
1 $585M (69)
2 218,000
4 18 months (army, air force)

ZAMBIA
1 Republic
2 English
3 290,586 sq miles 752,614 sq km
4 4,080,000 (68)
5 Lusaka 152,000
6 1964
Economy
1 $1175M (67)
2 $298 (67)
3 Copper, cobalt, tobacco, maize, groundnuts, fish
4 577 kg (67)
Defence
1 $20M (68)
2 4400
4 Voluntary

Index